A WATCHMAN SPEAKS

CONTINUED

Dedicated to those who have
received a love of the truth

RUSTY SMITH

PROSODY COMMUNICATIONS

A Watchman Speaks--Continued
Dedicated to those who have received a love of the truth

Published by:
Prosody Communications
Albert Lea, MN
www.prosodycommunications.com

Library of Congress Control Number: 2021910355
ISBN: 978-1-951357-06-1 (paperback)
ISBN: 978-1-951357-07-8 (eBook)

Printed in the United States of America and Around the World

CONTENTS

ACKNOWLEDGMENTS

This volume is the product of seeking the Lord every day, reading the Bible every day, the inspiration of the Holy Spirit, the instruction and guidance of the Lord, and obedience to His voice. It is a continuation of the discourses in the first book, A Watchman Speaks.

In this book, the reader may notice references to the chaotic times that have descended upon the material realm we find ourselves in now (2020, 2021). The COVID-19 pandemic, along with the social unrest of the last few years, has left the world in disorder and confusion and the USA a nation divided. We see many people anxious and afraid, losing hope, and turning away from God. Some are looking to the government, and believing man's social justice policies will bring them salvation. A perusal of the discourses in this volume will point out the truth. Man, through his power alone, cannot fulfill the needs of individuals or nations. Only faith in God and obedience to His commandments will bring the personal relationship with Him, which opens to us the Spiritual, reveals to us the truth, overcomes fear, and brings the inner peace that everyone seems to be so desperately seeking.

The only endorsement sought by the writer is the witness of the Holy Spirit to those who read it.

Thanks and blessings to everyone who takes the time and makes an effort to examine it.

Please note that italics in the discourses indicate scripture. Reference Bible versions are NKJV and ESV.

Sherry Gifford has again partnered with me by editing, typing, encouraging, and collaborating in every aspect of publication and the publication of the blog that contains its entirety found at www.christianrelationshipblog.wordpress.com. My thanks to Sherry.

Thanks also to Darin Johnson, who has so graciously handled the publication process.

FOREWORD

Throughout my life, the author (my father) has equipped me with both scripture and spiritual insight to navigate this world. He has been a straightforward guide for any topic, problem, or question that may arise – always with honest, straightforward life-giving encouragement through the unequivocal words of wisdom, love, and truth declared in the Bible. It is my joy to invite you to share in the revelations and journey given to him from our Heavenly Father.

Taste and see that the Lord is good!

-Julia Nagorski

A WATCHMAN SPEAKS

CONTINUED

455 UNCHANGING SPIRITUAL PARADIGMS

Our Creator has established all-encompassing, eternal truths that exist outside the dimension of time and the natural realm where a generation goes on eternally, and a covenant never ends or changes. These paradigms are only accessed by those who have entered the land of the living where the Creator dwells. There are no sinners or unbelievers abiding in this secret place of the Most High God.

The generation of Christ is the one that precedes his appearing as a man on earth and covenants which have ended or changed. The dispensations revered and understood by the carnal mind and the world's religions have no reality or influence in the Spiritual realm. They are confined to the understanding of the man of the earth and the boundaries the Almighty has established for the descendants of the first Adam.

The promises God has made to his chosen people apply to those who have become One Spirit with Him by becoming members of the eternal generation to which the eternal covenant has been revealed. If this sounds too exclusive, so be it. It is.

It is exactly what Jesus has told us. All the religious activities and extravagance will not allow anyone into the true kingdom of God. Those who would enter must do so as a child who has not known sin or forsaken the covenant of youth, for such is the kingdom of God. All who have reached the age of accountability and have knowingly transgressed against what he/she knows is right must die in order to regain true life. He who wants to save his life must lose it. Jesus gave His life to save us from our sin, and if we died with Him, we will also live with Him.

There is no other passage to the eternal generation of Christ than the death of the man of flesh and the birth of a new person who abides in Christ. Jesus' blood will cleanse the sinner, but it will not continue to cover the sin of the one who continues to live for himself and continues to sin after receiving the knowledge of the truth.

The covenant of faith demonstrated by father Abraham included hearing the voice of God, believing Him, and obeying Him. This is the covenant that encompasses all others and is eternal. We, as believers, enter that covenant by faith and so, too, become part of the eternal generation of the forefathers as well as Christ Himself through faith. There is no place for ongoing sin or for self-proclaimed sinners in this land where only the righteous abide. Those who have told us that we remain sinners after becoming new creations in Christ Jesus are liars attempting to build their own kingdoms, which are of this present world. Their inheritance will be according to their profession and their works.

The God and Father of all life desires an inheritance that loves Him and serves Him blamelessly, just as His Only-Begotten has shown us. The person who believes he/she can continue to live for him/herself and disobey the eternal law of God will never enter the land where He dwells or see His face.

456 IMMUTABLE LAW

Our Creator has established a variety of laws, all with a purpose and a reason. Still, the immortal, immutable law of the Spirit of life in Christ Jesus is the one that overcomes sin, death, and mortality.

Among the multitude who profess to know the Savior and call themselves Christians, there seem to be few who can confess the freedom from the dominance of the flesh and the sin produced by the lust of it.

This law of the Spirit not only frees the true believer from the law of sin and death but the power of the flesh altogether. Is this not what the gospel actually teaches? How is it that professional Bible teachers worldwide tell us that despite being born of the Spirit and becoming new creatures in Christ, we remain subject to our flesh, thus remaining sinners?

The real contention here is about who is really a Christian. The word of God is the real judge, and the opinion and doctrine of man and his institutions are worth nothing. Regrettably, eternity is in the balance for many who have believed the lie regarding ongoing sin and salvation. This subject cannot be taken lightly in the reality of eternal consequence.

A diligent search will reveal that God's salvation is from sin itself and not merely its consequences. What the professional religious leaders have done diligently has been an attempt to render the actual word of God, not say what it does say. When they are unable to pervert the exact words God has spoken through the Spirit of Truth, they are willing to compromise the truth by purposely mistranslating scripture to favor their false doctrines. This is most certainly true regarding humans being born sinners. Whose kingdoms are enlarged by such a lie?

The natural, carnal human is, in fact, a beast of the earth and bears that mark. He is the offspring of the man of dust. The person who is born of the Spirit and follows the immutable Spirit of life in Christ Jesus is able to fulfill the righteous requirements of that law. To live according to the flesh carries with it the sentence of death which is separation from God for eternity, while those who follow after the Spirit of God not only put to death the deeds of the body but are, in fact, the true sons of God and real Christians.

457 DISTANCE

The eyes of a fool are on the ends of the earth. Others look to outer space for the origin of the human race. How far have we actually come from our origin? Technology and knowledge of our environment are rapidly increasing, but where are we going? From where have we come?

True understanding and purpose of our existence seem no closer to being discovered than it was in the beginning of the records we have uncovered. Truth has always been here and is in plain few of the human whose eyes have been opened by his Creator. The thing that has blinded the descendants of the first man is sin. All of his offspring have followed in his footsteps by choice.

The actual answer to our existence and purpose is as near as our own heart. There have been countless people throughout the ages who have come to true understanding, which we all seek. It is not far off, although it may be mysterious. It comes by revelation of another dimension that cannot be comprehended through our biological senses or our carnal minds. Our Creator is not far off, nor is he hidden from the person who seeks Him diligently with his/her whole heart. All the speculation and natural ability must be set aside to enter the realm of true wisdom and understanding available in the Spiritual dimension where the Creator dwells. This is the land of the living where only the pure and blameless have access. This is the secret place where the Most High God Himself abides.

What is being described is very simple. A child can understand it, while the intellectual genius cannot pass into its reality. The only "distance" between what can be seen with biological vision and spiritual vision is humility and a pure heart.

Unless you are converted and become as little children, you will by no means enter the kingdom of heaven.

MATTHEW 18:2-3; 3:2

P.S. Can you really believe the little children described by Jesus are sinners?

458 THE SALVATION OF THE LORD

Unto him who orders his conduct aright, I will show the salvation of the Lord. Words provide us with a map to lead us to salvation. Nevertheless, its reality lies in experience. An intellectual assent or an unqualified belief based on man's interpretation of what salvation consists of will not produce God's actual intent.

The Lord's salvation has been established from the beginning. Many of the ancients understood its reality and knew the One in whom it exists. Long before Jesus appeared on earth to manifest His salvation, it was explained and given testimony by the writers of scripture. Today there are countless teachers and preachers proclaiming salvation to the masses, yet the evidence of the salvation described by the Holy Spirit is rare. There are many who proclaim, "Lord, Lord," but few who do the will of the Father and bear the virtues described in the Bible, who reflect the image of Christ and walk as He walked.

It should not be necessary to recite the fruits of the Holy Spirit or the works of the saints of old, but suffice it to say that the righteousness and holiness, purity, and faithfulness attributed to saints is difficult to observe in the vast congregations of self-proclaimed sinners which fill the world's tax-exempt institutions.

The true salvation of the Lord does not lie in a doctrine or an organization but in the Lord Himself. A sinner cannot abide in the Lord because He is holy and dwells in a place where no sinners are able to enter. While the blood of Jesus cleanses the sinner and covers his/her sins, it does not continue covering the iniquities of the person who lives according to the flesh and is not contrite with respect to ongoing sin.

Sin is the real issue that has separated the descendants of the first Adam from their Creator and is the reason the Father sent His Son to earth as a man to save people from their sin. This is not a theoretical or a positional deliverance from sin and its consequence, but true salvation from its source as well as the separation from God that results from disobedience to Him. There is no salvation outside of Christ, and there is no sin in Him. How can a person stand blamelessly before God if he/she refuses the salvation He has provided by creating them anew and making them new creatures in the image of the Savior?

His mercy endures forever for those who turn from their sin and follow His Spirit. Still, it is not extended to the person who tries to justify ongoing rebellion, blaming their flesh for an inability to obey the truth and the commands of God. It matters not who may have told us we cannot cease from the sin that so easily besets us. The Word of God remains firm and consistent. It applies equally to all without respect to persons or affiliations.

The salvation of the Lord is from sin itself and always has been.

PSALM 50:23

459 SEPARATION

Who shall separate us from the love of Christ? Shall tribulation or distress, or persecution, or famine, or nakedness, or peril, or sword? Yet in all these things we are more than conquerors through Him who loved us. For I am persuaded that neither death nor life, nor angels, nor principalities, nor powers, nor things present, nor things to come, nor heights, nor depths, nor any other created thing shall be able to separate us from the love of God, which is in Christ Jesus our Lord. Although not listed, viruses are included.

On the other hand, if sinners entice you to join them, do not consent or join with them. Come out from among them and be separate, says the Lord, even if they call themselves Christian sinners. Hello! The righteous should choose his/her friends carefully, for the way of the wicked (sinner) leads them astray.

When is a sinner not a sinner? Apparently, it occurs when he/she affiliates with those who believe they were born sinners and have no choice or control over their own desires and compulsions. How does this belief and philosophy reconcile itself to being born again and created anew in the image of their Creator? Hello!

The simple message here is to separate yourself from those who consider themselves pious and humble but remain sinners after being born of the Spirit and having been cleansed from all unrighteousness, yet refuse to walk blamelessly in holiness. What has the gospel told us? Have we who are born of God not been set free from sin and the power of the flesh?

This watchman is appealing to everyone who believes the gospel to separate themselves from the false church that teaches that ongoing sin is a normal Christian experience. It matters not how prevalent or popular this heresy is. It is the wide pathway that leads to death, and the institutions that are teaching it are indeed the harlot so often referred to in scripture. Amen.

ROMANS 8:35-39
1 CORINTHIANS 6:9-11
PROVERBS 12:26

460 WHICH WAY?

There is a way which seems right to a person but it ends in death. He who trusts in his own heart is a fool, but the person who walks wisely will be saved. God's ways are not necessarily our ways nor his thoughts necessarily our thoughts. The Almighty has given us commands that have no expiration date and warnings that never change.

There is no excuse for disobedience and no justification for rebellion. Certainly, God's laws are perfect and holy and Spiritual. Those who walk and live according to the flesh are not able to fulfill the righteous requirements of God's laws and statutes, because the carnal person does not have the ability to know or understand the way of the Spirit. The weakness of the flesh and the carnal mind are contrary to the Spirit and, consequently, the ways of God.

Our Creator's solution to this dilemma is the death of the natural man, which is only accomplished through faith in Jesus' finished work on the cross. Our old man was crucified in His sinless body on the cross, thus allowing a new sinless, spiritual person to rise with Him to newness of life. The person who can believe this reality and has experienced the miracle is now able to fulfill the righteous requirements of the law and walk in the ways of God just as Jesus has shown us. He has, in fact, told us that we are able to walk as He walked and do even greater things than He did as a man.

The Lord's ability to do all the miraculous things He said and did while He was on earth were the result of His total dependence upon the Holy Spirit, who is His Father. He is also our Father if indeed we are born of the Spirit. Faith is the answer to the understanding of the truth you are hearing. This faith consists of hearing the voice of the Father, believing what He has said, and then obeying what you have heard.

The ways of God are actually simple and attainable if they are not complicated by the religious professionals who would prefer to have the people of God depend upon them rather than the Holy Spirit. This is the answer to the haunting question regarding why there are so many denominations, cults and religious organizations.

Is what you have heard here not the true gospel?

GALATIANS 2:17-20

461 SUPERNATURAL WISDOM

The value of this wisdom is beyond any earthly treasure. Words used to describe this wisdom are primarily metaphor, because it emanates from a place outside the realm of human existence. This wisdom can only be accessed by those who have been chosen by the Creator to pass through the gates of righteousness into the Spiritual dimension where He dwells. Those who have a heart to know and understand such wisdom are gifted with her reality. This is where the true knowledge of God enables one to cease from sin and discern good and evil, truth and lies.

The natural man is able to observe the wonders of the physical creation which declare the existence of the Creator, but the actual wisdom through which it has all originated remains shrouded in mystery outside the biological boundaries of human understanding. This is where sinners dwell and humanity's natural wisdom prevails. This is where the fool stands with the purchase price for wisdom at the doors of the institutions of higher learning established by the hand of mankind, but the boundary established and guarded by the Almighty will not allow the mortal soul to enter. This is why we see the confusion of religion and the conflict created by its ignorance.

Little children do not understand such things, nor are their minds cluttered with all the complicated doctrines and jargon created by the blindness of the world. They are free to come to Jesus and to know His love. This wisdom is free and cannot be purchased at any price, nor can one return to its reality once it has been lost, without being reborn of the Spirit.

Are not the ways of God wonderful? He makes foolish the wisdom of man while revealing Himself and His wisdom to the poor and needy, the uneducated, as well as little children. All this right in front of the power brokers of the worldly wise.

Praise be to God and to the wisdom that only comes from Him!

LUKE 7:35

462 BLAMELESS

The one who is blameless in his way is the Lord's delight. The Lord has declared numerous people blameless throughout scripture. Many terms, metaphors, synonyms and descriptions are used to reveal those who have found right standing in His sight. These are the ones who abide in His presence and the holy place where He dwells. Wise, humble, righteous, upright, just, innocent, redeemed, chosen, faithful, saints, holy and overcomers are some references that come to mind. These are the ones who are not ashamed on the final day and are able to stand at the final judgment. They are pure in heart whose names are found written in the "Book of Life".

Many explanations and examples are given in scripture of those who have pleased their Creator and found favor with Him. Surely, we all desire to be members of this great throng who glorify our Savior. The records given to us by nearly every contributor to the Bible, both Old and New Testaments, reveal what pleases and displeases the Lord. Proverbs even gives us a list of things the Lord hates.

Obedience is very high on the list of things that please God, as well as the disobedience to His commands being one of the quickest ways to be condemned. The question arises as to whether or not we are able to keep and obey His commands. I have heard it said that we are not able, but what can keep us from being able? Why have so many through the ages been able to obey Him and please Him, while so many did not? And is it any different today? Really! Who possesses the attributes listed to the blameless that cause them to please our Savior while the seeming majority do not? Surely, the ones who do not receive the endorsement of our heavenly Father bear their own guilt. The Almighty has never changed nor have the requirements of knowing Him and pleasing Him. Without knowing Him, how can a person please Him? Does what another person tells us about Him and His ways actually constitute personal knowledge of Him? The point is that there is no substitute for a personal witness by the Holy Spirit that our heart is right with God and that we are pleasing Him.

Those who have told us to claim the promises of scripture and believe we are blameless before the throne of God while we continue to violate his righteous demands are actually condemning the ones who believe them to an eternity separated from the holy, loving Savior before whom we all must give account.

What say you? Are you really counted among the saints?

2 CORINTHIANS 13:5

463 EVERYWHERE/NOWHERE

Everywhere I look in the scriptures, I see the love of God displayed for His people, but nowhere do I see sinners associated with the kingdom of heaven or the place where God dwells. This is amazing in light of the fact that so many Christians call themselves sinners (proudly, I might add). The Psalmist declares that sinners shall not stand in the congregation of the righteous, but blessed is the man who walks not in the counsel of the ungodly (sinners).

The truth is everywhere to see, and the righteous follow it. On the other hand, nowhere do we see sinners following after the Spirit of God. There must be some disconnect in the reasoning of the one who calls him/herself a "born-again Christian" and yet a "sinner". A true Christian according to the gospel I read in the Bible says that Christ has set the believer free from sin, and those who abide in Him do not sin. How can this be?

The truth resides in the Spirit, while the lie resides in the world and the flesh.

Satan has blinded the eyes and the conscience of the proud religious leaders of this present age along with those who believe and follow their lies. The Word of God is not ambiguous regarding who we are in Christ or what He expects of those whom He has redeemed. The confession of the true believer along with his/her way of life is the reflection of the reality of the sinless life demonstrated by Jesus Christ.

Though sin is everywhere, so are the eyes of God keeping watch on the good and the evil. There is nowhere that the Spirit of God is not available to deliver the true Christian from the temptation to sin that so often presents itself. It is the overcomers who are actually saved and chosen in the end.

> *"Jesus answered them: Most assuredly I say to you. Whoever commits sin is a slave to sin, and a slave does not abide in the house forever, but a son abides forever. Therefore, if the son makes you free, you shall be free indeed."*
>
> *"But now having been set free from sin and having become slaves of God, you now have your fruit to holiness and the end to everlasting life. For the wages of sin is death, but the gift of God is eternal life in Christ Jesus, our Lord."*

"And you know that He was manifested to take away our sins, and in Him there is no sin. Whoever abides in Him does not sin."

ROMANS 6:20-23
1 JOHN 3:3-9
JOHN 8:34-36

464 HE IS COMING

Every eye shall see Him, and He will judge the world with righteousness. Whether you believe this or not has no bearing on the truth. He is coming to gather His Chosen to Himself, and those who know Him will receive their reward which he has promised to those who love Him.

The signs of his imminent return are manifest throughout the earth, and His judgments are already taking place among the nations. The wise among us are surely making preparations and getting ready. This preparedness is essential whether He comes today or further into the future, because it matters not if He calls us as individuals or if the final hour arrives for the whole world. Readiness is what He has commanded for all His people throughout the ages. Diligence is man's precious possession, and the true believer must be constantly vigilant and watching.

We who know the Lord have been commanded to proclaim His coming even before His incarnation on earth the first time. The ancients knew He would appear at an appointed time, just as we who are alive today. We are all of the same generation if we know the Lord.

We who do know Him should not fear but rejoice to know that He is coming which means the fulfillment of His great salvation. There is no cause to fear the unknown if we are abiding in our Savior now and have the assurance of His love. You may have expected more prognostication regarding His coming because of the title of this discourse, but the warnings and the reason to trust our great God and Savior should be of consolation to everyone who abides in His love.

MATTHEW 24:3 through 25:13
2 THESSALONIANS 1:3 through 2:17

465 BLESSED OR CURSED

Individuals as well as nations can reap blessings or curses based on adherence or rejection of the principles God has established. These principles are without appeal or compromise and are absolute. They are actually laws that cannot be violated without consequences. The blessings inherent in observing these laws are also its own consequence.

The wise person is able to see and understand the results of the unequivocal statutes the Almighty has established in the physical, moral and spiritual dimensions. The reality, as well as proof, of adherence or rejection manifest themselves in the lives of individuals, groups as well as whole nations. There are spirits involved throughout every blessing and curse.

If we pick a person, group or nation to analyze, there will be evidence related directly to the beliefs and works embraced by any and all of the subjects being observed. Examples of such sowing and reaping include religious, political, secular, cultural, and societal, as well as racial and national. How insightful must a person be to see the truth of Muslim nations or socialist and communist countries? What of sexually perverse groups such as LGBTQ affiliates and supremacy groups? These are a few of the more extreme examples that thrust themselves into the public eye. What of peace, love, tranquility, contentment and joy contrasted to conflict, hatred, confusion, discontent and misery? Are these things not obvious repercussions of good and evil? Are they not clearly the result of blessings and curses?

God is not mocked; whatever a person, group, or nation sows that will they reap. There is surely both good and evil, and truth is not subjective or relative. The one that thinks they can violate the principles of God and escape the consequences is ignorant and foolish. So it is for everyone who reject Him.

DEUTERONOMY 11:26-28

466 WHERE IS GOD?

His domain extends beyond the comprehension of man. In Him we live and move and have our being. There is no place outside of His sovereignty, yet He chooses how and where He will manifest Himself; and where He dwells there are few whom He chooses to approach His throne and few on whom His face shines. We know He has chosen Zion as His dwelling place, and Jerusalem where He has established His throne. But has He really limited Himself to a place on the earth for His glory to rest? His actual throne is in heaven, and earth is but His footstool.

How great is this God of Jacob, and how is it that some actually know Him in a personal way? He even chooses some to approach Him and learn directly from Him. Anyone who fears Him is able to understand these things and does not need another person to teach them to know God. It is a joy to talk about our Creator and His great kingdom and all His mighty works.

We who take the time to meditate on His wonderful works and diligently seek to know Him are rewarded with the understanding of His ways and His righteous judgments. Is there anything more fabulous and worthwhile that a mortal soul could achieve?

The location of the Almighty Creator, God, is directly related to a person's relationship with Him. He can be as near as our own heart or as far as the stars. It all depends on our individual relationship with Him, or if we are conscious of even having one at all. We are limited by our own values as well as His knowledge of who we are and, of course, His volition.

Draw near to God, and He will draw near to you.

ROMANS 10:6-8
JAMES 4:8
PSALMS 105:1-10

P.S. He is everywhere, even in the tiniest living creature.

467 MATERIALISM

Where your treasure is, there will your heart be also. Therefore, do not worry saying, "What shall we eat, or what shall we drink, or what shall we wear?" For after all these things the gentiles seek, for your heavenly Father knows that you need all these things. But seek ye first the kingdom of God and His righteousness, and all these things will be added to you. These verses portray our physical needs as well as spiritual reality.

The material realm is real and legitimate, but the love and desire for material things is idolatry. The person who has lost their life for Jesus' sake need not worry about the material things that people believe will bring them satisfaction. A proper spiritual perspective will allow the believer to choose righteousness rather than self-indulgence. The gratification derived from an abundance of material possessions is akin to the temporary pleasure of sin as well as the love of money.

A person cannot serve two masters, nor can he/she please the Savior and their lusts simultaneously. A choice must be made in advance of the day of reckoning. When the time comes, opportunity has ended. Not everyone who says, "Lord, Lord. . ." will enter His kingdom, but only those who have done the will of the Father. If this sounds absolute, it is because it is. The gospel has made it clear.

The love of things cannot be reconciled to the message of the gospel. Yielding to the lusts of the flesh is incompatible with abiding in Christ. Sin is not able to co-exist in the land of the living where only the righteous dwell.

Those content to be satisfied living in a material world and the kingdom of self-indulgence have no part in the eternal kingdom. They are as zombies walking about as corpses and the living dead; or as a beast of the earth without understanding. And so shall they die.

PSALM 49:16-20
HEBREWS 13:5

468 IMMANUEL

God with us. Jesus, the Christ, truly is God. Most people who call themselves Christians believe that. They believe that the miracles He did and all He accomplished as a man was because He was God. The fact is that He emptied Himself of His own power and totally subjected Himself to His Father. He only did the things He saw His Father doing. His power was that of the Holy Spirit, even the words that He spoke were what He heard the Spirit speak.

Jesus was truly a man that was born of a woman. Though God is His Father, he did not exercise His own power but submitted Himself to the Holy Spirit. He did everything to please His Father. If you can't see where this is going yet, I hope you will.

Many also believe that Jesus fulfilled the righteous requirements of the law for us. The word says that we, too, are able to fulfill the righteous requirements of the law that is not passing away by following after the Holy Spirit just as Jesus has shown us. This is also how we walk as He walked without sinning. This is how His righteousness becomes our righteousness. The mystery of God is understood by walking in the Spirit and obeying His voice. These things are made real by believing the gospel and then doing what it says. Jesus said that if we believe Him, we can do even greater things than He did.

Brethren, the real issue is faith. Faith without works is dead. Jesus demonstrated faith in all that He did as a man. So, too, did His apostles and disciples spoken of in the Bible. The Father gives the Holy Spirit to those who obey Him, not to sinners.

Are you ready to believe Him and separate yourself from the ones who don't? The Holy Spirit is calling us to walk in the fullness of the gospel and not the tax-exempt version of it preached in the churches and the electronic perversions of it.

The truth remains simple, and there is no need to go to a Bible school or a seminary to understand what the Spirit of Truth is saying.

If God is for us, who can be against us?

P.S. With regard to references, I hope every reader can recognize them.

469 THE MAN, JESUS, THE CHRIST

Jesus was, indeed, a man. He was born of a woman named Mary. She was a human being. Although a virgin at the time of conception, she remained so until after his birth. Jesus' father was a Spirit, and His conception was indeed a miracle. God, the Creator, is an eternal being and certainly does not have a mother. Yet there are many who believe Mary is the mother of God. The Spirit that inhabited the body of the Man Jesus is the Spirit who is His Father, but Mary is not a mother of that divine Spirit. The Spirit of Christ always was and had no beginning. The life of the man, Jesus, did. Can you see the error of those who call Mary the mother of God and pray to her as though she is God, also? She is no longer a virgin, nor does she sit in a place of dominion over the inhabitants of earth. Mary is certainly a blessed and holy woman, but nevertheless, merely a woman and not God.

My heart aches for the Roman Catholics who waste their time and effort praying to another human being who does not possess the power or the ability to answer their prayers. She is indeed an idol and a false God created by those who use her as another of their fables to capture the hearts of the simple and ignorant.

These Nicolaitans who reign over their captives and condemn innocent blood are being judged as you hear these words.

So says the Lord—amen.

P.S. Come out of her.

1 TIMOTHY 2:3-5
JOHN 3:6

470 CONTROL

Our land has been saturated with the innocent blood of the unborn. The forces of darkness have gained control of our Capitol and nearly all of our major cities. Most of our major corporate news sources have evolved to the point where they call evil good, and good evil. Perversion has risen to a level that exceeds the imagination of a righteous person.

The Almighty has turned His face away from our nation. Nevertheless, He has not forsaken those who fear Him and trust in His mercy. He remains in control in spite of all the wickedness that can be seen throughout the earth. He is coming to judge the world with righteousness and justice, and He has not forgotten those who serve Him. He has regard for His Saints, and their lives are precious in His sight.

There is a limit to the vileness and wickedness that the Creator will allow. The Lord is in control and will have the final say regardless of how dark and desperate the condition of mankind and the world appear.

Blessed are we who have put our hope and trust in Jesus. He will never fail!

HEBREWS 13:5

471 VACATION BIBLE SCHOOL (VBS)

This watchman has discovered a plot to corrupt innocent little children who have no knowledge or understanding of sin to believe they are sinners before they have the ability to commit sin. These VBSs are church-sponsored classes and are, in most instances, merely establishing the false doctrine they themselves have been taught. The teachers have been educated by instructors of Babylon. Most of them are well-meaning ambassadors of religious institutions.

I have heard the testimony of my own grandchildren after attending VBS that they learned they are sinners, even though they were not accused of any specific transgression. The teachers who believe that a baby is born a sinner, or even worse, a sinner from the time of conception, have not understood the truth regarding the actual choice an individual must exercise in order to commit a sin. Does this doctrinal error not constitute causing these little ones who inhabit the kingdom of heaven to sin? Surely, we have heard what Jesus said about the person who causes one of these little children of whom he spoke saying, "*For such is the kingdom of heaven*," to sin. There are no sinners in the kingdom of heaven.

If we take this heresy to its logical conclusion, the act of aborting unborn babies is doing the world a service by eliminating all these sinners. Of course, this notion is ridiculous, but no more so than the idea that any person can choose to sin and become a sinner before they have such ability. If one of these little ones, even the unborn, dies in a sinful state, can you really believe that a just and loving God would condemn them along with the sinners that have chosen to sin against Him?

No one is a sinner before they sin. And a little child does not have the ability to make the moral decision or choice that is required to violate or otherwise transgress the laws of God, unless he/she has been taught to hate by an actual sinner. Even then, they have not exercised their own volition in order to do it.

It is time for anyone who believes the gospel to turn from and separate themselves from sinners who refuse to repent and turn from sin. And certainly, do not let them teach your little ones.

If you are reading a Bible that translates Psalm 51:5, (which refers to the Psalmist's conception), in such a way that depicts the newborn as the sinner rather than the mother, get rid of it and find an honest translation that has not sacrificed the truth in favor of a false doctrine. To view an honest translation, see: KJV, NKJV, ASV, ESV, NASV and many others that have not been corrupted by the translators who love their false doctrines more than the truth.

This watchman has received the love of the truth. Amen.

2 THESSALONIANS 2:9-12
MATTHEW 18:1-7
ISAIAH 7:13-16
DEUTERONOMY 1:39

472 SOULS

The final battle for the soul of our country as well as the souls of humankind throughout the world has begun, and it is time for all of us who have been called by God to engage in what He has called us to do. If there is any doubt, ask the Lord to open your eyes.

The globalists and the One World Government advocates led by the spiritual forces of darkness are fully engaged, and their agenda is nothing less than world domination and the enslavement of mankind.

Government, religion, news media, military, education, medical and pharmaceutical, international corporations, as well as the majority of bureaucratic social dependents are all arrayed against us, who love liberty and freedom. True religious freedom along with free speech is being attacked as never before. The wealthiest among us have used their influence and resources to aid and support the oppressors.

If and when the US is submitted to international domination, the way will be cleared for the diabolical, one-world leader who is prophesied to come. What this means is the near end of the world as we know it. Fortunately for us who know the One whose kingdom rules over all, He will have the final word regarding the earth and those who dwell here. The final victory of good over evil has already been determined by the One who has the power to bring it to pass. I, for one, want to be on His side. The way to accomplish this is through obedience. There is no other substitute, not even pleading the blood. HELLO! So be it.

MATTHEW 16:24-28
PROVERBS 19:16

473 ERRORS

There are some who spend their time searching the scriptures for errors, not in translation or misinterpretation, but errors they feel God Himself has made. There are probably more of these critics than most of us can imagine. This watchman has heard them speak. Some are just ignorant fools, but most are highly educated and believe they have surpassed the understanding of those who actually believe what God has said.

The critics who believe they possess a superior intellect are willing to embrace theories and outright lies that put them in direct opposition to the Creator Himself. This is my idea of a real fool. Nevertheless, it is the Lord's opinion that matters. These fallible professors and theologians have crossed the line and embarked on a path that leads to death. Those who have followed them also love death.

The Spirit of Truth is rebuking some who have been tempted to entertain the error that has been mentioned. The wise response to Him would be to open your heart and ask the all-knowing God to lead you into the truth. It is He who inspired this discourse in order to call some who have wandered from the right way back to the path of life before it is too late.

JAMES 5:19-20
2 TIMOTHY 4:1-4

474 EVALUATION

The information we receive through our senses along with what we experience determines what we have to evaluate. What we think about is actually a choice with consequences. Some let their minds wander without taking control, while others discipline their minds to concentrate on things predetermined to edify.

Our Lord has admonished us and given us guidelines and instructions pertaining to what we choose and allow ourselves to entertain. Our response to Him is the evaluation of what He has said as well as our love for Him, and who we really are.

Thankfulness is a foundation for a proper response to everything, knowing that the will of God and His love for us is all for good. If we really are obedient to Him, we take every thought captive to the obedience of Christ and set our minds on things above where Christ is seated with our Father. This, of course, is only possible by following after the Holy Spirit and setting our minds on things of the Spirit.

If we are truly going to please our heavenly Father and walk as Jesus walked, there is no option other than obedience to the Spirit of Truth with whom we are one. Has this watchman gone too far and exceeded the gospel? Or, is the information that has been given in this discourse not the reality of the written word? We truly have a high calling in Christ, and it is He living in us and through us who will perform it.

The evaluation of the Almighty is the one that has, by far, the most significance and consequence. There is no substitute for having the mind of Christ and His perspective of all things, natural as well as supernatural. He is our life, and our all-in-all.

How great is our God? How wonderful are His ways? Though we try, we only get a glimpse of His glory and greatness. But let us continue to pursue Him wholeheartedly and evaluate ourselves in the light of His truth. Is this not our calling?

EPHESIANS 4:7-16

475 THE COOL OF THE DAY

The Lord still visits His garden just as He has always done. He is available to meet with us, and for the one who sets aside everything else in his/her life and seeks His face, the Lord Himself will reveal Himself and fellowship with us individually. I know this, because I practice it daily.

The beauty of the Creator and all of His creation can be seen by those who will take the time and the effort to observe His wonders. He is indeed calling His children to Himself to be where He is and as He is. Certainly, there is no higher calling. The majesty and magnificence of the works of the Creator surpass all the splendor of the grand cathedrals and all the works of human hands.

All the traps, nets, snares and pits put in place by religious practitioners and the lures of their delicacies of the world do not compare to the glory of our Creator. Their flattery and their smooth speech cannot compare to the excellence of the voice of the Spirit of Truth. Those who are captured by the voice of the immoral woman and her worldly beauty have been deceived by the one who deceived Eve in Eden.

If you doubt what you are hearing you must also doubt God's written record of mankind's journey. Nevertheless, He remains faithful and unchanged and has always loved those of us who fear Him and seek His face. Our God is worthy of all our praise and adoration, and His desire is for fellowship with those who know Him and love Him and walk with Him in His garden in the cool of the morning.

476 INSTRUCTION

Revelation is a form of instruction used by the Holy Counselor. Without it, the people cast off restraint.

Take firm hold of instruction, do not let go; keep her for she is your life . . . He who keeps instruction is in the way of life, but he who refuses correction goes astray . . . He who disdains instruction despises his own soul, but he who heeds rebuke gets understanding. . . The fear of the Lord is the instruction of wisdom, and before honor is humility. . . Cease listening to instruction, my son, and you will stray from the words of knowledge. . . Buy the truth and do not sell it, also wisdom and instruction and understanding. The point is made.

The instruction through revelation is the real form of it that the Spirit of Truth uses to take the things of Jesus and make them real to his saints. We who actually receive this form of instruction no longer require professional religious practitioners to guide us in their interpretations of truth or that of their worldly organizations. The anointing the chosen have received will teach us all things pertaining to life and godliness and how to abide in Christ. The anointing will not allow us to go astray or wander from the truth and the way of understanding.

The instruction we are receiving right now is being given to us in a way the carnal mind will stumble over and require an explanation that religion can confirm. The whole counsel of God and the truth of the gospel, along with the relationship that is not broken by sinful disobedience, is being established. The law of the Spirit of Life in Christ Jesus, along with the Spirit of Truth and the Spirit of Revelation are setting us free from the law of sin and death. Wisdom is instructing us in the ways of God and guiding us on the path of righteousness. This has all been foreordained by our Father for those who are chosen in his Son.

There is no other source of instruction where the riches of God can be discovered. It must come directly from Him—the Source of everything.

ROMANS 6:16-18
2 TIMOTHY 1:13-14
1 JOHN 2:26-27

477 COMMUNICATION

Words are an obvious form of communication, but the Almighty is not limited to words, even though He knows and understands every language used by every creature on earth and in heaven. God uses all our natural senses in order to speak to us but is not restricted to them, either. He speaks to and hears what is communicated through our spirits and even our hearts when we have no words.

The voice of God can be heard and seen in everything He has created. From thunder and lightning to great whirlwinds and earthquakes, His works are all speaking clearly to those who possess the wisdom and understanding to hear. There is no place and no language where His voice cannot be heard.

The real differentiation in how we are able to receive the messages the Lord is sending is based on our relationship with Him individually. Our Father communicates with His created beings as great masses, nations, groups, as well as individuals. The individual who actually knows the Great Creator personally is the one who understands the deep things and the mystery of God.

Wisdom calls out from everywhere, but only a selected few are able to discern the communication being sent. Certainly. any rational person would desire such intimate communication. Nevertheless, most do not. The fool prefers the voices of the world and the lies of the enemies of God. Even many of those who profess to know Him and claim to speak for Him are in delusion and remain in the outer courts of the place where the Creator dwells.

We do have the responsibility to respond to the Spirit of Truth if we hear His voice, but the one who is chosen for this honor must be given the ears to hear and the eyes to see. No one can take this honor for themselves. If you can hear what the Spirit of God is speaking now, the time has come to praise Him and give thanks. He inhabits the praises of His people.

478 ABORTION

From Roe vs. Wade to this hour, the voices of wicked and evil have prevailed in our land. It should be of no surprise to us that the forces of darkness seem to be prevailing in this nation (USA) against our Constitution, laws, and truth itself. The vast majority of politicians, judges, lawyers, bureaucrats, government employees along with most of the corporate media have their hands full of bribes and the blood of innocents.

Do you suppose the Almighty is unaware or does not care? His judgment is here and coming. The whole world, including the USA, has nearly run its course. Sin is a reproach to any nation, and God's definition of sin is prevailing around the world. He is, indeed, involved in social issues, but most of the greedy, self-seeking leaders, as well as those they represent, have become morally bankrupt, as well as monetarily.

The debts are coming due, and innocent blood will be avenged along with the injustice of the legal system and the corruption of the law enforcement bureaucracy.

Good will prevail over evil, just as light will prevail over darkness. Nevertheless, it will get exceedingly dark before the dawn comes. The love of many will grow cold because of the injustice and the unrighteousness that prevails on the earth. Sinners prevail even in the place the world recognizes as "the Church". And, why not? Even their babies are believed to be born sinners. Why not abort them and reduce their sinful influence on the earth? HELLO! You who believe the Lord's little ones who have not reached the age to discern good and evil are sinners; are you able to discern truth and lies?

If judgment begins with us first, what will be the end of those who have not received the love of the truth and do not obey the gospel? Will you be raptured out?

479 UNBELIEVERS

If the righteousness of the unbeliever exceeds that of the one who considers him/herself a believer, where does that leave the one who has named the name of Jesus Christ in the eyes of God as well as the world?

Is the one who calls him/herself a Christian but continues to lie and call him/herself a sinner better off than the unbeliever who does not lie? What does the gospel say of such things? It is clear that the person who says that they know God, yet does not obey His commandments, is a liar and the truth is not in him. Is God a respecter of persons? Does He really favor the one who uses Jesus' name and then puts Him to an open shame by continuing to sin? Is this one not, in fact, worse off than an unbeliever?

The professional would have us believe that God no longer holds the one who has called on Jesus' name accountable for sins he commits after that endorsement of belief. The fact remains that the wages of sin is death. Jesus did not come in the form of human flesh to free Adam's offspring only from the consequences of sin, but from sin itself. He came to put away sin in the flesh.

When unbelievers observe those calling themselves believers continue doing the things that unbelievers do, it causes them to blaspheme God for the hypocrisy of those committing sin and professing that they are forgiven, while the unbeliever is not.

The Lord looks on the heart. The heart of the one who is blameless before Him is the one who fears Him and has turned from his sin. Even though unbelievers may be foolish, how could a just judge hold them accountable for doing what they were created for? The truth is that no person is a sinner before they choose voluntarily to do it. No little child has that ability. In some ways, unbelievers have more wisdom than the believers who have believed they were born sinners, and, even after being born again, continue to be the same as before.

The time has come for those who believe the gospel to obey it and separate ourselves from sinners who don't believe it; that unbelievers may see the difference.

480 THE HILL OF THE LORD

Who may ascend into the hill of the Lord? Or who may stand in His holy place? He who has clean hands and a pure heart, who has not lifted up his soul to an idol nor sworn deceitfully. He shall receive blessing from the Lord and righteousness from the God of his salvation. This is Jacob, the generation of those who seek Him, who seek Your face. Brethren, this was and is the true Israel of God and the eternal generation of Christ.

Clean hands are the hands of those who have been crucified with Christ, ceased their own works, and allow Him to work through them. A pure heart is that of the person who has purified it just as He is pure--through faith and obedience. What is an idol? And how can a person lift up their soul to one, thus committing idolatry? An idol can be anything and covetousness is idolatry. To swear deceitfully comes easily to the one who is living according to the flesh and the lust of it. The person who is subject to bribes is an idolater and will swear deceitfully to satisfy their lust.

Scripture presents many scenarios regarding who may dwell with the Almighty, but none of them include the one who continues to be a sinner. The saints of God have not become saints through their own righteousness or their own good works but by believing God and obeying His Spirit. Can you hear Me, says the Lord? It is only by faith that a person may ascend into my holy hill and the place where I dwell.

No human clergy or institutional representative is able to give passage into the land where the Godhead abides. Only the Spirit of God can give passage through the veil and the gate into the Holy Place.

There is truly an eternal generation, and only those who have been born into it and abide in it have access to the inheritance of Christ and His kingdom.

PSALM 24:3-6

481 WHERE CAN WE GO?

And He said, "Therefore, I have said to you that no one can come to Me unless it has been granted to him by My Father." Then Jesus said to the twelve, "Do you want to go away?" But Simon Peter answered Him, "Lord, to whom shall we go? You have the words of eternal life."

The written letter kills, but the Spirit gives life. The Spirit of Truth is He who actually gives life to those who are able to hear His voice. He does not require a man or a woman to speak through, although He often does. The anointing He has given His chosen teaches us all things, and we do not need a human being to teach us how to know God or how to abide in Christ. It can be helpful to have a person who is truly anointed to help us and point us toward the real Shepherd of our souls, but it is He to whom we must go for salvation.

If we cannot actually find the Spirit of Truth, perhaps it is because we have not received the love of the truth. Why would this be? Is there a remedy? If a person is called by God and is being drawn to Jesus, the solution to receiving the love of the truth is to offer Him the sacrifice of our individual life, which is each person's reasonable service. Once the transaction is made, there remains no more question regarding whose life we are living and to whom we belong. The Holy Spirit is now able to share the eternal life of Jesus with us and manifest it with us. Praise God! The mystery is revealed, and the living gospel has become real and not theoretical. The written word has taken on life.

There is nothing greater or more important that a child and son of God can achieve than to be conformed to the image of Jesus and to walk as He walked.

Let the dead bury their dead.

482 APPEARANCE

Outward appearance and beauty are things with which the world is obsessed. Inner beauty and character are given token deference by the world, while the leaders of our political, religious, and commercial organizations seem to be obsessed with outward things such as race, color, financial prosperity and social standing.

The Lord looks on the heart and places value on things that cannot be outwardly observed. He takes delight in those who fear Him.

The appearance of earthly grandeur such as spectacular cathedrals and huge auditoriums filled with singing sinners are no more than a sign of the age in which we live. The great religions to whom the world's influential and wealthy leaders pay homage have little or no standing with the One to whom real power belongs. All this to say that we who truly know the truth must not join with those who seek after the things that are passing away and have no eternal value.

The things for which the worldly strive are of little value in the eyes of our Creator. The grandeur of earthly riches and worldly glory are but wood, hay and stubble in the eyes of God. We who know Him should know the truth, but many who name the name of Christ seem to be unaware of traps and lures that have been set to cause those who have been called to stumble and fall.

If a person is born of the Spirit, it is that person's responsibility to follow that Spirit. We are given a choice, and the choice we make will determine where and with whom we spend eternity. The appearance of Godliness may fool the world but will not fool the One who knows all the secrets of the heart.

483 EVANGELISM

I remember well the moment that the Holy Spirit came into my heart and lifted the burden of guilt and sin from my soul and filled me with the love of Jesus. I could not wait to tell the nearest person what my Savior had done. Everything changed, and my life was set on a new course. This is the testimony of many who have truly been born of the Spirit.

In the following days, there were numerous voices of well-meaning people telling me to go here or there and to listen to this and that and to read this book or that instruction manual. Religious people can be very aggressive in trying to recruit a newly regenerated, blameless babe into their franchised brand of Christendom. I truly was pushed around, but the Holy Spirit gave me a love and a hunger for the Bible itself. He has been faithful to this day.

To see a newly reborn babe who has experienced the redemption of Jesus is a pure delight, but this watchman has seen many such newborns recruited into cults, denominations, and even totally false organizations. Those who yield to these "separatarian" groups usually lose their genuine enthusiasm for Christ and His gospel in exchange for denominational doctrines and dogma. Once they become thoroughly indoctrinated, they are sent out as professional missionaries to disseminate the form of oftentimes false doctrines they have learned. Is this not a tragedy?

Hear Me, says the Lord. My doctrine is pure, and the one who actually serves me must be able to discern between the true and the false. There can be no compromise. The true evangelist chosen and sent by Me must be able to see what I am doing and hear My voice and not the voice of an organized religion. The salvation for which I gave My life is salvation from sin and death and Oneness with Myself, not an institution of man. The evangelism of the Spirit adds members to My kingdom and not the kingdoms of mankind's organizations. Man's organizations and denominations are of the world and will likewise perish with the world.

If you can hear Me, says the Lord, then surely you know what you must do and the message you must carry to those who have gone astray.

This is the final hour. I am coming for a spotless Bride.

484 FOOD FOR THE SPIRIT

For to be carnally minded is death, but to be spiritually minded is life and peace. He who sows to the flesh will of the flesh reap corruption, but he who sows to the Spirit will of the Spirit reap life everlasting.

Will so-called "carnal Christians" actually enter the place of eternal life? It appears not. To eat the food that nourishes our spirit requires knowing what it is and making the effort to secure it. *Jesus said, "The words I speak are Spirit and they are life." . . . Then Jesus said to them, "Most assuredly I say to you, unless you eat the flesh of the Son of Man and drink His blood, you have no life in you. Whoever eats My flesh and drinks My blood has eternal life, and I will raise him up at the last day. For My flesh is food indeed, and My blood is drink indeed. He who eats My flesh and drinks My blood abides in Me and I in him." He who abides in Christ does not sin.* Hello, Christian sinners!

Spiritual food often takes on the form of metaphors and parables, and must be Spiritually discerned. Without the Spirit of Life, the carnally minded are left in darkness, whether or not they call themselves Christians.

The positionalists must be so, because only the Spiritually minded are able to experience the reality of the spiritual metaphors regarding being seated in heavenly places and hidden with Christ in God. To actually be One Spirit with Him is just too much for the one living according to the flesh. In order to actually walk in all that the gospel has told us is unattainable for the carnally minded who live according to the flesh. For this reason, there have been produced doctrines depicting two natures and ongoing sin. Unless the old man (nature) has actually died and a new person has been born in his place, the reality of being "born again" is only theory.

This, brethren, is Spiritual food that produces life in the soul of the one who is able to really believe it and walk in it. The person who has actually overcome is now able to eat from "the tree of life" and drink freely from the "river of life" that flows from the throne of God NOW!

So says the Spirit of Truth.

485 SIGNIFICANCE

What is the significance of belonging to Christ? Much, in every way. In Him the mystery of the origin of life and all that exists is explained. Could not the Creator of everything seen and unseen become a man and walk the earth if He so chose? Well, He has; and now we have Him as a pattern of what mankind was originally intended to be.

All that the Creator created human beings to be has become a reality for those who have become one with Jesus. He not only showed us His Father's plan but has now made it possible for us who love Him to fulfill it as well. All things are possible for those who abide in Jesus. Is this not spectacularly significant?

Those who seek the Lord understand all things. This is the destiny of those who have become chosen in Christ to become all that we are meant to be. Could anything be more fulfilling or satisfying? Surely, God is making Himself and His ways known to those who diligently seek Him and obey His voice. There is nothing higher or more significant than experiencing the love of God.

I have written to encourage all of you who hunger and thirst for righteousness and truth to maintain your vigilance and hope. There is a hereafter, and God is faithful and will fulfill every promise to those who wait for Him and are faithful to the end. We have more trials to face, but our Savior will not leave us to face them alone. He reveals His strength through our weakness, and we glorify Him by believing in His promises and trusting Him.

The final conflict is near at hand, and the outcome is determined. Our faith will assure our personal victory over our enemies as well as His. He is mighty in battle, and there is no force that can prevail against Him.

Be faithful to the end, and your inheritance will be sure and significant.

486 FAMINE

The scarcity of truth in the public arena has encompassed the whole earth. The drought is the famine that plagues the masses throughout the world. Fear and confusion prevail among the inhabitants who dwell on the earth.

The thing that most grieves this watchman's heart is to see those who God is calling turn to the multitude of religious voices that emanate from the government-regulated churches and institutions. Also, the hosts of TV and radio evangelists and teachers, preachers, and prophets, who nearly all are proclaiming perversions and misappropriations of truth and salvation.

The truth is certainly available but only to those who have received the love of it and learned to receive it from its Source.

Nearly all the voices that are heard in the public domain are spreading lies and misinformation in an attempt to establish their own objectives. Those who listen to them and believe them are pawns in the grand scheme to give power to the forces that want to control humankind and the world.

If you can hear the truth being presented, there is no need to fear or be disillusioned. The Spirit of Truth is speaking now and will continue doing so to everyone who has put their trust in Him. He speaks directly to His chosen and has no need to use the voices of those who have gained control of mass media and social acceptance.

Information has never been more readily available, but truth has never been more difficult to find and discern. Without the Spirit who gives discernment, a person is helpless in the effort to escape the famine and the plagues that have come upon mankind.

Truth is a great gift, as is the One from whom it springs.

487 WILLINGNESS

Love itself goes beyond feeling to an act of will. *Your people shall be volunteers (willing) in the day of Your power.* Willingness and self-sacrifice are the qualifiers for true usefulness to God. No self-gratification or self-glorification is able to pass into the oneness with the Savior that makes a person an actual servant of God. Education and desire do not pass the test, nor does the approval of man.

If we are indeed willing to obey the voice of God, the ability to perform His will becomes His own ability to perform it in and through us. We all know that God's will is that we not sin. He is able to perform what His will dictates if we love Him with all our heart, soul, mind and strength. It is the power of Almighty God Himself who enables us to carry out His desire. Does the Holy Spirit not bear witness to this truth? Only a fool would dispute it.

Our will is the battleground where the Spirit and the flesh engage in conflict. *The flesh lusts against the Spirit and the Spirit against the flesh. If you live according to the flesh you will die, but if by the Spirit you put to death the deeds of the body (flesh) you will live. For as many as are led by the Spirit of God these are sons of God.*

What you are hearing is an invitation to pass through the "Gates of Righteousness", says the Lord. This is the gate through which the righteous must enter in order to abide in Christ and walk with Him. Superficial confession and intellectual believing assent to the truth will not produce the experiential confirmation needed to be chosen in Christ. A true hunger and thirst for righteousness and truth does produce the willingness needed to please our heavenly Father.

Anything less will not pass into the land where He dwells, and anything less will not permit people to be brethren of Jesus.

Without holiness no one will see God.

488 FEEDING SHEEP

Deliver those who are drawn toward death and hold back those stumbling to the slaughter. The Lord used this Proverb as a directive to me and has shown this watchman its application.

Commercial feedlots are set up to prepare animals (sheep) for slaughter. It is not dissimilar to the commercial institutional franchised religious organizations who are feeding their sheep processed food with little nutritional value. Just as the processed food sold at "fast food restaurants" and supermarkets, the processed doctrines shared by many of the religious franchises deliver instant gratification and a feeling of well-being but have very little eternal value.

The point is unless the sheep are turned away from sin and converted to righteousness, what they are being fed will not deliver them from slaughter and death. When sin is promoted as the inescapable condition and nature of a sheep, there is no escape. The Lord says that escapes from death belong to Him, as does the deliverance from the sin that is the cause of death. The professionals are lying in order to enlarge their flocks, in order to fulfill their lust for wealth and recognition.

What they are feeding the sheep who the Spirit of God is calling is food that inoculates them from the life-sustaining truth that can set them free from disaster. Sin is the poison that ultimately causes the destruction of the soul that is unable to cease and escape its grip. The franchised doctrines of the commercial feedlots will not produce the strength sheep need to escape their captors.

Truth is the remedy and the only means of deliverance.

Flee for your lives, sheep of God. The "Good Shepherd" is calling you out of the professional's pasture (feedlot) where you are being held captive.

With love—the watchman.

489 THE LIVING GOD

What a delight to speak of a "Living God", when we see the gods of the peoples and the gods of the nations who have no life in them dominate the world! The unseen God of true Israel is He who rules over all and has the real power and loves righteousness and peace. We who serve this God are they who are truly blessed.

Man's life is but a vapor, or a passing shadow, but those who know the "Living God" have hope and security that the rest of mankind has no knowledge of. Those who put their trust in the gods of this world are lost, and whatever hope they may have is false without substance.

We who know the God of the Bible have the confidence and assurance that everything taking place here on earth will work out for our good, because we love the "Living God" and he has told us it is so. There is nowhere else that a person can turn to find such comfort and rest in the midst of the turmoil that has come upon the world. The "Living God" is still available to the one who will seek Him with their whole heart, but the time is near when He will not be able to be found. This will be a time when all the false gods will be exposed for what they are, and those who serve them will be destined to remain without the life that can only be found and experienced in the "Living God".

In that day, multitudes will cry out "Lord, Lord", but He will not answer or open His door, because they refused to hear Him and obey His voice in a time when He could be found. This includes those who have known His name but refused to obey Him and do His will.

The "Living God" is a fearsome but loving God, not willing that any should perish, but many will, indeed, perish because of their own wrong choices and decisions.

Today is the day of salvation. There is no guarantee for tomorrow.

PSALMS 32:6
2 CORINTHIANS 6:2

490 TRUSTED STRONGHOLDS

A wise man scales the city of the mighty and brings down the trusted strongholds. The Lord has again used a Proverb to commission this watchman. The strongholds where many sinners find refuge and feel secure in their flesh is under siege as you read these words.

This stronghold is the many institutions of higher learning and their denominational offspring. The walls of these cities are fortified with lies and elaborate, complex doctrines and theories carefully crafted to make the word of God not say what it says. Those who subscribe to their heresy are rewarded with a license to continue sinning without receiving the penalty for sin. The security they offer is no more than the lie the serpent spoke to Eve in Eden, *"You shall not surely die". . . "Has God indeed said?"*

The real enemy that seekers of truth and righteousness face is the one who disguises himself as an angel of light. His perversion has filled the strongholds with doctrines and fables, and he has sent out his ministers disguised as preachers of righteousness to deceive those whom the Holy Spirit is drawing to Jesus. The Lord is calling many who have been lured into these strongholds and places of artificial security.

The true salvation of God is in Jesus and the place where He dwells. There is no refuge there for the person who has not overcome the dominance of their flesh. Freedom is in Jesus, and there is no sin in Him.

If anyone is able to hear and understand what is being said, you have a responsibility to make the truth known and to deliver those drawn to death. This is a deadly serious battle, and we who know the truth must engage.

Sin is the issue and the very reason Christ came to earth.

ROMANS 8:1-4

491 EXPOSURE

Exposure of lies by the illumination of truth is one of the weapons God has supplied to the soldiers of righteousness in His army. We who have received the love of the truth are commissioned to use the truth to defeat the forces attempting to make it of no effect. The forces and the armies have gathered from Washington, D.C. to Rome in the political realm as well as the spiritual.

This watchman and those who believe him are among the forces of righteousness taking a stand in order to expose the tyranny and heresy going on in the public arenas of the world. Our enemies are the forces of darkness attempting to subvert and eliminate the power of truth. We who love truth are on the winning side of the conflict regardless of how dark it gets; though many of us may have to give our lives in the struggle, Satan will be crushed under our feet shortly.

In the end the righteous will be exalted and the wicked and all sinners will be exposed along with their lies. The masses who have believed them will join them in the place for the devil and the false prophets as well as "the Mother of Harlots".

The fulfillment of the prophecy is near, and the battle is taking place as you read these words. The souls of mankind are in the balance, and true righteousness and holiness are on trial, just as Jesus was on trial before the political and religious leaders of His day. We, too, are on trial as all the holy prophets and believers who have known God throughout recorded history.

Let us be sure we have put our faith and hope in the place of true safety and salvation.

Everything shall be made known (exposed).

2 CORINTHIANS 4:1-6
MATTHEW 10:24-26

492 TREADING

The battle is on, and the saints of the Lord are his chosen weapons of war. He has told us that we would tread down our enemies. *Behold, I give you the authority to trample on serpents and scorpions and over all the power of the enemy. . . . You shall tread upon the lion and the cobra, the young lion and the serpent you shall trample under foot. We are not helpless victims with regard to sin or the enemies of righteousness.* Our power is in Jesus, just as our salvation. He is the true Shepherd.

For the idols speak delusion; the diviners envision lies and tell false dreams; they comfort in vain. Therefore, the people wend their way like sheep; they are in trouble because there is no shepherd. My anger is kindled against the shepherds, and I will punish the goatherds. For the Lord of Hosts will visit His flock, the house of Judah, and will make them as His royal horse in the battle. From him comes the cornerstone, from him comes the tent peg, from him the battle bow, from him every ruler together. They shall be like mighty men who tread down their enemies in the mire of the streets in the battle.

Are you up for it, brethren? The Good Shepherd is moving, and those who hear His voice must follow. We are engaged, whether we like it or not, and He will honor those who follow His Spirit.

Let the saints be joyful in glory; let them sing aloud on their beds. Let the high praises of God be in their mouth and a two-edged sword in their hand to execute vengeance on the nations (denomi) and punishment on the peoples; to bind their kings with chains and their nobles with fetters of iron; to execute on them the written judgment—this honor have all His saints.

The fence is teetering, and those sitting on it have but a short time to answer the call that the Spirit is making before it collapses.

You can only serve one master.

PSALMS 60:11-12

493 CRISIS

The watchman is crying, "Wolf, Wolf", and the crisis is not imaginary. The signs of the end can be seen at every level of nature and humanity. The breakdown of nations and borders are unprecedented as are the calamities of nature.

The wolves and the beasts of the earth have surrounded those who love righteousness and truth while the religious are in delusion regarding the knowledge of God and the truth of the gospel. There is but one place of refuge from the impending disaster coming upon the whole world. Those who crave power and wealth are willing to destroy the USA and all of humanity to satisfy their lust.

Jesus is coming, but it will be a day of darkness for everyone who has taken His name in vain. The eagles have gathered, and the violent are attempting to take the kingdom by force. The bloodthirsty who serve the flesh would destroy the "true Israel of God" in order to further their own kingdoms and their own glory. If you have eyes to see, they are all around us, singing and flattering God while serving themselves. His anger is near the point of ending the world as we have known it.

The wicked who have made plans to control the world and all of humanity will be consumed by the indignation of the Almighty, while we who love His appearing will receive our reward and our inheritance.

Be ready; you know not the day or the hour.

494 PIOUS BEASTS

There is a generation that is pure in its own eyes yet is not washed from its filthiness. There is a generation—O, how lofty are their eyes! And their eyelids lifted up. There is a generation whose teeth are like swords and whose fangs are like knives to devour the poor from off the earth and the needy from *among men.* Is this not the same generation that crucified Jesus? They are still here, and their religious delusion is unchanged.

Beasts of the earth are they who bear the mark and the image of the man formed of the dust. They have been here since the first generation and the first murder. They are metaphorically depicted as wolves, bulls of Bashan, roaring lions and bloodthirsty beasts. These beastly impostors are capable of making long, elaborate, rehearsed prayers in order to demonstrate their piety and devotion.

Fervent lips with a wicked heart are like earthenware covered with silver dross. He who hates disguises it with his lips and lays up deceit within himself. When he speaks kindly, do not believe him, for there are seven abominations in his heart; though his hatred is covered by deceit, his wickedness will be revealed *before the assembly.* These are the flattering voices we hear from the beasts whose right hands are full of bribes. They are dogs that continually howl, because they are hungry for the food that satisfies their flesh and their hungry mouths.

Any who do make gifts to them are surely aware of their tax-exempt government-sponsored standing and their recognition by the world. They are peddlers of the gospel and have sold their souls to fulfill their lust. Yes, they are indeed sinners, but not members of the Body of Christ.

Sinners do not abide in Him.

495 TYPES

The first shall be last, and the last shall be first. The older shall serve the younger. There is a pattern well-established in scripture that portrays Messiah.

Adam betrayed his Creator and lost his relationship and his place in the Lord's Garden. His firstborn son, Cain, violated the law that was yet unwritten and killed his younger brother, Abel, because he was angry that God received Abel's offering and not his.

Abraham was a type of the Father. He had two sons. The first was Ishmael, who was born to a concubine. His second son, Isaac, was the son of promise born to his wife. Isaac also had two sons. The first was Esau; the second was Jacob. God loved Jacob but hated Esau.

The paradigm continues throughout the Bible with the sons of Joseph, the kings of Israel on up to the birth of Jesus. All these examples of first and last, younger and older are actually types of flesh and Spirit. They are all types of the first Adam and the "last Adam", who is the primary subject of all of scripture. The first Adam was the flesh man of the earth who forfeited his inheritance to fulfill the lust of his flesh. Jesus, the "second and last Adam" is the Spiritual Son who is also the "firstborn" of a new race of spiritual human beings that are born of God.

In Christ, the first Adam's offspring are put to death and the "last Adam's" Spiritual offspring arise with the ability to always do the things that please the Father, just as Jesus did and has shown us.

That which is born of flesh is flesh; that which is born of Spirit is spirit. Dead is dead. In Adam all die. In Christ all live. The flesh comes first, and then the Spirit. If we who are born of the Spirit walk in the Spirit, we will not fulfill the lust of the flesh.

This is the heart of the gospel and the plan of the Father.

Sin shall no longer have power over the one born of God, who walks in the Spirit as the "Firstborn of many brethren" has shown us. Jesus has restored, through His obedience, what Adam lost through disobedience. We, too, are given the right as well as the ability to maintain the relationship that Adam lost. Jesus is the "Tree of Life" and has given us access to Himself through His Spirit.

We now have a choice to follow the "first Adam" or the "last Adam". *If you live according to the flesh you will die, but if by the Spirit you put to death the deeds of the body, you will live. For those who follow after the Spirit of God, these are the sons of God.*

Let the dead bury their dead, says the Lord. You follow Me. You can choose the type you will follow.

496 FRUIT

You shall know them by their fruit. Whatever a person sows, that they shall also reap. This is true in all realms of existence. The violence and the tyranny we see in liberally controlled cities, counties and states in America are glaring examples of the fruit of their beliefs and managements. What these people are reaping is the judgment of God in response to their wickedness. Only a fool is unable to see the direct correlation between the liberal philosophy and control and the unrest and destruction taking place.

When observing the pandemic, any objective person is able to see where the worst of it has struck. This is not an accident. If it were planned to punish bad behavior and mismanagement it could not be more accurately targeted. The Almighty does not need to be defended. Wisdom is exonerated by her children, and justice for man comes from the Lord. God's laws are absolute and cannot be broken without consequence.

A person's religious persuasion, political views, and even race have no bearing on the law. A person will reap what they sow, and if their fruit is rotten and detestable, there is a reason. On careful examination of the person whose life is miserable it is usually of their own making. There are not nearly as many victims as liberals and special interest groups would have us believe.

Right is right, wrong is wrong. Truth is not arbitrary, and lie are lies no matter what persuasion, gender, color or race of the one speaking them. It is the Creator who establishes what is right and wrong, good and evil. He is the only One with the power to enforce the edicts He has made. He is doing it whether anyone can see it or not.

The idea of petitioning God to be on our side is futile unless a person actually knows His will. If a person has wisdom, he or she will make every effort to be on the side of God. The opinion of fools is worth less than nothing, and anyone who believes there is no God is certainly a fool.

PROVERBS 11:31; 14:34
LUKE 6:43-45

497 RESISTANCE

Resistance can lead to life or death depending on who or what a person is resisting. If a person is submitted to the Lord, he/she has the power to resist the devil and he will flee. On the other hand, if a person resists the Holy Spirit and will not relent, eternal death is inevitable.

He who is often rebuked and hardens his heart shall suddenly be destroyed without remedy. I have witnessed a person close to me resist truth in favor of lying spirits come suddenly to a mental breakdown from which she has not recovered.

Pharaoh resisted the God of Jacob to the extent that his whole country was ravaged, and the firstborn of every family and every animal was killed. When Paul contended with the religious leaders of his day he declared, "You always resist the Holy Spirit; as your fathers did, so do you."

As believers, resisting temptation and the deceitfulness of sin is the way to abide in Christ and hold the beginning of our confidence steadfast to the end. God is faithful not to allow us to be tempted beyond our ability to resist, and with the temptation will provide a way of escape. There is no justification for sin if we abide in Christ.

Daniel, as well as Shadrach, Meshach, and Abed-Nego, certainly resisted the power of the king who believed he had the power to kill them, but their God overruled. The list could go on, and many of the Lord's saints and prophets have resisted unto death, including Stephen and most of Jesus' first apostles.

Those who resist the will of God have always hated those who resist wickedness and sin. This phenomenon is glaringly obvious in society today. We who love the Lord are the people called to resist the tyranny and lawlessness that has risen to power in our midst. We are the standard of righteousness the Lord is raising against the enemies of God.

If not us, who?

HEBREWS 2:10-11; 4:14-16

498 ANTICHRIST

The mystery of The Antichrist is not so mysterious to the one who is able to identify the many antichrist spirits among us who have been here from the beginning. The spirit of antichrist is the spirit that denies that the Son of God came to earth in the flesh. This is the one who sits on the throne in his or her own temple.

Antichrist is but a type and an image of the spirit of a person who is energized by Satan and has become his or her own god. This spirit is not unique in its declaration that Jesus has not come as a Man in the flesh. This spirit bears the mark of the beast on the hand and forehead of its host.

The actual incarnation of Antichrist, the individual man, is near, but he should be of no surprise to anyone who knows the Savior. There is but one true Savior who has appeared in human flesh to save His people from sin and death. He will also appear again soon, and His appearance will destroy the Antichrist by the power of His Spirit.

All the prophecies will be fulfilled, and the fearsome Antichrist will be revealed by the brightness of the Lord's coming with His saints and His holy angels.

We are not to fear the Antichrist or the multitude of antichrist spirits we must face. Certainly, Jesus has conquered them all, and we are merely waiting for the manifestation of what Christ has already accomplished. Is a great mystery not herein revealed? Praise God!

You need not spend money, buy books, go to endless seminars, listen to endless sermons speculating about the Antichrist and who and where he is. If you abide in Christ, you will understand it all soon enough.

Let the God of Israel be magnified!

2 THESSALONIANS 1:3-12; 2:1-12

499 THE SPIRIT OF ANTICHRIST

The spirit of antichrist is the spirit of a person which would diminish or negate what the Son of God accomplished as a man. To be clear, Christ came in the likeness of sinful flesh to put away sin in the flesh. "Whose flesh?" you may ask. Certainly not His own; He knew no sin.

The spirit that would have us believe we cannot be free from sin while in a human body is the same spirit that confesses that Jesus did not come in the flesh, thus denying that what He was sent to do was a failure. Can you see the error of the one who tells you that you can be a Christian and still be a sinner? This may be hard to hear, but such a person actually has a spirit of antichrist.

Many well-meaning preachers and teachers of the gospel have been deceived into believing the lie that Satan has perpetrated into the doctrines of countless institutions and denominations who are teaching their followers that they remain sinners after being set free from sin. I have heard it and seen it. The indisputable truth is that a person who has been born of the Spirit of God has been set free from sin.

Sin is what separates a person from the life of God. The one who sins willfully after receiving a knowledge of the truth has no more sacrifice to save them from their sins, but has only the expectation of judgment. It is not possible to be one Spirit with Christ while being one spirit with antichrist.

I'm aware that what you are hearing sounds radical, but what does the Bible really say? A person must be trained to make it not say what it does say.

Let us stick to the simple truth.

1 JOHN 3:4-9; 4:1-3

500 INNOCENCE

The newborn baby is considered by most to be innocent in spite of Babylon's teaching that they are all sinners. When these newborns enter the world, everything is new to them, and all that they experience is shaping who they are and who they will be. These little innocent ones surely respond to love. When the time of accountability comes and they follow the way of their earthly parents and choose the way that ends in death, every one of them needs a savior.

Those who God calls find such a Savior. He renews them and they become "born again". This birth is supernatural and their new Father is God Himself. Everything becomes new, and old things pass away. This is the miracle that restores the innocence of the newborn baby. Their sins are washed away, and they have become new creations. These innocent new babes are free from sin and the dominance of their flesh and their former nature inherited from their first parents. They now have received the nature of their new Father, God Himself.

If this newborn babe obeys his/her new parent, they need not return to the sinful ways of the old person, who is now dead. Innocence and blamelessness are now a reality that must be maintained with great diligence. This new person will go astray if he or she is careless or lured off the path of righteousness.

There are countless representatives of established religion who will counsel these newborns that they remain sinners in spite of the fact that they are new creations born in the image of their Creator. What you are hearing is the reality of modern Christianity and the published doctrine of nearly all denominations and established institutions. They are exposed as you read these words, and no newborn, spiritual babe needs to lose their newfound innocence because of the lie of Satan and his ministers disguised in religious garb.

Ultimately, each one of us must stand before God and give account of what we have done with what he has given us. He has surely given us everything that pertains to life and godliness, which includes His very nature.

Sin is a choice and we are and will be held accountable for our choices, whether we call ourselves "Christians" or not.

Pleading the blood or blaming our teachers will not change the reality of whether we have obeyed the voice of God and abided in Christ or not.

In the end only innocence and blamelessness are what counts.

501 TRADITIONS

Traditions can be beneficial if they promote and build a personal relationship with our Lord. Daniel had a tradition of praying to God facing toward Jerusalem three times a day. He was certainly blessed by God. Wisdom tells us that the person who listens to her (wisdom) watching daily at wisdom's gates and waits at the posts of wisdom's doors is blessed. *For whoever finds wisdom finds life, finds favor from the Lord.* This, too, is a tradition this watchman has observed to great benefit.

Traditions initiated by many of the institutional churches and taught by clergy have a detrimental effect on personal relationship and ongoing fellowship with the Lord. Many such churches have established hierarchies of Nicolaitans who stand above their congregations, putting themselves in the position of a mediator between the laity and the Lord. Both the deeds and the doctrines of these Nicolaitans are something Jesus hates. These multi-level professionals are actually discouraging those who hunger and thirst for righteousness and truth from developing relationship with their Savior for which their soul yearns.

Traditions which are observed without real understanding, true devotion and heartfelt enthusiasm are of no value. The list of useless traditions carried on by religious hypocrites is extensive and disgusting, as is their liturgy and the bogus sacraments they observe.

Come out of her, My people that you do not partake of her sins and receive of the plagues coming upon her.

There is but one mediator between God and man, the Man Jesus Christ.

MATTHEW 6:7-8
MARK 7:6-9

502 MEDITATION

If we are able to slow down, and if we are willing to take time out and think on the things of God and meditate on what He has said and his wonderful works, our spirits are enabled to escape the limits of the natural as well as the confines of time. What is being spoken of is a place where revelation is the norm, and Spiritual understanding and discernment become reality.

Is this not the place where the Lord has told us that we are seated with Him and hidden in God? We are being called to this heavenly place where the perspectives of the material world fade into temporary and passing significance, and our flesh takes on a subservient existence. This is the place where sin loses its deceptive quality, and the tempter has no access.

As we meditate on what God has said and done, His power and authority, His greatness and glory overshadow everything in the natural, biological creation. When our minds and hearts are set on heavenly things and things of eternal value, the riches of the world and our temporary existence in it become what they really are—passing distractions and insignificant wastes of our devotion and energy.

Has our Creator not told us to think and talk of Him continually? He surely knows what is best for us. Our labor here on earth is only for the subsistence of our bodies that will return to dust, while the spirit within our bodies will go on into eternity. If the work done in our bodies is Spiritual and is actually being performed by Christ living through us, those works have eternal value and will follow us into eternity.

This admonition should surely give us pause to meditate and set our minds on things above where Christ is seated with God.

PSALMS 63:6-8; 77:11-14; 19:14; 119:97-104
1 TIMOTHY 4:15-16

503 ALL LIVES MATTER

The Creator, the God of all creation, takes delight in His created beings and is an impartial judge rewarding every individual according to their deeds. There is no way to escape the just reward of His hand. Jesus gave His life for all mankind and makes no distinctions based on color or origin, although He does show favor toward those who fear Him and speak the truth in their hearts.

To base value or worth on different groups because of color or social status is an injustice to every individual person. This type of bigotry is the work of fools void of honesty and wisdom. Any person who allows himself to be identified and evaluated according to the group or community in which they reside has succumbed to the lie of the one who would divide and oppress whole groups of people for their own selfish and evil agenda.

Each individual person has unique and intrinsic value based on the Creator's design. The person who denies his or her uniqueness, and the personal responsibility to God for it, has lied to him/herself in his/her own heart. The salvation that the Almighty has provided for all people is the escape from lies and spiritual death.

What person in their right mind would choose to be part of a group filled with hatred and rebellion rather than one filled with love and righteousness where color or origin have no influence? This is precisely the choice each one of us is being given by our Creator.

Truth will prevail and every lying tongue will be cut off.

So says the Lord.

P.S. The only group worth being associated with is the one which has become One Spirit with God!

DO UNTO OTHERS MATTHEW 7:12

504 WHEN YOU PRAY

The fervent prayer of a righteous person avails much. Who can actually gain audience with the Almighty? How can we know that He hears us and will answer our petitions? There is really no point in praying at all if there is no chance that God will hear.

When you pray do not be like the Gentiles (uncircumcised in heart) who think they will be heard for their *much speaking*. Do you have a rosary? Do you pray to the dead on behalf of the living? There is but one God and one Mediator between God and mankind. If we are to be heard by the Lord, our request must be according to His will. Then we have assurance that He will hear us and respond to our petitions.

So, who can actually approach His throne and enter His dwelling? *He who has clean hands and a pure heart who has not lifted his or her soul to an idol.* The Most High cannot be bribed, and a vow to attend church services is an insult. The Lord wants your whole heart and your whole life and all that you have and are. Can anyone actually believe that they will be heard because of repetitions, prearranged prayers void of any real significance?

The notion of praying to the dead for the dead is about the most absurd, religious nonsense imaginable. Anyone who really wants to be responded to by the Lord must know and believe that He alone is God, and the rewarder of those who diligently seek Him.

What is being said here may seem faith threatening or disingenuous, but it is, in fact, the truth spoken in love to all who have been misled and deceived by religious spirits and doctrines of demons. The Lord's ears are open to those who love Him with all their heart, soul, mind and strength.

The Almighty is capable of hearing and answering every prayer made to Him only without the help of departed saints and icons and religious clergy. He waits for the prayer of His anointed and chosen ones, and they are His delight.

This discourse is dedicated to God's called-out ones who remain in Babylon.

1 JOHN 5:21

505 DEAD WORKS

The works initiated by the carnal mind and performed by uncrucified flesh are but wood, hay, and stubble, as well as chaff blown away by the wind. The time has come to evaluate all that we think, say, and do. This is what our Lord is requiring of His chosen. This is not complicated for the one whose life is hidden in Christ and is following His Spirit.

Religiously directed busyness is usually carnally directed to keep the fleshly-minded busy in an attempt to make them feel like they are pleasing God. The fact is that only the things initiated by Him please Him. If we have entered His promised rest and ceased our fleshly endeavors, we are able to perform the works that will follow us into eternity. The anointing of the Holy Spirit and obedience to Him is the only way to delight our Savior. This is precisely how Jesus pleased His Father and how we are enabled to walk as Jesus walked.

This is truly exciting to us who have been chosen to do it. What you are reading is an example of such anointing. This watchman did not choose this course by his own initiative or because of natural ability. The Lord has commissioned me to instruct and encourage those whom He is calling to Himself. If you are indeed chosen, the gates of righteousness along with the mysteries of God are open to you, and you are able to enter the "land of the living" NOW. Your position is real, and only your physical body must wait for transformation when Jesus makes His appearance.

The Lord says, let the religious positionalists speculate about the things of the Spirit and the future of the dead church, but you follow Me and trust Me. If you abide in Me, you are secure, and your fate is assured. The one living according to the flesh has no such assurance nor the promise of eternal life regardless of what a pastor may have said.

Jesus is the way, the truth, and the life. He is the only way to the Father in heaven.

506 WHERE ARE THEY?

The professional theologians, professors, the worldly wise, the wealthy, the influential, the debaters of this age, along with the princes of Ecclesia are surely not abiding in Christ nor have they understood His ways or entered His rest. They are mostly all on the outside trying to convince humanity that they know the way into the kingdom of heaven. They are actually barriers and hindrances to those who hunger and thirst for righteousness and truth who have their hearts set on pilgrimage.

Most of the entire religious system that the world knows as the "church" is but a façade covering a diabolical scheme to perpetrate the sin Jesus died to free us from, and to make us think we are right with God while not observing his most elementary command. The clergy are trained to take captive the poor and needy and are largely successful in luring them into their traps. They don't realize the nets they have spread have also captured themselves.

From outside the true "Body of Christ" the religious decoys seem to have merit, but as a whole they represent confusion which is Babylon. There is no hope for her. She is destroyed along with all her merchants and those fornicating with her. If you have eyes to see and ears to hear, you know this is truth.

Righteousness as defined by God is the way into His kingdom, and there are none righteous who continue to sin and do not change. Sinners will not be able to stand in the judgment but will be cast down and will never enter the place or experience the things God has prepared for those who love Him.

It is not really so difficult to see who is where if you know God.

507 THE LAST DAY

"The last day," "the day of the Lord," will be a fearsome day for the inhabitants of the earth. What a person believes does affect what they do. There are many elaborate and complex theories and much speculation produced by the carnal minds of religious practitioners. The "Mind of Christ" is far less complicated and reveals truth by revelation.

What has the Lord actually said about His second coming and His appearance before all Creation? Precise times and dates remain a mystery, but signs and events abound. Nevertheless, Jesus has told us that He would come unexpectedly; every eye would see Him. Paul has told us that we who remain on earth when He appears will not precede those who are in the grave. Jesus said, "This is the will of the Father who sent Me that of all He has given Me, I should lose nothing but should raise it up at 'the last day,' and this is the will of Him who sent Me that everyone who sees the Son and believes in Him may have everlasting life, and I will raise him up at the 'last day.'" Does this not indicate that the "last day" is the day of His appearing, second coming, and the catching away of those who are ready and waiting?

His "second coming," His appearance, and the "last day," as well as the "Day of the Lord" all seem to coincide.

The "last day" is the end of earthly time and all the systems of the world we have known. We will all be thrust into eternity, and the final judgment for all who have lived on earth will occur. Every person will be judged according to the works they have done. This includes those who have been given the opportunity to be conformed to the image of Jesus or not.

What we believe definitely will be revealed by the mark each person bears on their forehead and hand. Are we earthly beings (beasts), or are we heavenly beings (citizens of heaven)?

There will be no place to hide and no excuses given voice. Sinners will not be able to stand in the congregation of the righteous.

508 RECOGNITION

This watchman is excited to be able to respond to some questions I have often heard but had no actual scriptural response. I have heard people ask if they would see their loved ones and friends in heaven and how would they recognize them.

The Lord has told us who abide in Him to no longer know one another after the flesh but after the spirit. When the apostles asked Jesus to show them the Father, his response was, *"If you had known Me, you would have known My Father also; and from now on you know Him and have seen Him . . . Have I been with you so long and yet you have not known Me? The one who has seen Me has seen the Father."*

We who abide in the Spirit are able to know and recognize one another after the spirit even now. Think about it! Where is our true fellowship? Who are the ones we truly want to associate and fellowship with? Are they not our brethren in the Lord?

Spiritual things must be spiritually discerned, not only here on earth but also in heaven. The journey that begins here will certainly be expanded and intensified when we leave our mortal bodies behind. If we are indeed seated in heavenly places now, surely, we who know as we are known will have the ability to recognize and appreciate our loved ones and friends in that place. Unfortunately, only those who abide in Christ now will be there; those who have become one Spirit with Him.

Eye has not seen, ear has not heard the things God has prepared for those who love Him, but He has revealed them to us through His Spirit who dwells in us.

We know that when Jesus appears, we will recognize Him, because we will be like Him. The person who has this hope should purify him or herself just as He is pure. Wow!

LUKE 24:13-32
2 CORINTHIANS 5:16

509 EQUITY (WITHOUT APOLOGY)

Justice for mankind comes from the Lord. The sea is raging and the people clamoring for equity, but nowhere can it be found on earth. Truth has become relative, and the multitude of self-interest factions all pursue what is right in their own eyes.

Where can righteousness and justice actually be found? God has established such a reality in Jacob, the true Israel of God, the Body of Christ, His true church. This is not "pie in the sky" of which I speak but an actual, spiritual people who have believed the truth and submitted themselves to it. Naysayers and detractors may mock and slander such a proclamation, but such scoffers are but fools demonstrating their ignorance.

Hear Me says the Lord. I am the "Just Judge" who renders to each individual person the recompense for their deeds. There is no escape and no shelter outside of the absolute truth. What you are hearing is the truth, and no amount of rebellion and conjecture will change it. I am a merciful God; justice is the foundation of my throne. Only through humility and submission to My Lordship is a person able to enter this place where truth, equity and justice prevail.

Jesus Christ has made the way, and He is the only way into the kingdom of peace for which every soul yearns no matter how loud and boisterous the voices of opposition may be. Their baseless demands and threats carry no enforceable validity. They will all be cut off and silenced in the grave.

Can you hear Me?, says the Lord. There is no plan formed against Me that will succeed. The earth is Mine, and I will prevail. The only hope for those who dwell on the earth is to embrace the heavenly solution.

PSALM 103:17-19

510 GREATNESS

How do we measure greatness, and how many are actually able to recognize it? How great is the One who has the ability to speak everything that exists into being? To what can we compare such a person? Yes, He is a Person and has made Himself known to those He has chosen to reveal true greatness.

Everything we are able to know and experience in the realm of the natural creation declares the greatness of our Creator, but it does not stop there. It is only the beginning of the revelation of true greatness. There is a whole other dimension of creation that beckons us to enter into and participate in. This is the Spiritual dimension where the Creator dwells and actually encompasses all that we are able to discover through our biological senses. Is this not exciting?

There is a host of great human beings who have accomplished impressive things by human standards, but how do any of them compare with the wonder of life itself? The greatest Person to ever walk this earth, supposed by the people of his day to be a mere carpenter's son, was actually the Creator Himself who took on human form in order to reveal the essence of the greatest Person that has existed throughout eternity. His chosen ones are able to see Him and know Him. How great is this? How absolutely glorious is this revelation? The mystery of life itself is revealed to those who love this greatest of all beings that exists and in whom we have our very being.

To understand and know the Creator's love and purpose is surely the greatest thing any created being can experience. Really, what can be compared to the greatness of the God who possesses all power and authority who was willing to sacrifice His own life that we might know Him? Surely, He deserves our total devotion and adoration.

I say let's give it to Him!

Words fail to describe the greatness of our Lord and Savior, but we try. What greater things can we do? Actually, to obey Him is the highest thing a person can do to prove his or her love. This is what Jesus has shown us.

HEBREWS 1:1-4
COLOSSIANS 2:8-10
PHILIPPIANS 2:5-8

511 FOUNDATIONS

All the foundations of the earth are unstable. A sure and stable foundation is kin to true wealth and eternal treasure. A spiritual foundation consists of things that cannot be seen with the natural eye nor built upon by human effort. While earthly metaphors are used to describe eternal structures, they are only figurative symbols of heavenly reality.

Love, truth, righteousness, justice and mercy are the foundation of the "Throne of God" and His kingdom; while peace, joy, wisdom, understanding, prudence, and discernment are a few of the unseen but solid realities of a spiritual foundation. What is built on this foundation will last forever, while the things built on earthly foundations are temporary and of little value.

The words of Jesus were always Spiritual, and though often metaphorical and spoken in parables, they were of eternal value and of supernatural origin and must be Spiritually discerned. The carnal mind may interpret these metaphors and relate them to the natural world in which we live, but they always go beyond the limits of carnality.

Unless a person actually transcends the natural realm, he or she will remain within the boundaries and confines of the world, which is passing away. Jesus is the cornerstone of the Spiritual foundation upon which all the multitude of Spiritual cities, places, people, kingdoms and events described in the Bible are built. Jesus is the actual Word of God who is manifested in the flesh to show us the way through the "Gates of Righteousness" into the realm from which He came. Unless we enter through and abide in Him, we do not have eternal life and will perish along with our biological flesh, the world, and the earth we inhabit.

His words are Spirit and truth and are the foundation of eternal life. Are you coming?

512 THE REAL PROBLEM

The real problem in a word is *carnality.* We have all been born into it, but those called by the Spirit of God have been given an opportunity to escape its boundaries. Because we have been called does not necessarily mean we have escaped the death sentence to which we were subjected. Many who are called have been captured by carnal impostors disguised as Spiritual instructors sent to bind us to our flesh and our carnality. If they are successful in their mission, we will remain bound by our flesh and continue our existence as sinners.

Our Creator is testing our hearts in order to know who really loves Him, and to those who do, He endows a love of the truth. This is the point where those who have been called become chosen. Those who actually love unrighteousness more than God are sent a strong delusion and are left under the tutelage of the carnal instructors who would bind them to the earth, the flesh and to sin. It is heartbreaking to see, if one is able to see it, for it is the truth, and only God can make the way of escape. This watchman is but one voice sent to warn the called-out ones, and he labors continually sounding the trumpet the Lord has provided.

The carnal mind is the enemy of God, and those who defend its carnality are the emissaries of the one who desires to destroy our soul. To expose this diabolical plot is what the servants of God have done throughout the ages. The call of the Lord is a call to righteousness in order to escape the snares of sin and death.

The labor of the righteous leads to life; the wages of sin to death. "*The righteousness of the upright will deliver them, but the unfaithful will be caught by their lust. Therefore, the ungodly shall not stand in the judgment nor sinners in the congregations of the righteous.*"

ROMANS 8:5-11

513 TEAR DOWN/BUILD UP

The commission given to Jeremiah applies to the watchmen of this present age. What must be torn down are strongholds consisting of false doctrines, erroneous interpretations and translations of the Bible, along with traditions, fables and outright lies. Even the least aware among us must realize that the multiplicity of doctrines, denominations and cults cannot be the true doctrine of Christ. What has not originated from revelation from the "Spirit of Truth" is not of God and must be torn down and replaced with actual truth. You may ask who has the right or the power to decide. The answer is simple, albeit controversial. The answer is God.

His word and His Spirit both interpret and make commentary on themselves and render truth and the will of the Lord. Whatever does not live up to this standard is destined for destruction. Anyone unable to accept this is in error and delusion. Debate is for the carnal minded who have not partaken of the mind of Christ. The truth is in Him, as is His true Body, the true Church. Whatever is not is counterfeit and reprobate. This is where sinners who believe they are Christians abide, and will abide if they do not receive the love of the truth.

Jesus came to save people from sin, not in sin. Sin has no place in Him nor in the one who abides in Him. The lie is coming down, and righteousness is being built in its place. The Lord's chosen are able to do His will and obey His commands. Those who teach otherwise are the false teachers and prophets who have been prophesied to come in the last days. They are here, brethren, and they have filled the pulpits and airways throughout the earth.

Righteousness and truth will prevail, and all liars will be condemned and put to shame.

Sin is a reproach to any people and will not go unpunished, regardless of whether they call themselves Christians or not.

2 PETER 2:1-3

514 HERE AND NOW

Questions often arise regarding salvation as to when and how certain aspects apply. There is considerable controversy among the religious in this regard. The Lord's response is in accordance to each person's level of faith and their relationship with Him. Nevertheless, the use of tense and position are extensive in His word. He has made quite clear the terms and the timing of the salvation He has provided. The Spirit of God esteems belief in what He has said as righteousness. Belief is an essential part of faith.

Actual experience of salvation is subjective and can be the confirmation of the reality of the words spoken about it. Many who put off certain aspects of salvation do so because they are unable to see the reality of them in their own lives. Hence, we have whole denominations and schools of theology centered around subjects such as dispensationalism, positionalism, and rapture theories, as well as sin and its place in the life of so-called believers.

When salvation actually occurs and how it progresses in a person's life is a major force in how that individual lives out his or her life while on earth. Without getting theologically technical, this watchman would encourage anyone who loves the Lord and the truth to diligently and carefully examine what the Lord has actually said about every aspect of His great salvation without the help of trained professionals and religious commentary. Every person who knows the Lord and has received the love of the truth has also received an anointing that will lead them into the truth about every aspect of salvation.

You may discover that the only thing we are waiting for is the transformation of our mortal bodies. The rest of salvation, including righteousness and freedom from sin, is here and now.

Believing and obeying the voice of God is the key of faith that opens the gate into His kingdom NOW!

2 CORINTHIANS 6:2

515 INDIVIDUALITY

The uniqueness of every person allows them to make choices based on their own conscience and the integrity of their own heart or lack of it. This individuality includes every aspect of a human being both biological and spiritual. This uniqueness can be a source of pride for many as well as a source of a feeling of inferiority to others.

The establishments of the world have cast whole nations, races, groups and cultures into factions that wicked and greedy power brokers have learned to exploit for their own lustful purposes. For any individual to allow him or herself to be categorized with a group and be lumped in with a certain philosophical or belief system is an error of the proud who have been lied to, flattered, and manipulated by those who want to exploit them.

The person who allows himself to be categorized in such a way has relinquished their freedom to think and choose as an individual and to fulfill who the Creator has designed him to be. If you watch or listen to the corporate news sources, this is painfully obvious to the one who is able to think and choose independently.

There is truly a conspiracy to overthrow and wipe out liberty, freedom and individuality by the consortium of globalists who want to control all of humanity and the world. To understand this gives the individual the ability to resist the forces assembled to bring it about. It does not matter who or where you are, the truth is the best defense against the tyranny that is taking place throughout the earth.

Please say AMEN! Pride comes before destruction and humility before honor.

516 PEACE

Peace seems to have eluded most of the world. The chants of "Peace, Peace" can be heard from pulpits and microphones, but its reality appears to be out of the reach of most people. Troubled waters have flooded the majority of large cities throughout the earth, and the countless, self-serving factions are pointing their fingers at one another.

Peace is right where it has always been. *The kingdom of God is righteousness, peace and joy in the Holy Spirit. . . Therefore, let us pursue the things which make the peace and the things by which one may* edify *another*. Is this not simple? Is it not the truth that anyone with a pure heart can understand? What is being described is a place, a land where love and good will toward all is a reality. Yes, there is such a place, and it is in the heart of those who know God and obey Him.

All the turmoil, wars, unrest and violence are the result of envy, greed, selfish ambition and the rejection of truth. Who can say it is not so? The establishment of peace begins in the heart of the individual who actually desires peace and pursues it honestly.

Jesus is referred to as the "Prince of Peace". We who know Him are partakers of the peace which passes understanding. Anyone who claims to know Him but does not have peace within has been deceived. Abiding in Christ will produce the fruit of peace and joy that cannot be found anywhere in the world.

What most people really desire can only be found in relationship with the Author of peace that has always been here and does not change. The world and those who dwell on earth remain subject to the storms of nature and life that are without hope of ending or resolution, even in death.

God's way is the right way to find peace.

517 SOCIAL CLASSES

What do social classes have to do with spirituality and eternal life? In reality, very little. So why are class and racial divisions so numerous among those who call themselves Christians? Is the true "Body of Christ" not but one body? So why do we observe all these factions? The answer is based in the carnality and bigotry of those who are taught to believe they are Christians but do not know Christ.

Confession without the reality of the indwelling Holy Spirit is the delusion sent to those who have not received the love of the truth. Such impostors and hypocrites that fill the pews and auditoriums of buildings and gatherings proclaim what they call the gospel without true understanding. Falsehood and lies will not produce the fruit of righteousness and true spirituality. This deception only produces further carnality and sin. Though these followers of the flesh may flatter God with their mouths, their hearts remain far from Him.

How do you respond, O inhabitants of the flesh of the earth? Do you really believe that you are redeemed from the consequence of sin while living according to the flesh and its lusts. This battle between flesh and Spirit is the battle of the ages.

Jesus' coming in the likeness of sinful flesh and dying in the flesh has put away sin in the flesh once and for all for those who believe Him and follow His Spirit. Any other interpretation of what He has said and done is a lie. Whether the carnal mind is able to receive the truth or not, the reality remains the same.

So what effects do societal class and cultural status really have in the kingdom where Jesus is King?

Is this not a profound question that demands a response?

JAMES 2:1-7

518 FLESH MERCHANTS

Merchandisers abound in the world. They are sent out by the established institutions of religion, small and large. While they speak of righteousness and holiness, they make their appeal to the lust of the flesh, the lust of the eyes, and the pride of life. These merchants of fleshly origin defend those who are carnally minded and dominated by fleshly desire by teaching them that even if they sin, God understands and has made provision for them to maintain a favorable standing with Him, without actually obeying His commandments or following His Spirit.

These flesh merchants would have us believe that even though a person may be living and walking according to the flesh, their salvation remains secure and they will not die because of some mysterious, intellectual assent to isolated passages of scripture relating to believing and confessing, yet not obeying. The Spiritual application of scriptures leaves the one who continues to sin and calls himself a sinner without further provision for his rebellion and disregard for the redemption the Lord has provided for sin and its consequence.

Let's reason together. Why did Jesus take on human flesh? And what did He accomplish by living a sinless life, shedding His blood, dying, and then rising from the grave? Was it not to free us from bondage to the flesh, sin and death? How can a person continue to sin and claim to have been freed from it?

The real issue is whether a human being (as Jesus was) can live according to the Spirit here on earth, or must we continue to be controlled by the desire of our fleshly bodies? What does the Bible say? If a person believes the gospel according to the flesh merchants, freedom from sin is for another age and we must remain sinners controlled by the lust of the flesh, the lust of the eyes and the pride of life.

We all have a choice!

ROMANS 8:12-14
REVELATION 18:9-24
1 JOHN 2:15-17

519 BELIEF/UNBELIEF

Response is a good indicator of whether a person believes what they have heard or not. When the Almighty speaks a clear and unambiguous command or statement of fact, faith responds immediately, while unbelief may give an affirmative reaction while trying to figure out a way to make what God has said into something that does not require an immediate action or personal commitment.

The real issue is based on the actual relationship of the person who is being evaluated. Belief is based on a person's faith and trust. The one without such virtue will attempt to disguise their unbelief by complicating what God has said and even make it appear to apply to another age or circumstance not at hand.

To disbelieve what the Lord says is often a path of least resistance which avoids the criticism of others who do not actually believe. Consequently, many large congregations and theological seminaries have risen to try and prove their reasons for not believing the simple truths that the Lord has spoken. Many of these truths have been referred to in past discourses, and many of them carry the weight of eternal life and salvation from sin and death. Without true belief and love of the truth, unbelief brings a curse of delusion on the offenders.

To actually believe the truth is a gift given to those who have been chosen in Christ and are spiritually able to confess that He has come in the flesh. He came to put away sin in the flesh and actually does for those who believe Him. Those who don't believe what He has said and done have built elaborate doctrines and fables to hide their sin and unbelief. They have turned reality to theory and caused the things God has given us to experience now into a future hope without the foundation of truth.

We are called to believe, but if we don't, the fault lies in the heart of the unbeliever, not God.

2 THESSALONIANS 2:9-12
JOHN 8:31-32
MARK 9:23-24

520 NEGLECT

Therefore, we must give more earnest heed to the things we have heard lest we drift away. For if the words spoken by angels proved steadfast and every transgression and disobedience received a just reward, how shall we escape if we neglect so great a salvation, which at the first began to be spoken by the Lord and was confirmed to us by those who heard Him, God also bearing witness both with signs and wonders with various miracles and gifts of the Holy Spirit according to His own will?

What will become of the person who is spiritually lazy, who has allowed himself to neglect the true gospel in favor of a false gospel which is less demanding and requires less commitment? The one who is careless of his way will die, says the Lord. Does salvation not require diligence and constant vigilance? If we examine ourselves to find out if we are really abiding in the faith once delivered to the saints, will any of us be content to call ourselves sinners?

This watchman knows the answer to the question and also the content of the true gospel and the whole counsel of God. Salvation cannot be taken lightly or casually or left to professionals who are trained in carnal institutions. Unless we are able to hear the voice of the Spirit of Truth ourselves, the enemy of our soul will find a way to deceive us.

To love the truth requires full commitment and observance of it. There is no place for trusting the carnal understanding of those who have been trained and paid by institutions with a vested interest in capturing your soul in order to enlarge their own kingdoms. To neglect the truth of what you are hearing may well cost you your soul.

All are warned! This is not a game.

521 GOD CANNOT LIE

Not only can the Creator not lie, but He hates all lying. Who is a liar and the father of it? He is the same one who appeared as a serpent in Eden and deceived the woman. What we are left to face is to determine what is the truth or a lie.

Of course, there is only One who can be trusted for the discernment to recognize the vital reality of the truth. He is the One who cannot lie. Whatever He says is so. To add or subtract from what God has said is an offence of great magnitude and consequence. There are many who have made this error and twisted the truth because they lack the fear of the Lord and covet the adulation of humanity above the approval of God.

Who are these deceivers, these offspring of Satan? It is alarming to see them, because we have been taught to respect and revere them. That does not change the reality of the truth. How can the Almighty allow such a thing? Why did He allow Eve to be deceived? The Lord has a purpose for all that He does, and whether we understand His motive or not is not the real issue. The real issues are belief, trust, faith and obedience. After all, God is in charge, and He can do whatever pleases Him.

Do we love Him? His greatest commandment instructs us to love Him above everything else. Surely, this is not beyond our capability if we really do fear Him and give Him what is reasonable for Him to expect. The person who realizes his place as a created being will do the will of the Creator. It is His will that we obey His voice which has clearly told us not to sin. If this is His will, would He not give us the capacity to obey Him?

Surely, He has, and the true gospel explains it in detail. Nevertheless, the deceiver has produced an alternate gospel that has made provision for the flesh to disobey the stated will of God and not die. This deceiver causes those who will believe His lie to question the Lord's will and command and yet not suffer the death that results from disobedience.

When a descendant of Adam and Eve is called by the Spirit of God and is born anew of His Spirit and given a new life and the very nature of their Creator, is it unreasonable for God to expect this new creature to obey Him and follow His Spirit? The liar would try and make us believe we are not really new creatures who have been given the ability to obey the voice and commandments of God, but we already know he is a liar and so are all those who mimic his lies. These are the ones who would steal our salvation and destroy our souls, because they have not received the love of the truth.

No lie is of the truth! Regardless of how a lie is packaged and delivered and given credence by the world's version of the gospel, the truth remains the same.

2 CORINTHIANS 11:3-4
HEBREWS 6:16-20

522 QUEST

The Lord has commissioned the quest of which I speak. Why he requires witnesses such as myself remains somewhat of a mystery. Jesus spoke of "the few" and among the masses in the great sea of humanity, those who actually hunger and thirst for righteousness and truth really are the few of which he spoke.

The joy and satisfaction of finding a true saint of God is one of this life's great rewards. It brings a level of fulfillment that the Lord Himself looked forward to as He faced His own death on the cross. He died for all, yet only the few have realized the extent of His great sacrifice and His love. They are the chosen, the elect with whom He shares His inheritance.

The desire for purity of heart and true holiness is a gift given to those who seek the Lord with their whole heart. Such were the fathers of the faith with whom we who now share their passion have been joined. Our communion transcends all nationality, culture, history, language, ancestry and every worldly influence. This, brethren, is the work of God and His plan for all who love Him.

This knowledge/understanding is a great reward in itself. Many have been invited to this great supper, but regrettably, there are but few who respond to the call. This great feast is in the land where only the righteous dwell and where Jesus has gone before us to prepare a place for those who love Him.

Is He not a wonderful Savior and God?

LUKE 14:15-24
MATTHEW 20:15-16

523 PRETENSE

Pretense cannot be found in Jesus nor in truth. Pretense is produced by pride. Among those naming the name of Jesus and calling themselves Christians (Christ-like), pretense has found deep roots. Most religion is built on pretense and the approval of the world and its governments.

Our Lord is looking for more from His children. His true Body is the manifestation of Himself on earth, and though spiritual, it is the reflection of Himself. How are we doing, brethren? Can the true "Body of Christ" be seen in the multitude of steepled buildings that are called churches? Do those preaching and teaching what they call the gospel while simultaneously calling themselves sinners really produce pretense-free disciples? The answer is obvious, as is the pretense of such doctrine.

The grand cathedrals that endeavor to reflect the kingdom of God and His glory have only succeeded in demonstrating the pretense of the institutions they represent. The glory of God far exceeds the pretense of mankind's effort to establish their own kingdoms and glory. The pretense of outward righteousness and holiness is betrayed by the testimony of the victims of religious leaders and clergy and all those who have disgraced the name of Christ by their hypocrisy.

The day is at hand when all pretense will be judged, exposed and brought to shame by the Righteous Judge who is impartial and without pretense. He is the One who knows every heart, and there is nothing hidden from His sight. All the things that pretense attempts to hide are being brought to the light for all to see.

1 CORINTHIANS 4:1-5
2 CORINTHIANS 4:1-6
MATTHEW 23:27-28

524 AS HE IS

Love has been perfected among us in this: that we may have boldness in the day of judgment; because as He is, so are we in this world. . . . God is light, and in Him is no darkness at all. . . . But we know that when He is revealed we shall be like Him, for we shall see Him as He is, and everyone who has this hope in Him purifies himself just as He is pure. . . . For whom He foreknew He also predestined to be conformed to the image of His Son that He might be the firstborn of many brethren. . . . He who says he abides in Him ought himself to walk just as He walked.

What can we say to these things, brethren? Can we justify ongoing sin as the one who does not know the truth? And you know that He was manifested to take away our sins, and in Him there is no sin. Whoever abides in Him does not sin. Whoever sins has neither seen Him nor known Him.

So how do we see Him? And, furthermore, how do we see ourselves? Was the psalmist of a higher standing than we who have become "One Spirit with Christ"? Hear Him: *I was also blameless before Him and I kept myself from my iniquity. Therefore, the Lord has recompensed me according to my righteousness, according to the cleanliness of my hands in His sight. With the merciful, You will show Yourself merciful; with the blameless one, You will show Yourself blameless; with the Pure you will show Yourself pure; and with the devious You will show Yourself shrewd.*

How has the Lord shown Himself to those who continue to sin calling themselves sinners, having taken His name in vain and casting His word behind them? This is no small issue! Truth will prevail regardless of what the legion of professionally trained commentators say.

Only those who abide in Christ now will be with Him when He appears again! His reward will be with Him.

JOHN 20:21
MATTHEW 5:14-16
REVELATION 22:12-14

525 WITNESSES

The Lord has chosen witnesses from every generation to join the eternal generation of those who love Him and are faithful to Him. The enemies of God have devised shrewd schemes to reduce the testimony of the Spirit of Truth down to the earth to be spoken from the ground. The clever schemes of the religious rulers are crafted to capture the sheep in the pasture of God and make them their own.

The witnesses of God have given testimony throughout the ages and are doing so now. Truth prevails even now in the midst of the confusion and the flood of unrighteousness that has covered the earth. The blameless whose hearts are right with God remain in the land and the pasture where the voice of the "Good Shepherd" can be heard. Those who are following the earthly impostors are being led into the pit where sinners and all the enemies of God are headed.

The witnesses the Lord has raised up are still proclaiming His righteousness and love for all who have ears to hear. They are joined by a great cloud of heavenly witnesses who have preceded us and have given testimony of the righteousness of faith.

Though the lie of the religious seems to justify those who continue to sin, their end will not be with the blameless and the faithful who have actually trusted their Savior to deliver them from the one thing that can separate them from a true relationship with the great Creator. Regardless of how innocuous the religious professionals portray sin to be for those who believe them, death remains the result of ongoing sin.

This is the testimony of every true witness throughout scripture and history.

The soul that continues to sin shall die.

526 WASHING AND COVERING

The shedding of blood signifies the death and the putting away of the flesh of the one who sheds it. Jesus, the Christ, is very unique and special, because even though he was every bit human he is also the Son of God. His blood possesses the supernatural, Spiritual power to wash away sin and to cover it eternally. Is there more that God has intended for the blood of Jesus to accomplish?

There seems to be some misunderstanding among the religious who believe this blood protects them from all sorts of afflictions and onslaughts of the enemy of our souls. What Jesus' blood actually accomplishes when properly applied is in no way diminished by limiting it to what the Father has purposed it to accomplish. Nevertheless, to try and make it apply to the works of the Holy Spirit is putting faith in an unintended, unscriptural and ignorant application.

The spiritual task of cleansing away sin and permanently covering sins is only obscured by the misappropriation of it. To plead the blood in biological terms reflects a misunderstanding of the work of the Spirit. To claim the power of Jesus' blood to cover the willful ongoing sin of a person who has received the knowledge of the truth is not only wrong, but also destructive. The fear of God will keep us from such error if we have it.

Turning Jesus' blood into a carnal fable is like praying to dead saints to win God's favor. The Lord cannot be bribed, neither will He respond to foundationless proclamations of ignorance. The blood of Jesus is sacred, mysterious and wonderful, but it does not go beyond what the word of God has stated; particularly with regard to willful, future and ongoing sin.

HEBREWS 10:26-31
EPHESIANS 1:7

P.S. The shedding of blood symbolizes the putting away of the flesh, not its preservation.

527 WORDS

The words of the Lord are pure words like silver tried in a furnace of earth, purified seven times. . . .Do you see a person hasty in their words? There is more hope for a fool than for that person. . . .Idle words lead to poverty.

Words are something we all use and have in common, but how we use them can be the difference between life and death. Words are used to convey truth and lies. They are like weapons or tools to be used for good or evil depending on the one using them. The person whose heart is filled with love speaks words that convey and promote love. The person whose heart is filled with hatred speaks words that convey and promote hate.

The words a person uses reflect the condition of his or her heart. *Out of the abundance of the heart, the mouth speaks.* This truth should give any thoughtful person pause to consider the words they use and how they use them. Motive behind the words we use is a reflection of who we really are and what we really believe. This should put the fear of God in our hearts and cause us to pause and think before we speak. God is judging every person according to the words they speak.

Listen carefully and you will hear the truth of what is being said as well as the source of its content. Politicians and special interest groups surely expose their motives and bias. And the religious broadcasters also clearly reveal their true motivation as they continually plead for gifts, tithes, and donations. These all betray the truth for the bribes they covet to establish their own kingdoms and influence.

The Lord surely sees all this selfishness and hypocrisy, and though the wheels of justice turn slowly, all the words each person speaks will be called to account. SELAH!

MATTHEW 12:33-37

528 SPEAKING "THE WORD"

This word refers to "The Word of God." Because a preacher quotes the Bible and builds a case to support his or her pet doctrines, does this constitute speaking the "Word of God"?

The "Word of God" is living and powerful, but if it is not ministered by the Holy Spirit, it brings death. Yes, the written letter kills but the Spirit gives life. The point is that unless the one preaching the word is anointed by the Holy Spirit, which most preachers claim to be, they may well be ministering death. The actual anointing is exclusive to those who have received the love of the truth and make no compromise in favor of denominational or institutional doctrines.

The pure truth is the Word that has not been corrupted by bias, carnal understanding, mistranslation, and misinterpretation of what the Holy Spirit has spoken. What the Lord is saying is that people's opinions and prejudices are worth nothing, as is much of their preaching and teaching.

A purposely mistranslated version of the Bible is used to further promote false doctrine in place of truth. An example of such heresy is Psalm 51:5, as translated in the latter version of the NIV and many others. The final judgment of such dishonesty is severe. God is watching over His Word, and He knows the one who has received the love of the truth and those who have not.

Again, opinions here are of no value and only serve to confuse those who may be hungering and thirsting for righteousness and truth.

Is it not high time to turn from the preachers of denominational and all factions promoting their own version of "The Word"?

It is painful to see it.

PROVERB 30:5-6

529 TO BE

To be carnally minded is death, but to be Spiritually minded is life and peace. STOP! SELAH! The Lord is saying that to be Spiritually minded is not optional for the person who desires to please God and abide in Christ.

Let this mind be in you which is also in Christ Jesus . . .And do not be conformed to this world but be transformed by the renewing of your mind. . . . Take every thought captive to the obedience of Christ. . . Pray without ceasing . . . We have the mind of Christ. Does God's word not thoroughly confirm the absolute necessity of being spiritually minded? Because the carnal mind is enmity against God.

To be seated with Christ in heavenly places is precisely what being Spiritually minded consists of. This is the place from which what you are reading has originated. The idea that we can please our Heavenly Father by going to a church building on Sunday and participating in religious activities is the deception taught by the enemy of our souls. The person who knows God and walks in His ways does so 24/7. This is what abiding in Christ means.

If what is being said sounds too radical, consider what Jesus actually said and did. *But you are not in the flesh but in the Spirit if indeed the Spirit of God dwells in you. Now if anyone does not have the Spirit of Christ, he or she is not His, and if Christ is in you, the body (flesh) is dead because of sin but the Spirit is life because of righteousness.*

The carnal mind and carnal religious activities do not produce the righteousness of God. Only the Spirit can do it.

We are given the choice to walk by faith or by sight, but not both. Our *minds* are the battleground where the conflict between flesh and Spirit is taking place even at this moment.

ROMANS 8:5-10

530 FOR WHOM IS THE LAW?

The law is for sinners. HELLO! Are there sinners in the "Body of Christ"? Not according to the Bible. Although the sinners who live according to the flesh are unable to keep the law, we who abide in Christ and live according to the Spirit are able to fulfill the righteous requirements of the law without being subject to it. Who is the fool who will debate the Holy Spirit?

Apparently, there are whole denominations, institutions, organizations and churches who do dispute what God has said. These professionals would have their followers believe they remain sinners but are no longer under the curse of the law. They have crafted elaborate doctrinal theories that proclaim sinners to actually be saints.

This seems nonsensical, but it is what these carnal, intellectual, religious clerics have done. Rather than directly confront the truth, they have devised doctrines and fables that make the Bible not say what it actually says. Multitudes subscribe to their deception, because they take pleasure in their sin and prefer the lie over the truth. An excuse to continue being a sinner yet still be saved from eternal torment has great appeal to those who love their sin more than God. Having a cover for their unrighteous behavior and remaining positionally blameless and above the law is the really big lie Satan has succeeded to introduce into modern carnal theology.

If anyone who has subscribed to this heresy is able to hear and understand the truth, the time has come to make your calling and election sure.

Time is short, and today is the day of true salvation.

ROMANS 21:13
1 TIMOTHY 1:8-10
DEUTERONOMY 28:15-68

531 THE DOCTRINE OF CHRIST

Whoever transgresses (sins) and does not abide in the doctrine of Christ and does not have God . . . Afterward, Jesus found him in the temple and said to him, "See, you have been made well. Sin no more lest a worse thing come upon you." How do the popular doctrines of the day square up with the actual *"doctrine of Christ"? . . . And Jesus said to her, "Neither do I condemn you; go and sin no more."* The true doctrine of Christ does not make provision for the person following after the desire of their flesh to abide in Himself.

The apostle, John, speaks of the "doctrine of Christ" when he makes the unequivocal, unambiguous statement: And you know that He was manifested to take away our sins, and in Him there is no sin. Whoever abides in Him does not sin. Are all these Biblical quotes not sufficient to discredit the false doctrines that seem to allow the sinner to continue on sinning and remain in right standing with God?

The professionals trained in this erroneous form of doctrine would also have us believe that infants are born sinners and just continue on through their lives as sinners, even if they are born again and have become new creations in Christ.

Sin is the primary issue and the one thing that can separate us from God. If the enemy of our souls can convince us that we can continue to sin and still go to heaven, he will succeed in destroying our souls.

There will be no apology given for telling the truth with regard to sin and salvation.

ROMANS 13:11-14

532 CEASE

It is essential that we enter the Sabbath of the Lord. This is where our flesh becomes subject to the Spirit of God and we cease our own works. *For He who has entered His (God's) rest has himself also ceased from his own works as God did from His.* This is where sin has been conquered and eliminated. This is where God's work is accomplished through the one who has ceased his or her own work thus ceasing the sin produced by the lust of our flesh.

There is no double standard in this place of rest. All who enter are chosen and overcomers. Everyone who is able to enter has been crucified with Christ, and it is He who is working through the lives of those submitted to Him. These saints have been freed from sin just as He has told us. *And having been set free from sin, you became slaves of righteousness.*

There are also many (most) of those using the name of Jesus Christ who have not entered that promised rest and cannot cease from sin. They are unable to enter the Lord's Sabbath because of unbelief and disobedience, and they heap up teachers who will help them try to justify and absolve them of their ongoing sin, telling them that Jesus' blood covers all sin, even future.

Without true understanding of the Bible and the salvation that God has provided from sin, *they are unable to come to a knowledge of the truth and remain laden with sin . . . they are spots and blemishes carousing in their own deceptions while they feast with you, having eyes full of adultery and that cannot cease from sin, enticing unstable souls.*

In my effort *to deliver those drawn toward death and to hold back those stumbling to the slaughter,* I have concluded that mingling with those who call themselves sinners and Christians simultaneously is not fruitful. The Lord has released me from the pain of such effort.

Those whom the Lord grants a love of the truth must come out from among those who are unable to cease from sin and call themselves sinners.

HEBREWS 4:11-13

533 FORMAL RELIGION

This religious crowd has made a mockery of Jesus' great sacrifice and what He accomplished by reducing it to the irreverent understanding of those who have trampled under foot the actual meaning and purpose of His shed blood as well as His death, burial and resurrection. These reprobates have turned Jesus' accomplishments into a cheap form of grace that allows sinners to dominate a worldly imitation of the true Church.

The Lord certainly sees all these things and has cut them off from the land of the living and allowed them to continue on in their religious delusion.

The Lord's mission was to save His people from sin. Satan and the formal religious crowd of Jesus' day found a way to kill Him and supposedly defeat His mission. Of course, the Lord outwitted them and supplied the great salvation that is now available to those who obey Him.

Satan has never stopped trying to kill, steal, destroy and lie. The religious crowd of modern day has been duped into believing that Jesus' great sacrifice and shed blood give blanket immunity to those who continue in disobedience to God.

The Lord requires absolute obedience. He always has. The idea that sins are forgiven and covered in advance of their willful insurrection is the big lie of Satan and his human offspring. Jesus' blood is sacred, and no unrepentant sinners have access to its supernatural cleansing power. Only those who turn from and totally reject their iniquity and *walk in the light as He is in the light* will be cleansed of unrighteousness.

If you think this watchman speaks on his own, please read your Bible without the sanctions and oversight of formal religion.

HEBREWS 10:26-31
1 JOHN 3:8-9

534 IN VAIN

Moreover, brethren, I declare to you the gospel which I preached to you which also you received and in which you stand, by which also you are saved if you hold fast that word which I preached to you—unless you believed in vain. Taking the Lord's name in vain is not what is commonly believed.

Those who have called on the name of the Lord and have been saved but then disobey Him and do not walk in His ways are the ones who have taken His name in vain. There is no point in confessing the name of Jesus Christ if a person goes on as a sinner and brings shame and reproach to His name. The person who does such a thing is not humble as so many have been taught, but rather has become reprobate.

To be born of the Spirit and then live according to the flesh is exactly the vanity that ends in death. *Brethren, if anyone among you wanders from the truth and someone turns him back, let him know that he who turns a sinner from the error of his way will save a soul from death and cover a multitude of sins.*

Truth is always better than a lie, just as righteousness is always better than vanity and sin. To defend a sinner is the vain exercise of a fool who hopes to justify his or herself of their own vain misuse of the holy name they have taken in vain. Jesus did not shed His blood in vain, but those who continually plead His blood over things and situations for which His blood does not apply do so in vain and make themselves look like vain fools to the one who understands the reality of what Jesus' blood was shed to accomplish. This vanity diminishes the actual purpose of what God has accomplished.

The vanity of the modern church and the pretense of those who consider themselves believers and support vain doctrines and teachings are laboring in vain. *Unless the Lord builds the house, they labor in vain who build it.* The Lord does not engage in vanity nor does He bless it. His salvation is from sin, not in it.

It is vain to even think that Jesus will save those who have taken His name in vain and persist in the delusion that they are pleasing God while they remain sinners. This is the epitome of vanity.

To speak the truth in our own hearts pleases our Savior and is the beginning of escape from the path of vanity on which the world and its false churches trod. The knowledge of God, and understanding His ways and walking in them, is the path that leads away from using His name in vain.

EXODUS 20:7

535 TO THE END

But the one who endures to the end will be saved. If a professional pastor who teaches the doctrine of eternal security is asked if a person can lose their salvation, most will reply with an ambiguous and dishonest discourse on how it is not possible. Well, it is possible, and the Bible says so multiple times. It is the overcomer, the faithful, the righteous, the blameless and those who are without sin who will be saved in the end. While the trained professionals may tell us that all these things are positional, they are indeed actual and the essence of the elect.

Many who claim to know Jesus and flatter Him on Sunday have rejected the true qualifications of sainthood and salvation, slandering anyone who believes in true holiness. This watchman has seen it and heard it. Nevertheless, in the end every person will receive the just reward for what they say and do.

While we are not saved by our works and deeds, they are the proof of whether or not we have actually been saved. SELAH! The person who says they know Christ should be walking as He walked; in righteousness and truth and certainly not as a sinner with a false sense of humility.

The end of every life will declare the truth regarding the content of the book each of us contains. Yes, we are books which our Creator reads and by which everyone will be judged in the end. A true fear of God will fill the book with a record of righteous deeds and a life of obedience to the God who we claim to love and worship. The Lord desires only the worship of those who do so in Spirit and in truth. The person unable to cease from sin is incapable of such an expression of love and adoration.

How can anyone escape who will not obey the gospel and truly repent of their self-centered existence?

2 PETER 2:9-22
1 PETER 1:3-9

536 FREE

Whom the Lord sets free is free indeed. Jesus frees the ones who trust Him from a master which would destroy our souls. The depth, height, and breadth are determined by a personal understanding of what the Lord has actually done through His great sacrifice of Himself. Even the shallowest understanding will give a person a new start in life. As in the parable of the sower and the seed, different levels of freedom may be realized and subsequently produce life, which is freedom, from a dormant seed.

The seed who has come to life is the one called to partake of the generation that has continually flourished from the beginning. It is by faith that a person becomes eligible and able to walk in the total freedom Jesus has supplied. Believing what God has said is the work that leads to the absolute freedom that is obtainable through faith.

Where else can we find deliverance from the prison of flesh into which all humans are born? Jesus has made a way for those held captive by their flesh to put their own fleshly, carnal existence to death and take on a new life that is free of sin and the resulting death that it produces. This is not myth, fable, speculation or theory; it is the reality of the gospel and the freedom we who love the Lord and the truth have been given.

Victory over the enemies of our souls has already been accomplished for the ones who understand the reality of the freedom that Jesus has set forth.

The person who really loves the truth and hungers and thirsts for righteousness and truth is now free to partake through faith.

HEBREWS 11:1-3
JOHN 8:34-36

537 MARKS

Every person born of a woman has a mark, even two. A mark on the forehead and the hand are the marks that symbolize and identify the one to whom that person belongs and serves. These marks are the symbol of what a person believes and the work they do. Is this not simple? Each individual can be identified by the image they are conformed to.

There are but two choices we have to select from, and our final choice will determine where and with whom we will spend eternity. SELAH! This should surely give us pause if we are not sure whose mark we bear. One is that of the man of the earth, the first Adam; the other is that of the Man from heaven, the second and last Adam, Jesus Himself.

The choice God has given us is to try and hang onto and save the life into which we were born or to let that life die and take on the life of Christ. *He who tries to save his life will lose it, but he who loses his life for My sake and the gospel's will find it. . . Jesus' words are Spirit and truth. . . That which is born of flesh is flesh; that which is born of Spirit is spirit . . . If you live according to the flesh you will die, but if by the Spirit you put to death the deeds of the body you will live. For as many as are led by the Spirit of God, these are sons of God.*

Does this not simplify and explain the mystery of marks and image for the one who has a heart to know?

ROMANS 8:5-11
REVELATION 13:16-18
EZEKIEL 9:3-6
REVELATION 7:3

538 THE LAST DAY

The last day is "the day of the Lord" when time as we know it will end. This is the day when Jesus has told us: *Most assuredly I say to you unless you eat the flesh of the Son of Man and drink His blood, you have no life in you. Whoever eats my flesh and drinks My blood has eternal life, and I will raise him up at the last day. For My flesh is food indeed and My blood is drink indeed. He who eats My flesh and drinks My blood abides in Me and I in him.*

The Spirit of God has told us through Paul: *Behold, I tell you a mystery: we shall not all sleep (die) but we shall all be changed—in a moment in the twinkling of an eye at the last trumpet. For the trumpet will sound and the dead will be raised incorruptible and we shall be changed. For this corruptible must put on incorruption and this mortal must put on immortality.*

These scriptural quotes should put an end to the erroneous notion that the Lord will catch away (rapture) some fabled church before the end of time. *Immediately after the tribulation of those days, the sun will be darkened and the moon will not give its light; the stars will fall from heaven and the powers of the heavens will be shaken. Then the sign of the Son of Man will appear in heaven; and then all the tribes of the earth will mourn, and they will see the Son of Man coming on the clouds of heaven with power and great glory, and He will send His angels with a great sound of a trumpet and they will gather together His elect from the four winds from one end of heaven to the other.*

Be ready!

1 THESSALONIANS 4:13-18
MATTHEW 24:29-31

539 DESPERATION

The days of total despair and desperation are looming just beyond the horizon. We have been warned by numerous prophets, apostles, and even Jesus Himself of the tribulation to come. It is coming upon all those who dwell on the earth who lack humility and the fear of the Lord.

Where do you dwell? Are you *seated with Christ in heavenly places? Is your life hidden with Christ in God?* Do you have a place in the Spiritual "Body of Christ", *being conformed to His image, being brought to the unity of the faith and of the knowledge of the Son of God to a perfect man to the measure of the stature of the fullness of Christ; that we should no longer be children tossed to and fro and carried about with every wind of doctrine by the trickery of men and the cunning craftiness of deceitful plotting, but speaking the truth in love may grow up in all things into Him who is the Head—Christ—from whom the whole body joined and knit together by what every joint supplies according to the effective working by which every part does its share causes growth of the body for the edifying of itself in love.*

This is what the Holy Spirit is doing as you read these words. There is no time left for partaking in dead religion and fellowship with those living according to the flesh unable to cease from sin. We are either citizens of heaven or earth, but not both. All the woes, plagues, pestilence and curses described in the Book of Revelation are coming upon those who follow after their flesh and reject the genuine salvation from sin that Jesus has provided.

When the flood arrives and the fullness of the time of the Gentiles is completed, there will be no further opportunity to be heard by the Father.

I truly hope everyone who hears this message will escape the coming flood of desperation which will cover the earth.

The only place to find shelter and to hide is in Christ! (the secret place of the Most High God)

REVELATION 3:10-13

540 IN AND OUT

Moses came to a place at the age of 120 years old where he was no longer able to go out and come in. There may well be a similar place in the life of a person who is also chosen by God where double-mindedness can keep that one from constantly abiding in Christ. This is what God's elect are commanded to do. This is the place where sin becomes a thing of the past, and our fleshly desires have lost their power.

If a person has entered into this holy place where we meet with God, is there really a reason for us to go out again? Abiding in Christ is not optional for anyone whose intention is to please God. Single-mindedness is the state of mind where *every thought is taken captive to the obedience of Christ and we pray without ceasing.*

The Lord does not expect anyone to be able to live up to His expectations without completely trusting in Him and following His Spirit. To the carnal mind, all these things are beyond the realm of reality. Henceforth, we have doctrines and whole denominations and institutions which have devised ways to bypass God's commands and expectations and remain in a hypothetical place of good standing and righteousness.

I am aware that what you are hearing is a constantly recurring theme, but it is critical for the salvation of the soul. To be double-minded is the same as trying to serve two masters. Without total commitment to the ways of God, any hope of pleasing Him is no more than a fantasy. He requires us to speak the truth in our own hearts. There is no substitute for truth, regardless of what any professional Bible scholar may say.

REVELATION 3:12-13

541 SIX THOUSAND YEARS?

Could there be some kind of misunderstanding? This watchman has not entered the controversy because wisdom will not allow it.

The Lord not only knows the beginning from the end; He is the beginning and the end. He created everything that can be seen from things which do not appear. What does appear to the natural eye is but a temporary construct designed to test and prepare created beings for eternity.

The age of the planet earth or the numerical age of the people inhabiting it is of little consequence in what the Creator has purposed for those to whom He has revealed Himself and who have come to know and love Him. Revelation of truth far exceeds carnal understanding of the age of the earth and the human race. The knowledge of God produces righteousness, but the knowledge of the written letter without the discernment of the Holy Spirit only produces death.

Life is in the same Spirit that hovered over the formless void at the beginning of the physical creation, and now recreates fallen human beings, making them new creations with divine natures and a spiritual union with the One who created all things seen and unseen.

If you are wondering yet where this discourse is going, the answer is nowhere, just like the age controversy. While it contains a good measure of truth, it will not settle things that the Lord prefers to remain as mysteries. AMEN!

PSALM 131:1-3; 90:1-6

542 FOLLY

Folly is exhibited on the public stage and portrayed as though universally accepted. The folly we see has crossed the border of reason and sanity into the dark depths of insanity.

Nowhere can this folly be more prominently displayed than on the stages of the huge auditoriums where women have replaced men and preached a gospel to the crowds of mesmerized sinners who believe they can please God without obeying Him. This folly is so prevalent that most preachers and teachers of the Bible believe they must subscribe to this new version of the gospel in order to maintain their income and the congregations they have established as their own kingdoms.

Going back to the secular display of folly, we can see politicians willing to endorse special interest groups, policies and outright lies to maintain their own power and financial empires. A voice of truth and reason is difficult to find and is usually being drowned out by the voices of folly.

What we are witnessing is the destruction of morality and perversion of truth in both the secular and religious realms.

The Bible itself is the place where truth and sanity can be found if you are able to secure a translation that has not been perverted, also. God can be trusted, and so can His word if we have received the love of the truth. We have been warned that many deceivers would come and their deception would grow worse and worse; all the more reason to draw near to God and abide in Christ.

Folly may be the distinguishing characteristic of the era in which we find ourselves, but our Lord is raising a standard in the midst of it to which everyone who loves truth, righteousness, justice and Jesus is being called to engage. Sinners must forsake their iniquity in order to be part of this standard. Saints are congregated in much smaller crowds than sinners.

MATTHEW 7:13-23

543 GIFTS

Every good and perfect gift is from above and comes down from the Father of Light with whom there is no variation or shadow of turning. The person with a pure and thankful heart is better able to see the grace of God. The gifts He has bestowed on every one of us come from His benevolent heart of Love.

Life itself is most likely the beginning of the gifts each of us receive. Jesus is the One who gives light to every person coming into the world. The pure heart of a newborn child is a gift and a testimony of the Lord's own purity. *Behold, children are a heritage from the Lord. The fruit of the womb is a reward.* The wicked who destroy this reward before it can even see the light will face severe reprisal.

The gifts we receive are meant by our Creator as blessings with which He expects us to glorify Him. Unfortunately, most human beings choose to use them for selfish reasons and their own glory. The person who has joined himself to Christ and become One Spirit with Him will, by the divine nature he has been given, glorify the One who has given the supernatural life he has received by living that life for Him.

The list of gifts could go on indefinitely, and many of us would point out the gifts of the Holy Spirit. He is the real gift and the individual gifts He bestows are intended to bless the "Body of Christ" and not that individual only. Some believe these gifts are their own and attempt to use them selfishly. This is an error we see prevalently among those who choose religion rather than relationship. Surely, God sees and will reward every person according to their works.

1 CORINTHIANS 12:4-11+

544 ENTICEMENT

The Lord is calling us to Himself to be as He is. The voice of wisdom can still be heard in the midst of the enticing voices of seduction and confusion. *If sinners entice you, do not consent.* Their greed will slay them along with those who join them. The enticing speech of a seductress has slain many wounded victims who have yielded to her smooth words.

Blessed is the person who endures temptation, for when that one has been approved, he will receive the crown of life which the Lord has promised to those who love Him. The enticing voices that offer salvation without the death of the body of sinful deeds has captured countless sinners who want to be saved but still be able to enjoy the pleasures of sin. *But each one is tempted when he is drawn away by his own desires and enticed. Then when desire has conceived it gives birth to sin; and sin when it is full grown brings forth death.*

I am sure you have heard it but not so sure it has been identified for what it is. This is actually a life and death situation, and ignoring it carries a verdict of death. No matter how smooth, how enticing or how biblically sound ongoing sin is presented, it is contrary to the truth of the gospel. Yielding to temptation after receiving the knowledge of the truth leaves a sinner with no more sacrifice for their sin.

A truly contrite heart turns from temptation and sin, and if the person with such a heart walks in the light as Jesus is in the light, then His blood will cleanse that person from all unrighteousness. There is no recourse for the person who makes provision for the desires of the flesh and the sin it produces.

ROMANS 13:14

545 FEAR (REVISITED)

The Lord is speaking of fear. Fear is a double-edged sword. *The fear of the Lord is the beginning of knowledge and wisdom. . . . The fear of man brings a snare, but whoever trusts in the Lord shall be safe . . . . The fear of the Lord is to hate evil; pride and arrogance and the evil way and the perverse mouth. . . . And do not fear those who kill the body but cannot kill the soul but rather fear Him who is able to destroy both soul and body in hell . . . Who is the person who fears the Lord? That person He will teach in the way He chooses. He will dwell in prosperity and his descendants shall inherit the land. The secret of the Lord is with those who fear Him and He will show them His covenant.*

Fear has overtaken the whole world and displaced the peace that existed in much of it: a debilitating fear that causes torment and despair. *Yea, though I walk through the valley of the shadow of death I shall fear no evil for You are with me. . . God is our refuge and strength a very present help in trouble. Therefore, I will not fear.* It certainly appears that we are given a choice with regard to whom and what we fear. Only a fool would choose the fear of circumstance and uncertainty rather than the rock-solid and unchanging fear of the Lord.

Faith, of course, is the deciding factor in our choice and our well-being. There is much more that could be said, but it should not be necessary for anyone to make the choice to fear the Lord or to fear "fear" itself.

Fear is a big deal, isn't it?

PROVERBS 14:26-27

546 ASSURANCE

Faith is the vehicle by which assurance is obtained. Faith requires absolute obedience to the voice of God in order to function. Any assurance of salvation a person may be clinging to without the assurance given by the witness of the Holy Spirit and the word of God is "pie in the sky". The flesh merchants of religion offer an assurance of redemption based on partial truths and fables that bind their captives to the present world.

Jesus unequivocally came to deliver His people from their sins and this present world. You may have heard this before, but what is the reality of it? The mass indoctrination of the multitudes that attend church on Sunday and participate in huge religious gatherings of self-proclaimed sinners certainly do not reflect the truth of the gospel once delivered to the saints by Jesus and His apostles. So, what are we who love the truth to do?

The answer lies in diligently seeking the Lord and the fullness of His counsel. The assurance that we seek is found in Oneness with Him. There is no substitute for the relationship that comes from abiding in Christ. This is where the assurance and the confidence of salvation is originated and maintained. It is also the place where the command to cease from sin becomes a possible reality. The person who continues to sin and believes they are a sinner cannot have this assurance of salvation regardless of their indoctrination.

Let the dead bury their dead. You follow Me. . . .If the blind lead the blind they will all fall in the ditch.

ACTS 17:30-31

547 REFUGE

Everyone is looking for refuge, but there are few who actually are able to find the secret place for which they search. Many will try to enter the place of true security without the confidence to actually pass through its gates. The wealthy fool trusts in his/her riches for refuge from the tempest. The common person believes the lies and promises of governing and religious leaders who have no real power.

The Lord is our strength and our deliverer, a very present help in the time of trouble. The verses regarding the refuge, protection, deliverance, a hiding place and covering are numerous throughout scripture, but there are qualifications for anyone who would claim them as their own. Many have been taught that belief and confession of Jesus' salvation without the fruit of true righteousness and holiness gives them access to God's refuge. Nevertheless, without the confidence and assurance of true and living relationship with Jesus, the promises are empty.

No person living according to their flesh will possess the peace or the assurance provided by the witness of the Holy Spirit to actually experience the security and refuge promised by the Lord.

There is a way that seems right to a person but ends in death. Partial obedience to the ways of God does not please Him, as Balaam has shown us. So, too, partial faith and double-mindedness will not produce the assurance and refuge every person desires. Total commitment and obedience that leaves no room for conscious sin is the blamelessness required by the Lord for any person to dwell with Him in the safety of His presence.

EPHESIANS 4:17-24
HEBREWS 12:12-17
JOEL 3:16-17

548 FROM WHERE—TO WHERE?

Every individual who has heard the call of the voice of God has been called from where they are to a new and different place. Obedience to this call is the beginning of a journey of faith that, if a person continues on in obedience to the voice of God, will end in paradise.

Where we have come from is the place where our biological senses predominate our lives. Where we are called to is another dimension where our natural senses submit to the Spiritual guidance directed by our invisible Creator, who is calling us into the realm where He dwells. We are clearly instructed to leave our old lives behind and move on to newness of life. Obedience through faith is clearly the path on which the Spirit of God is leading. Only a fool would believe that Christ would lead us into sin on this narrow path on which He leads.

The person who turns back to the place from which they have come or listens to voices other than God's can wander off the way which the Holy Spirit is leading. It is our individual responsibility to obey the voice of the One who originally called us from the world that is perishing into the glorious liberty to which we are called.

This liberty and freedom lead to the place where only the righteous may enter and dwell. It is the land where Jesus has gone before us to prepare a place for those who love Him and obey Him. There is no accommodation in this place where the blameless are called for those who have turned back to the place from where they were called. The person who still loves the place from where they were called will certainly be allowed to return and stay there, but we who have received the love of the truth and the new life we have been given will surely be given the ability to prosper there.

2 CORINTHIANS 5:16-21

549 EDICTS

Edicts have come down on both the citizenry of the carnal nations and the Spiritual nation of which we have a part. These edicts are coming from self-proclaimed authorities who do not have the legitimacy needed to make them.

Most of these self-proclaimed authorities are no more than political and religious bureaucrats who have succeeded in making themselves more important and powerful than legitimate dignitaries.

These illegitimate edicts come in many forms from medical, ethical, moral and subjective, to laws created by the bureaucracy that has no right to make them. This is all the result of fear, panic and insecurity brought on by forces who want to destroy prosperity, take away freedom and make slaves of free people.

It is actually a form of tyranny and rebellion brought about by those seeking power over others. The tyrannical forces that would be dictators and enslave all of humanity have raised their heads and made themselves known. Though they lie and attempt to hide their true motivation, the discerning among us have uncovered the diabolical schemes they are near to bringing about. Truth is our defense against them, and God is on the side of justice; yet, in the Creator's plan for mankind he does allow the wicked to momentarily prosper. He judges harshly those who use His name and have taken it in vain. We are witnessing such judgment in our nation and throughout the earth now. Kings and dictators can only prosper if God allows, and the multitude of princes in our country is the direct result of the wickedness the people have embraced, particularly in the large cities. It may well be time for the prudent among us to hide themselves until the tempest has passed.

The Lord has promised that the righteous will see the demise of the wicked.

PSALM 37:1-20+
PROVERBS 22:3

550 SIGNIFICANCE

This Jesus is the stone rejected by you builders which has become the cornerstone. And there is salvation in no one else for there is no other name under heaven given among mankind by which we must be saved . . . Therefore, God has highly exalted Him and given Him the name which is above every name so that, at the name of Jesus every knee should bow in heaven and on earth and under the earth, and every tongue confess that Jesus Christ is Lord.

It is truly amazing to hear people constantly use His name as a curse word and worse. Equally distressing is to hear religious people use His name as some kind of gimmick to attempt to produce self-glorifying miracles. The name of Jesus, the Christ, is the most significant and wonderful name a person can utter. It is sacred, and anyone who has even elementary wisdom will use it reverently.

To use Jesus' name in vain (vainly) is foolishness that exceeds reason. How can a person escape the repercussions of the mindless and careless use of a name so significant? Many will weep and howl when He appears and they realize their folly. What is being explained here is an attempt to turn some who may hear to stop and really think about the name that is above all others.

In Jesus dwells the fullness of the Godhead bodily. His name represents the power and authority of the Creator Himself.

MATTHEW 28:18

551 MEANING

The meaning of life can be known and understood. *Those who seek the Lord understand all. . . The eyes of a fool are on the ends of the earth.* The essence of the meaning of life may be found in the Lord's great commandments. *You shall love the Lord your God with all your heart, soul, mind and strength. And love your neighbor as yourself.* SELAH!

Jesus is the model. He always obeyed the voice of His Father. He never sinned. At the end of His life, He had the testimony that He had completed everything His Father had sent Him to do. As He died, He said, "*It is finished.*" We who have been given a new life and become one Spirit with Him and are told to *walk as He walked;* is His Father not our Father? If we can hear His voice, is there a justifiable reason not to obey it? This new life we have received, is it not His?

Though our lives are diverse, can the Almighty not direct each one to do the work and complete the tasks for which He has created us? Most of us have been taught that we are not able to perform such a feat, but the instructors have lied and contradicted the words of scripture and the voice of the Holy Spirit. *We can do all things through Christ.* And this certainly includes obeying Him.

So, the real meaning and purpose of our existence is to glorify our Creator by loving Him above all others and loving our fellow human beings as ourselves. This really is simple, and anyone who has a heart to do it can!

ROMANS 13:8-10
2 CORINTHIANS 10:4-6
JAMES 2:18-24
1 CORINTHIANS 7:19
JOHN 7:14

552 FULFILLMENT

Those searching for fulfillment from things of the world along with peace and rest will fall short of their desire. Even in noble things, there is no lasting satisfaction, because everything that can be accomplished in the natural realm is temporary and vain.

Those who diligently seek the Lord according to His terms are the few able to enter His rest and experience the peace and fulfillment of which He has spoken. The disobedient, sinners, and those without the necessary faith to enter His rest cannot achieve their hoped-for desire. Belief without the obedience produced by faith will leave the one who is searching without the resources needed to achieve fulfillment.

Mankind has been designed by their Creator to only reach their full potential and realization of who they are through a real and living relationship with the One who created them. Artificial and superficial goals and achievements only leave a person looking for a further reality. To understand this will free a person to search for spiritual and eternal fulfillment of which the Bible speaks.

Why go on any further searching the earth or even outer space for the things that only exist in another realm? Only in the Spirit can true riches be found or even be discerned. Scripture has told us all these things, but there are only few who have ears to hear and eyes to see.

DEUTERONOMY 10:12-13
HEBREWS 3:7 through 4:11
JOHN 3:11-12
2 PETER 3:11-14

553 THE STING

Sin, of course, is the sting of death. The persons who fear death do so because of a regard for sin in their hearts. The unknown is actually not unknown for the one whose heart is blameless before God. The pure in heart possess the assurance of favor and security in death. The sinners, even the ones who are taught that all their sins are covered despite the continuation of sinning, may confess that it has no hold on them, but the fact remains.

The Lord has made provision for the truly contrite sinner to come to a place of right standing with Himself, but the one who does not honestly repent and cease from sinning is lying to themself and to the rest of creation. *God will not be mocked,* and those who call themselves sinners in an attempt to appear humble are in reality mocking the claims of the gospel.

The truth is recorded in the books, and only the truth will cancel the "sting of death". Every person has the witness in their heart of blamelessness or guilt regardless of what they may have been taught to believe. There is no reprieve from the sting of unforgiven sin or the death that it creates.

Believing the truth and obeying it is the remedy for a person's heart to experience freedom from death and its sting. The alternative is dreadful and is the destiny of the soul that continues to disobey God. SELAH! Is the pleasure derived from sin really worth the cost? Most of us would say no, but at the same time, many look for a doctrine or teacher that would absolve them from the consequence of its continuation.

2 THESSALONIANS 2:9-12
1 PETER 3:10-12
2 PETER 1:3-11

554 EARTH

Earth is the dwelling place of the biological creation and the home of the carnal-minded and all who live according to the flesh. The Lord has presented and offered an alternative residence for the person who will believe Him and obey Him. It is a land where He Himself dwells. It is the place from which Jesus came to earth, and to which He returned when His work on earth was finished. We have been invited.

The temporary nature of earth leaves the natural human being with only the hope of a beast of the earth. The religious teachers and preachers would have mankind remain content to abide and trust in our natural state in order to serve themselves. The Spirit of God is calling us to the land where only spirits live, and the influence of our flesh has been made subservient to Himself. Though we may have heard a similar message in the past, the Lord would have us re-examine the status of our hearts and minds.

The things we can see are temporary while the things we cannot see (with our natural eyes) are eternal. To whom is our supreme loyalty, and where is our citizenship? These are serious questions and demand honest answers.

Brethren, we are near the end, and we must be ready. We must not allow all the distractions of the world to cause us to veer off course.

2 PETER 1:12-13
2 CORINTHIANS 13:5-6

555 GODLINESS (NEW CREATION 101)

Godliness, holiness and righteousness are qualities the Lord has commanded of His chosen. How is it that organizations bearing the name of Christ teach that sinners are the chosen ones who share the nature of the Holy God? Are these things not diametrically opposed?

The whole purpose of God in salvation is to free the sinner from sin. The idea that godliness is some positional standing without substance in a person's life is both wrong and blasphemous. How could such deception and acceptance as truth possibly become one of the elementary teachings of the gospel?

Godliness is to be like God, which is exactly what His great salvation has provided for. Jesus came to save sinners from their sin and both show the way and make the way for those who would believe Him and trust Him to walk as He walked and fulfill and obey the commandments of God.

If what you are hearing sounds too radical and unscriptural you need to return to the gospel recorded in the Bible without the help of organized religion and paid professionals. What is being spoken of is basic truth. If a person is unable to see it and hear it, that one has been indoctrinated by the ungodly or has not received the love of the truth.

Certainly, anyone who hungers and thirsts for righteousness and truth will rejoice in the freedom from sin and death that Jesus is providing. The way of the sinner is hard and leads to death. The way of the godly leads to peace, joy, love and heaven itself. The time has come to question what all the tax-exempt "church" daughters are teaching and where they are trying to lead those called to be as Jesus.

ROMANS 8:28-29
1 JOHN 2:5-6; 3:5-7
EPHESIANS 4:21-24
HEBREWS 12:14
2 PETER 1:3-4
PSALMS 86:1-2

556 DOUBT

To know the voice of God, to hear it and believe it, and then to steadfastly obey it produces the faith and confidence that does not allow doubt to gain a foothold. In Eden, the clever serpent was successful in causing Eve to doubt the word the Creator had spoken directly to her and her husband. We all know the story, and it exemplifies the seriousness of doubting the word of God. Things have not changed to this day. Faith and confidence are the results of hearing, believing, and obeying the voice of God.

If any of you lacks wisdom, let that person ask God who gives generously to all without reproach, and it will be given to him, but let that person ask in faith with no doubting, for the one who doubts is like a wave of the sea that is driven and tossed by the wind, for that person must not suppose that he or she will receive anything from the Lord; that person is double-minded and unstable in all his or her ways.

If a person believes they are a sinner, tell me how that person could possibly expect the Lord to respond favorably to a petition they make.

In order to overcome doubt, a person must be able to stand blamelessly before God and have a pure heart. This is not possible for a sinner or one who has not believed what Jesus' sacrifice has accomplished.

I write these things to you who believe in the name of the Son of God that you may know that you have eternal life. And this is the confidence that we have toward Him, that if we ask anything according to His will, He hears us. And if we know that He hears us in whatever we ask, we know that we have the requests that we have asked of Him. . . . We know that whoever has been born of God does not keep on sinning, but he who has been born of God keeps himself and the wicked one (who deceived Eve) does not touch him.

Doubt may present itself, but if our minds are stayed in Christ, it will not have the power to overcome our faith.

HEBREWS 4:14-16
JOHN 1:4-5
REVELATION 3:20-22
MARK 11:22-26

557 TECHNOLOGICAL THEOLOGY

This watchman has observed many who choose to establish their theological and doctrinal beliefs based on a constant yet changeable search of internet commentary. While this use of technology has nearly endless information and opinions, truth is largely obscured and perverted. This form of religious technology leads to uncertainty, doubt, and confusion.

The Holy Spirit and God's revelation of truth is the only reliable application of scripture. Life is in the Spirit and most likely not on the internet. The Lord can certainly use the internet, but unless the actual voice of God can be heard by its users, deception is most likely inevitable. The abundance of professional counselors who can be bribed and influenced by prejudice and bias will nearly always produce lies and perversions.

Where will any person end up who does not learn to discern truth and hear the actual voice of God? He says that everyone must work out their own salvation with fear and trembling. The comfort of false prophets, teachers, and commentators leads to death.

The point is that no government, religious or secular, can lead its followers into the love of the truth that only the Spirit of God is capable of doing.

PSALM 25:1-5

558 WHAT IS

The reality of what is and the actuality of where we are in the grand scheme of the Creator's plan is near completion. The whole world is on the course of destruction. There is little an individual can do beyond changing their own heart and mind. Our faithful Creator has made the way of escape from eternal death, but there seem to be few who have a desire to go His way.

While the great sea of humanity rages and flounders looking for relief from the obvious disaster occurring before our eyes, there is a person who is being prepared to take upon himself the place of God and deceive the whole world into submitting to his evil reign over the earth. Yes, he is the human manifestation of the lawless one who has lied and caused destruction on the earth from the beginning. He is the antithesis of the One who loves His whole creation and is the one who has been prophesied to appear in the last days before the end.

Antichrist is the diabolical opposite of the Lord, who is love and has offered salvation to all who love the truth. His spirit and his followers have been here from the beginning. His hatred and violence have plagued humankind from the time the first man gave him license by rejecting the commandment of the Creator.

The Almighty has set a limit on the tyranny we now see on the earth, and we are drawing near to it. What is—is this: The manifestation of the rebellion of the human heart and the rejection of legitimate authority. Rest assured that God remains in control and will save those who love Him. The just Judge is at the door, and no one will escape His justice.

GALATIONS 6:7-10
MATTHEW 24:4-14
2 THESSALONIANS 2:3-12
1 JOHN 4:1-6

559 BURDENS

If the burdens we attempt to bear are too heavy and beyond our ability to successfully carry them, there is something wrong. *Jesus said, "Come to Me all you who labor and are heavy laden and I will give you rest. Take My yoke upon you and learn from Me for I am gentle and lowly in heart, and you will find rest for your souls. For My yoke is easy and My burden is light".* His promise is true, so what is wrong cannot be the Lord's fault but must lie with the one who is overburdened.

The promise does not apply to sinners or anyone who does not trust the Lord or believe Him. The dilemma that most of us face is one of misunderstanding or false belief in what is required to enter His rest and partake of His yoke. What right does a person who goes on sinning after being forgiven and cleansed have to claim the Lord's promises or to be relieved of the burden of sin? Only the misinformed can have such hope or expect such relief.

The fact remains that there is a place of rest where the people of God are able to enter through faith. Those unable to enter cannot do so because of unbelief and disobedience. The person who does not understand this is the one who continues to live his or her own life and has not lost it for the Lord. This is only complicated for the person who is trying to understand spiritual things using their carnal mind. Jesus' words are Spirit, and they are life for those who are able to hear them; so, too, are nearly all the promises of God.

To be carnally minded is death but to be Spiritually minded is life and peace.

HEBREWS 3:18 through 4:3

560 REVIVAL

Revival meetings and fundraisers share elevated emotional and evangelical pleas for prayer and financial support. While finances may be more subtle, they are usually connected to the plea for the blessing of spiritual renewal and awakening. This is a somewhat shocking indictment, but careful observation will reveal this as common practice among the 501c3's.

Public requests and pleas for money are so common among TV, radio, and other forms of electronic religious ministries that their voices can be heard nearly nonstop. The revival they seek and the blessings they promise are highly suspect and obviously self-serving. These are the peddlers and flesh merchants who have used the gospel as a means of personal gain.

The broadness of this accusation is because of the widespread misuse of Jesus' name and the disingenuous use of the gospel.

If the Spirit of God genuinely moves in a person's heart and in a group, the result will be one of true repentance and lives that are permanently changed. The excitement of the moment will translate into true holiness and righteousness rather than a return to sinning and a need to confess the same transgressions over and over. True revival will cause permanent change that does not require an annual or semi-annual repeat of being stirred up and resaved.

Whole-hearted giving is the way of life for those who have become chosen and does not require constant fund-raising drives to sustain ministries that are appealing to a basically self-centered constituency who are living according to the flesh. All these charlatans will disappear just as they have appeared, and their followers will have to move on to yet another one to tickle their ears and give them temporary solace.

2 TIMOTHY 4:3-4
2 PETER 2:1-3
ISAIAH 57:15

561 COMMON SENSE

Common sense is a companion of the power of reason and even wisdom. It can look at the sky at night and know there is an intelligent Creator, and during the day, can hear His voice in all that He has made. The fool cannot or will not acknowledge such obvious revelation.

The governors and authorities of our large cities seem to be void of the endowment of these invaluable gifts. So, too, are the religious leaders who extol sinners as the foundation of their earthly kingdoms. *Those who call evil good and good evil are an abomination to the Lord.* So, too, are they an affront to common sense and a sound mind.

The idea that centralized authority can justly govern a people and have no fear of God and no regard for His judgments and commands epitomizes folly. This is where the politicians and theocrats are attempting to lead the whole country.

Common sense and justice will build a nation up, but the anarchy and disregard for law and order will surely destroy society and the whole culture that has produced the peace and prosperity that most of us have enjoyed and is the envy of most of the world.

Those who lack common sense and integrity are facing the death of hope in the future as well as eternity. The time has come for those who have the common sense to know right from wrong and left from right to stand up. This is the hour that may be the last opportunity to do it.

PROVERBS 14:33-34

562 OPINION

There is no shortage of opinions or points of view in the world today. A person with a rational mind may have an opinion with some merit and value if it is aligned with truth, but an irrational fool's opinion is worth less than nothing. These foolish opinions have gained wide circulation throughout the earth in the current time of confusion and upheaval. *A fool takes no pleasure in understanding but only in expressing his or her opinion.* Our city streets are full of such foolishness and ignorance.

A fruitful land is being set ablaze by the opinion and demonstration of those who have no understanding of what they are doing. They don't even seem to realize that they will find nothing to eat amidst the rubble of what they have destroyed. If they are allowed to continue in their folly, even those who have a measure of rationality and common sense will suffer.

While freedom of speech allows even the insane and self-destructive persons to voice their opinions, if they are permitted to implement them, the fruitful land will become a wasteland where tyranny and lawlessness will rule the streets.

Unless the Almighty intervenes, we will surely know that His judgment has come upon this nation because of those whose wicked opinions have prevailed. We can but hope and pray that it will not be so. Preparations must be made.

The prudent sees danger and hides himself but the simple go on and suffer for it.

PROVERBS 1:7; 10:8,14,20-21; 12:15; 14:8, 16; 13:16; 28:26; 29:11
2 THESSALONIANS 2:9-12

563 IDOLS AND FALSE GODS

Almost anything can be an idol or a false god if it is given that status. Even noble things and worthwhile endeavors can be elevated to a place in a person's heart beyond their devotion to our Creator. SELAH! We know the Lord's first and greatest commandment, at least I hope so. It is quite literal, but even so, it may need highlighting. It is easy to pass over without any real contemplation or serious deliberation.

As I watch people, even those who claim to be believers, I see them elevate a host of things higher than the Almighty God. From my vantage point can be seen nearly all of humanity putting the love of things, money, ideas, traditions, beliefs, other people, hobbies, lies, special interests, causes, pets, and of course, the list could go on. The point is that the Lord Himself is the only thing (Person) that deserves to be first in every person's life. This is not some idealistic goal or ambition. It is the command of God. To fall short is to miss the mark completely and not be able to stand blameless before Him. What you are hearing is a wake-up call to all who have called upon His name and taken it as God.

The Lord God demands and deserves to be first and highest in every person's life. If anyone misses this or doesn't believe it, they have missed the meaning of life and the reward that has been prepared for those who love Him. Meditation and honesty are in order here!

Our time is short.

COLOSSIANS 1:9-14; 3:5-6
LUKE 10:25-28; 14:25-27
1 CORINTHIANS 10:19-22
1 JOHN 5:20-21

564 WORRY

I have heard people ask if it is a sin to worry. The Lords says: *Whatever is not of faith is sin.* This is certainly to the point! If we allow ourselves to worry and be anxious, we are demonstrating a lack of trust. This is a major issue throughout scripture. Without trust, faith has no foundation, and we reap the scourge and torture of worry.

The whole issue can be settled by steadfastly believing God at His word. The assurance of the Holy Spirit and His witness of God's love should be totally sufficient to overcome the worry and anxiety and doubt that arises due to the lack of faith.

Some people actually believe that worry is a virtue and proudly proclaim how they worry. Have you heard it? If we believe the truth and take the Lord at His word, there remains no place for the nonsense of worry. What can, or does, it change? Its effect can be paralyzing and prevent a person from the trusting relationship with our Savior which He, as well as we, desire.

If we are following after the Holy Spirit and walking in footsteps of Jesus, worry has no access to our consciousness or our lives. To entertain worry is foolishness and disobedience.

I think no more needs to be said.

MATTHEW 6:25-34

565 VISUALS

When you see . . . we have been given visual signs that will accompany the end times and the Lord's second coming. They come with cautions and warnings as well as admonitions. The signs prophesied from ancient times are appearing in the nations, the environment and the heavens. They are here for all who have eyes to see. The "*abomination of desolation*" and the appearing of antichrist are not as many have imagined and are being brought into focus in this hour.

Lucid descriptions and vivid pictures of the last days are being revealed in metaphors and revelations through watchmen and prophets throughout the earth. What is happening worldwide has happened on a limited scale throughout history, but the worldwide scale of the phenomenon taking place now is universally cataclysmic and catastrophic.

The Lord has described His Bride to us in detail. She is a Spiritual entity consisting of faithful overcomers who have made themselves ready to meet Him. She is holy and pure, wearing spotless, white garments. She has been chosen from among all who have ever lived on earth. She is not from Canaan, nor does she mingle with the daughters of Canaan. Her appearance is dazzling, and her countenance is glorious. She is a delight to her Husband and never causes Him shame.

Does this description of the "Bride of Christ" sound like the multi-factioned conglomeration that calls itself "the church" on the earth today? You know! The seat of antichrist is in the midst of her temple and is being exposed as you read these words. The throne on which he (and she) are seated is here on the earth. The throne on which Jesus is seated is in heaven. Can you see them? When they can be seen, the conflict of the ages can also be seen.

I hope you know what to do; and also, every reader is among the chosen in Christ.

MATTHEW 24:15-31
REVELATION 21:9-14; 3:1-6; 4:1-11

566 DELIGHT

In what does our soul delight? And, even more significant, in what does the Lord's soul delight? *As for the saints who are on the earth, they are the excellent ones in whom is all MY (my) delight. . . Trust in the Lord and do good; dwell in the land and feed on His faithfulness, delight yourself also in the Lord and He will give you the desires of your heart . . . But the meek shall inherit the land and delight themselves in the abundance of peace.* This is a spiritual land where only the righteous dwell, and there is no ongoing sin. This is where the saints of God have entered His Sabbath rest and ceased their own works.

Those who delight in the ways of God are His chosen in whom He delights. They are His own special people. They are special because they have taken on the image of the firstborn of the new creation, who is Jesus and have become His brethren. They always obey Him and do the things that please Him. Their prayers are His delight, but the prayers of the wicked are an abomination to Him.

Herein we see the contrast between the truly meek and humble who actually submit to the Lord and those who, calling themselves sinners (which they are) believe that this confession demonstrates their humility, thus pleasing God. Not so! Only true holiness, righteousness and obedience please Him and give Him delight. False humility is no better than any other form of hypocrisy, and *sin is a reproach to any people.*

To sum up what delights the Lord is all the things that Jesus did as a man and is doing through the lives of those who abide in Him now and in whom He abides.

GALATIANS 2:17-20
1 TIMOTHY 5:20

567 TECHNICALITIES

The laws produced by natural man are filled with technicalities and minute details, which are able to subvert justice and negate its enforcement. Not so with heaven's justice. In the end every person will receive absolute and righteous justice based on their works and deeds. *Justice for mankind is from the Lord.* The theology lawyers have devised technicalities by which those who do not fulfill the righteous requirements of God's commandments can escape the justice the Lord has decreed. These technical arguments will not prevail in the final judgment. In fact, they will not even be given a voice. These theological technicalities are foolishness in the eyes of the Just Judge.

The commandments of God are not ambiguous, and the penalty for disobedience is no more equivocal. In His love and mercy, the Lord has provided an escape from the penalty of disobeying Him. This mercy has come to us through the great sacrifice of Jesus Christ and His shed blood. What God has required of everyone who has partaken of this grace and mercy is to turn from the cause of the death sentence that has been stayed.

If any person rejects the requirements God has put forth to realize the benefit of His abundant provision, that person will die. The theological lawyers have devised doctrines by which a person who has been redeemed and forgiven can continue in the sin and disobedience from which they were delivered and not suffer the penalty for what they do. There are whole institutions, organizations, denominations and churches which have subscribed to these diabolical technicalities.

*Anyone who has rejected Moses' law dies without mercy on the testimony of two or three witnesses. Of how much worse punishment do you suppose will he be thought worthy who has trampled the Son of God under foot, counted the blood of the covenant by which he was sanctified a common thing and insulted the Spirit of Grace? For we know Him who said, "Vengeance is Mine," says the Lord. "I will repay," says the Lord. And again, the Lord will judge His people. It is a fearful thing to fall into the hands of the Living God . . . While they (*theological lawyers*) promise them liberty, they themselves are slaves of corruption; for by whom a person is overcome (*believers*) by him also he is brought into bondage; for if after they have escaped the pollutions of the world through the knowledge of Jesus Christ they are again entangled in them and overcome, the latter end is worse for them than the beginning; for it would have been better for them not to have known the way of* *righteousness than having known it, to turn from the holy commandment delivered to them.*

Do these scriptures leave room for the loopholes the professionals of Ecclesia have devised to allow their captive sheep to disregard the truth for the sake of their godless doctrines and denominations?

Awake to righteousness and do not sin for some do not have the knowledge of God. I speak this to your shame.

GALATIANS 6:7-9
REVELATION 20:11-15

568 INSOLENT DERISION

We are witnessing an insolent and rebellious incursion on the streets of our major cities that is astonishing. These anarchists deride everything decent and righteous and break every commandment of God and rule of law with apparent impunity. Can these fascists prevail? They are all Democrats. A presidential election is near, and if the USA falls completely into the hands of those who hate her, what will become of the rest of the civilized world?

Those who trust in the Lord will not be forsaken by Him, but what of the rest of mankind? It seems as though lawlessness has a chance of overcoming the rule of law. If this occurs, we can be sure that the balance of good and evil has finally tipped in favor of the wickedness that has been gaining strength for many years, and the favor of the Almighty has turned away.

It is certainly time to seek His mercy for this nation and the world, but without His intervention the end of everything that is upright may be near the prophesied end. Even if society completely breaks down, we who trust the Lord will have a refuge in the midst of the tribulation, just as Noah and the faithful of Jerusalem in the day of Babylon's conquest.

When the whirlwind has passed the wicked will be no more . . . Those who call evil good and good evil will be silenced along with those who have insolently derided those who love peace and truth. In the final hour God's judgment will be seen by all, and His righteousness will prevail.

Nevertheless, it is good for us to seek the preservation of the good things that have been able to withstand the onslaught that has come upon civilization.

The end is already determined.

REVELATION 17:13-14

569 ONE LIFETIME

Every human being has one lifetime to live in their natural body. The amount of time allotted to each person may vary, but every moment counts. We are here for a reason and each of us will give account of what we have done in our fleshly bodies to our Creator. SELAH!

Jesus Christ, of course, is the supreme example of a life that was perfectly lived, while his time was only approximately thirty-three years. Most of us are only part way into our lives at that age. By that time, we have hopefully discovered why we are here and where we are going. Unfortunately, most people have no idea. They spend their resources just surviving. The example that Jesus has given us is what each individual has been created for.

This may sound far-fetched or idealistic, but it is nevertheless what our Creator has intended that we are on earth to be and do. Those whom the Spirit has called have been given the opportunity to become children of God and fulfill our purpose. We who actually become chosen in Christ are the ones who are able to do it. This again, may sound idealistic and unrealistic to the carnal mind, but to the one who has become One Spirit with Christ, it has become the life that we live.

When our life on earth in a biological body ends, the person who is the brother or sister of Jesus just steps into an existence free of the distractions and encumbrances of the flesh. This is an exciting prospect and makes for a fulfilling and meaningful life here on earth.

What you are hearing is the truth of the gospel and the hope given to us in God's word.

Let's get on with it!

1 JOHN 4:17-19
1 CORINTHIANS 6:17,19-20
ROMANS 8:28-30
GALATIANS 2:20

570 SPEAKING TRUTH

Speaking truth begins in our hearts. If we are not honest with ourselves, how can we be truthful with anyone else? And how can the truth be discerned by a person who does not even speak truth in his/her own heart? The Lord requires the person who would abide in His presence to speak the truth in his/her heart.

Those who have believed lies have stored them up within themselves, and when they speak out of the abundance of their hearts lies will proceed from their lips. There are multitudes of churchgoers who are doing this very thing. One who is able to discern truth can hear the lies in nearly every sermon and broadcast. In most cases, what began as a move of the Spirit of Truth has deteriorated into the deceptions of the human heart.

Those who have received the love of the truth are the chosen ones who are able to hear and discern truth and also walk in it. Is this not the truth? The hearts of those who have not received this love have been sent a strong delusion from God that allows them to be deceived in their own hearts and in their own minds and continue on in the deception and unrighteousness the lies produce.

The solution to this dilemma is repentance from the deceitfulness of sin and a truly contrite heart. The love of the truth is bestowed on those whose hearts have become blameless before God and abide in the Truth, who is Jesus. The person who has lost his/her own life for Jesus' sake will understand what it means to speak the truth in his/her heart and in every circumstance.

PSALM 15:1-5

571 BUILDING

The Lord is a builder. He is building a metaphorical house as well as a whole city. He is building it with precious living stones. One by one, he skillfully places each stone. *For every house is built by someone but the builder of all things is God. Now Moses was faithful in all God's house as a servant to testify to the things that were to be spoken later, but Christ is faithful over God's house as a Son and we are His house if indeed we hold fast our confidence and the rejoicing of hope firm to the end. . . Beware, brethren lest there be in any of you an evil heart of unbelief in departing from the Living God; but exhort one another daily while it is called today lest any of you be hardened through the deceitfulness of sin. For we have become partakers of Christ if we hold the beginning of our confidence steadfast to the end.*

The altar constructed to offer sacrifices to God by ancient Israel was built of stones that were not hewn by human hands. So, too, the altar on which we sacrifice is a spiritual one of which the carnal person cannot participate. *We have an altar from which those who serve the tabernacle (flesh) have no right to eat. Then one of the seven angels who had the seven bowls filled with the seven last plagues came to me and talked with me, saying, "Come, I will show you the Bride, the Lamb's wife." And he carried me away in the Spirit to a great and high mountain and showed me the great city, the Holy Jerusalem descending out of heaven from God having the glory of God. . . The construction of its wall was of jasper, and the city was pure gold like pure glass. The foundations of the wall of the city were adorned with all kinds of precious stones . . . But there shall by no means enter it anything that defiles or causes an abomination or a lie, but only those who are written in the Lamb's Book of Life.*

What is being built is clearly a spiritual house and city. It has no earthly headquarters and no carnal leaders or authorities. There is no entry for anyone who has not sacrificed their life on the spiritual altar and lost it for Jesus' sake.

Where are the sinners who continue to serve the earthly tabernacle?

1 PETER 2:4-12

572 WHEN NO ONE CAN WORK

I must work the works of Him who sent Me while it is day; the night is coming when no one can work . . . You are the light of the world; a city that is set on a hill cannot be hidden nor do they light a lamp and put it under a basket but on a lampstand, and it gives light to all who are in the house. Let your light so shine before mankind that they may see your good works and glorify your Father in heaven. . . . I am the light of the world. The person who follows Me shall not walk in darkness but have the light of life. . . . As You have sent Me into the world, I also have sent them into the world.

The pattern is obvious. *Then I heard a voice from heaven saying to me, "Write: Blessed are the dead who die in the Lord from now on". "Yes," says the Spirit, "that they may rest from their labors and their works follow them. . . . I have been crucified with Christ; it is no longer I who live but Christ lives in me.* The time to work is short, and the point is that it must be done while we have the liberty to do it. The darkness is coming, and the visionaries are speaking. When the prophesied darkness has come, all work will be underground and far more treacherous to perform.

The path of the just is like the shining light that shines ever brighter unto the perfect day. The way of the wicked is like darkness; they do not know what makes them stumble . . . God is light, and in Him is no darkness at all. If we say that we have fellowship with Him and walk in darkness we lie and do not practice the truth, but if we walk in the light as He is in the light we have fellowship with one another, and the blood of Jesus Christ, His Son, cleanses us from all sin.

The forces of darkness are here and coming. The darkness that will cover the whole earth is at hand, and the true "Body of Christ" has work to do while we are able.

AMOS 5:13-20

573 MORE ABOUT HOPE

The heart filled with hope is one able to withstand despair and all the forces that come against it. Real hope based on truth and faith in God and His word is a force that cannot be defeated. Hope is able to rise from the most devastating calamities and the darkest circumstances.

We are living in an age when the person without the hope that comes from knowing the Lord can easily slip into depression and despair. When the foundations of law and order are crumbling before our eyes, and the security we have always known is disappearing, the hope that a person has is the real assurance of well-being that stands firm in the face of disaster.

Genuine trust in the Lord gives an immutable hope that is as unchangeable as the One in whom we trust. Is this hope not more valuable than silver and gold and all the things that the world can offer? Real hope is built on a spiritual foundation that cannot be seen with the natural eye nor comprehended with the carnal mind. The person who has a pure, blameless heart in the sight of God is the one who is able to possess such hope. It is a gift from the Creator who has all power in heaven and on earth. It is the result of abiding in Christ and being one with Him. Where else can any human being go to find such hope and joy in the midst of chaos and anarchy?

Hope in the Lord!

PSALM 31:24
HEBREWS 11:1

574 BABYLON

The heavenly view of Babylon is not the same as the carnal, earthly, and universally accepted understanding of who and what she is. Babylon is a metaphorical woman who is an adulteress, a whore and a mother. Her place on earth is also metaphorical along with her merchants and those fornicating with her. The career theologians and doctors of theology have, for the most part, missed her dominance in the world and the confusion she instigates. Babylon's reality and her identification are mysterious and diabolic, as well as treacherous. In her resides the cunning and deception of every false religion along with the tyrants that want to rule the world and enslave humanity. This metaphoric woman is the epitome of all that is wicked and evil that opposes the rightful place of God over His creation.

Her reign is near the end, and the Almighty will destroy her and her influence over mankind in short order. He has commanded the true Israel of God to repay her double for what she has done. The Lord's instruments of war and conquest are His people, and His command is to repay her double for her treachery and murder. The war we are in is spiritual, as are the weapons supplied to us by our Commander in Chief.

Only by revelation can she actually be seen and understood. Anyone can read about her (Babylon) in Jeremiah Chapter 51 and Revelation Chapters 17 and 18. If the Lord reveals her to you, you may well be overwhelmed by the magnitude of her dominion.

If you have a part in her kingdom, the time has come to get out and run. Her judgment is at hand.

JEREMIAH 51:6-10+
REVELATION 18:4-6+
PSALM 149:4-9

575 EDOMITES

Jacob I have loved; Esau I have hated, says the Lord. Why? Historically, these two sons of Isaac were twins, Esau being the firstborn. Metaphorically they represent the conflict between flesh and Spirit that spans the entire history of mankind. The record of the struggle between Edom and Israel is a parable that continues to this very day. The characters are metaphorical types of the first Adam and the second and last Adam. Listen now, and the whole story will be explained from the vantage point where those who have become brethren of Jesus are seated with Him in heavenly places.

Esau represents the man of the earth formed of the dust. He is a beast of the earth and lives according to his flesh. Israel (Jacob) is a type of the Man from heaven and lives according to the Spirit. They represent two nations which have been in conflict from the beginning. *The flesh lusts against the Spirit and the Spirit against the flesh.* The carnal man (Esau) is the enemy of God. The Spiritual man, Jacob, is a type of Christ the Son of God. Esau has hated Jacob ever since he supplanted Esau and tricked him into selling his inheritance as the firstborn son, much as the serpent tricked Adam out of his inheritance.

The parable deepens. These Edomites are the offspring of Esau, and Israel is the offspring of Jacob. They represent (are types of) a fleshly nation and a spiritual nation, the firstborn and the younger. Thus the saying: *The older shall serve the younger* and *the first shall be last and the last shall be first . . . First the fleshly and then the spiritual.* This paradigm fills the scriptures.

In the era in which we live, the conflict continues in the form of religious rivals that are no more than descendants of Esau and Jacob. The Edomites are the pretenders who falsely claim to be disciples of Jesus, but in reality, follow after their flesh and carnal understanding of Spiritual things. The true Israel of God consists of the chosen who have become one Spirit with the firstborn of the Spirit and His brethren.

The Edomites constantly attempt to reduce Spiritual truth down to the ground and would destroy the Spiritual nation if they were able. These Edomites have filled the earth with their flesh doctrines and their churches. They are tax exempt and sanctioned by worldly governments. The true Israel of God, which is the true "Body of Christ" remains a spiritual people who are not of this world system.

I hope you all can see them and will choose to follow the second Adam.

1 CORINTHIANS 15:35-49; 2:10-16
GALATIANS 4:22-26, 28-31

576 DILIGENCE

Diligence implies personal responsibility and work. The effort and labor involved in order to be diligent requires commitment and faithfulness. *But the day of the Lord will come like a thief and then the heavens will pass away with a roar, and the heavenly bodies will be burned up and dissolved, and the earth and the works that are done on it will be exposed. Since all these things are thus to be dissolved, what sort of people ought you to be in holy conduct and godliness looking for and hastening the coming of the day of God because of which the heavens will be dissolved being on fire and the elements will melt with fervent heat? Nevertheless, we according to His promise look for new heavens and a new earth in which righteousness dwells. Therefore, beloved, looking forward to these things, be diligent to be found by Him in peace without spot and blameless and consider that the long suffering of our Lord is salvation.*

Can going to a church service once or twice a week and attending a Bible study actually qualify as being diligent? Biblical qualifications require giving the totality of our lives and resources to the Lord in service to Him. Constant prayer with our minds set on heavenly things always engaged in the work of the Lord is the diligence of which the Bible actually speaks.

How do we measure up to the real standard of diligence that Jesus has exemplified for us?

1 JOHN 2:3-6

577 DO OR DIE

It is not the person who hears, or even believes, the voice of God who is justified, but the one who does (obeys) His voice that is justified. Is this not what the Bible actually says in both Old and New Testaments? Does this not explain why every person is judged by their works? *Show me your faith without your works and I will show you my faith by my works.* Are we not saved by faith? *Faith without works is dead.* Disputation of these Biblical truths is meritless.

The one who believes the commandments of God lives by (does) them. Keeping the commandments of God is what matters. Obedience to His voice is what He requires and always has. Ask Adam; ask Moses; ask Balaam; ask the young prophet who was slain by the lion. God is indeed loving and merciful, but the person who does not obey Him will die. What of the person who takes His name in vain?

The soul that sins will die. What of the person who sins after coming to a knowledge of the truth? What of the person who does not abide in Christ; the one whose sins have been forgiven and who then denies the Lord, what is that person's end? What of the person who wanders from the ways of God disobeying the truth and embraces the delusion sent to those who take pleasure in unrighteousness? The Lord has made His ways well known and has commanded us to do (obey) them.

It is clearly His will that His people not sin. Has the Lord not told us and shown us how to do what He has commanded? The whole issue of doing His will is found in the love of the truth and obedience to it. *It is the Spirit who gives life, the flesh is no help at all. The words I have spoken to you are Spirit and life . . . . If you live according to the flesh you will die, but if by the Spirit you put to death the deeds of the body (flesh) you will live. For all who are led by the Spirit of God are sons and daughters of God.*

This is the answer to doing the will of God and how not to die. God's ways are actually simple. It is the carnal mind of the flesh that complicates what God would have us do.

ROMANS 8:6-14
PROVERBS 12:28
2 CORINTHIANS 3:4-6

578 MOTHERS AND QUEENS

From the dust of the earth came the first man. Is the earth not a mother of the natural man? From the rib of the first man came the first biological mother of the human race. All the mothers who have followed have also come from mothers. Most all earthly creatures have mothers, and every one has significance. Mothers are genetic females, not to be confused with genetic males. The son is referred to as him, and the earth is referred to as her. Grooms are men, brides are women. How could anyone become confused?

The multitude of mothers made reference to in the Bible are all born of women who were fathered by men—some good and some bad. A good mother is always one who respects and loves her husband and nurtures and loves her children. The good ones build up their houses, while the evil ones tear them down. Examples of both are prevalent.

In the spiritual and metaphorical realms, there are also a host of mothers, wives, and also adulteresses. They, too, are identified as virtuous or wicked. The bride of Christ is, of course, the epitome of virtue, and the heavenly Jerusalem is described as the mother of the true children of God. Jezebel, on the other hand, has a multitude of children. She knows the depths of Satan, who is also the serpent who deceived Eve in Eden. She is a murderess, as is the mother of harlots, who blasphemes God and kills His servants.

All these mothers are not hard to identify. There are also mothers who are queens, both on earth and in heaven, both legitimate and illegitimate. Some are given the status of goddesses, but only the true "Bride of Christ" deserves the title of "Queen of Heaven". All others are impostors and lesser gods. Those who worship them are idolaters. Those who pray to them are fools.

JEREMIAH 44:15-23
REVELATION 2:20-24; 21:9-12
GALATIANS 4:22-26

579 MORE TO LEARN

Until we fly away and time is no more, we have lessons to learn and things to add to our experience on earth. Though we may have regrets, we can learn from them, but the mind which abides in the place where the Lord has instructed His people to dwell has a continual peace. Instruction is the way of life to turn one away from the way of death.

The person who obeys the voice of the Spirit of God is learning His ways constantly, and His knowledge is infinite. Carnal inquisitiveness and curiosity may continue throughout a person's life on earth, but does not necessarily prepare them for eternity. What the spiritually minded person learns are lessons of eternal value. *To be carnally minded is death, but to be Spiritually minded is life and peace.*

Choice is a constant factor in learning, and if our choices are instructed by the Spirit of God, there need not be any sin in our lives. This is the significance of *taking every thought captive to the obedience of Christ.* If you can hear the voice of God, you are being taught (learning) how to walk in freedom from sin. Is this not what the truth of the gospel instructed us to do?

How will anyone escape who has not learned to obey the gospel and neglected the great salvation the Lord has provided? Learning the truth is the result of loving it. There is no salvation outside of abiding in it. What is being spoken is serious instruction and a profound lesson. While there are many more things to learn and take to heart, there are not many of greater importance.

COLOSSIANS 3:1-7
PHILIPPIANS 2:5-8
2 CORINTHIANS 10:4-5
PROVERBS 1:2-7

580 GOD'S WILL

Can we really know the will of God? How did the Man, Jesus of Nazareth, know? Some might say that Jesus Himself is God. This is true, but he was a man with every passion and desire of every other human being. He had His own free will yet walked a sinless life. He was tempted in every way that we are, yet never sinned. *Jesus prayed, saying, "O, My Father, if this cup cannot pass away from Me unless I drink it your will be done. . . . And again, Father if it is your will, take this cup away from Me. Nevertheless, not My will but Yours be done.* Is there really a difference between the man, Jesus, and those who have been born of the Spirit of God and become His brethren, One Spirit with Him in whose lives are no longer their own but His? Jesus, of course, is the only begotten, but are those of us who are born of God and bear His image not also God's sons and daughters?

There are many who say, "Lord, Lord," but it is not necessarily they who inherit the kingdom of heaven but those who actually do the will of the Father. Has He not made His will known? Is He not still making it known today? Does endless worship and flattering words substitute for actually doing the will of God? *If we say, "I know Him," and do not obey His commandments (we) are lying and the truth is not in us, but whoever keeps His word, truly the love of God is perfected in that one. By this we know that we are in Him. He or she who says they abide in Him ought themselves to walk just as He walked.*

Jesus always did the things that pleased His Father. Can anyone tell me that this is not possible for the person who is now abiding in Christ? The truth is not ambiguous, nor is the will of God! What value has the prayer of the one who knows not the will of the Father and does not walk in it? *Love has been perfected among us in this: that we may have boldness in the day of judgment; because as He is, so are we in this world . . . Now this is the confidence that we have in Him, that if we ask anything according to His will, He hears us. And if we know He hears us, whatever we ask we know that we have the petitions that we have asked of Him.* Just how important is it to know God's will? Does not salvation itself depend on such knowledge? A diligent study of the scriptures without the assistance of professional commentary and teaching will yield the truth regarding God's will and His salvation.

If anyone has received the love of the truth, the will of God will be revealed.

2 PETER 3:9
1 JOHN 2:15-17

581 MIRACLES

Everywhere I look I see miracles. They are supernatural, and though they appear in the realm of nature, their source is beyond what the natural human being can see and are initiated from a spiritual dimension outside of the visible. The miracles that are visible to the natural eye receive the most attention and acclaim, but the miracles that are not readily observed are of even greater significance.

It is no small thing that the works of the Creator can be seen by anyone who has eyes. Yet there remain many who will not even acknowledge Him. The greatest miracle I have experienced is when the God of creation revealed Himself and His love to me and completely changed a life headed toward destruction and gave me a new life with Himself at the center.

Physical healing and miracles are exciting and wonderful and let us know that the Lord is actually near and is concerned with the welfare of mankind. They also confirm what He has spoken and done. To be obsessed with the physical miracles performed through people who concentrate on them can be (and is) an error in judgment and spiritual discernment. These miracles are meant to glorify the Creator but also to test people's hearts. The purpose of the Father is to separate those who love Him from those who put the miracles in the place where God Himself belongs.

Aren't His ways wonderful and beyond the reasoning capacity of the carnal mind?

JOHN 9:1-3
MARK 8:25
LUKE 18:41-43
JOHN 2:23-25; 6:26-40

582 SUFFERING

Although he was a son, He learned obedience through what He suffered . . . The Spirit Himself bears witness with our spirit that we are children of God and if children then heirs—heirs of God and fellow heirs with Christ provided we suffer with Him in order that we may also be glorified with Him. . . . Since, therefore, Christ suffered in the flesh arm yourselves with the same way of thinking for whoever has suffered in the flesh has ceased from sin so as to live for the rest of the time in the flesh no longer for human passion but for the will of God. The will of God is obvious with regard to suffering and sin. How much scriptural evidence do we need in order to acknowledge the truth about what our Father expects of us? Self-denial and suffering for the sake of righteousness could not be much more prominent in the gospel. There are some among us who believe Christians should not suffer and even more who believe that sinning is a normal part of the Christian experience.

How could the church have slipped so far into degradation? The standard established by Jesus and His early apostles was and is the standard which was set for all time. Suffering is part of the established normal experience of those who would follow Christ; and freedom from sin was and is what Jesus came to earth to accomplish. How can anyone honestly study the gospel and miss it? For that matter, the whole of scripture.

1 PETER 4:12-19

583 SHOULDA, COULDA, WOULDA

Many of us know the things we should have done but didn't and the things we would have done, but they were inconvenient, as well as what we would have done but just couldn't find the time. HELLO! Excuses and reasons abound for not fulfilling the righteous deeds and worthwhile projects we have put off and forgotten.

We have not learned these things from the Lord. He would have us revisit our past procrastinations and reset our minds and will to do what is right when we see it. The time allotted to each of us is short, and the Lord will demand an account of every one of us based on the gifts He has given us and our abilities. *To whom much is given much is required.*

The lost of the world are coming out as never before, and darkness is covering the earth. Love requires us to have hope, to share it and not hide it because of a fear of mankind and what they might think. This is basic truth and what everyone who knows the Lord should do. He does not expect us to do what we could not do, only what we would do if we really loved Him.

This admonition is both timely and appropriate for those who may have become distracted or complacent in their relationship with Jesus. When time is no more, our opportunity to do what we should, could and would do will end with it.

MATTHEW 25:14-30

584 FORGIVENESS (HD)

Who has not needed forgiveness? The one who needs it must be prepared to give it. God is the only Person who has no need to be forgiven, but even so, there are many who mistakenly believe they have legitimate grievance against God. This is something that can keep a person from ever knowing Him. Everything that the Almighty does is done in righteousness and love. He is totally just.

Does the Lord actually forgive the person who does not repent of his/her sin and turn from it? Some would have us believe that God forgives us in advance when our hearts have no contrition and no real intention of ceasing the transgressions of which we are guilty. This is a mockery of Jesus' sacrifice and shed blood. The idea that God forgives future sins in advance is as preposterous as believing that everyone will be saved from the torment of eternal separation from our Creator.

The person who holds animosity toward God or any other person is not capable of receiving forgiveness him/herself. This is more devastating than any virus. The person who is incapable of forgiving is also incapable of knowing the love of God that surpasses all others. We all have one chance to get it right, and that is while we are here on earth. The time and ability to forgive and receive forgiveness will end when our journey here on earth has ended.

Let's get it right!

PSALM 51:17
MATTHEW 6:12; 5:23-24; 6:14
1 JOHN 1:9
EPHESIANS 1:7

585 VIOLENCE AND THE BLOODTHIRSTY

The violence in our cities is easy to see; the violence from the pulpits not so easy. What is being addressed are the lies of professionals who are actually bloodthirsty. Considering that blood is the life of all flesh, the Lord looks at those who feed on, promote, and follow after the flesh the bloodthirsty of which He so often speaks. He describes them as having *teeth that are swords and whose fangs are knives to devour the poor from off the earth and needy from among mankind.*

In the heavenly realm the poor and needy are they who are dependent on God having no resources of their own. The bloodthirsty are they who would dissuade the poor and needy from their total dependence on God to trust in their flesh. You will not hear them say so outright, but this is what their contrived doctrines produce. This is what the leaven of the religious leaders of Jesus' time did and why Jesus called them whitewashed tombs full of dead people's bones.

The violence of the false doctrines of the bloodthirsty that causes the righteous to stumble and go astray is extremely violent in the eyes of the Lord. Those who commit such offenses are they to whom Jesus pronounced: *Whoever causes one of these little ones who believes in Me to sin, it would be better for that person if a millstone were hung around their neck and were drowned in the depths of the sea. Woe to the world because of offenses! For offenses must come but woe to the person by whom the offense comes.* No lie is of the truth, and no lie will go unpunished. It is the transgressions of the professional religious leaders of our day that are leading multitudes astray. The conflict and the confusion we see today is God's judgment on the perversion of the gospel and the idolatry and sin that results.

The love of the truth is the solution to the scourge of the violence of the pious, bloodthirsty ways of those whose eyes are lifted up but are not cleansed of their filthiness.

PROVERBS 30:12-14
PSALM 11:1-7

586 COMPLACENCY

There are many calling themselves Christians who remain complacent in the face of disaster. Because the affliction that has come upon the world's masses has not reached their doors, they imagine that it will not. The day is coming when the plagues that have come upon all those who dwell on earth will cover the earth as a great flood; unless the self-proclaimed sinners who believe they are Christians enter through the gates of righteousness and come to a true understanding of the gospel and obey it, their end will be as the rest of the world.

The Lord's chosen people are a holy nation, and no sinners are included in His inheritance. Only the righteous are among those who dwell in the heavenly places where the Lord Himself is seated. Those who dwell on the earth are the ones who live according to the flesh and have confidence in it. They are the complacent who say they trust the Lord, yet refuse to obey Him. The day of reckoning is near and will reveal the truth of every heart.

When the flood has consumed the earth, the Lord will no longer respond to those who would not listen to Him when He spoke and gave warning in advance.

This is a call to seek the Lord while He may be found.

PSALM 32:6-11
PROVERBS 1:20-33

587 THE SHADOW OF DEATH

The shadow of death is cast upon the world. The leaders can see it but have no idea what to do about it, while all the opportunists scheme to take advantage of it in order to advance themselves and their wicked endeavors. The Lord is still on His throne as He was at the time of the flood. The evil plans of the underworld of demons and their human pawns are short-lived and will come to nothing.

The great kingdoms of the world and their leaders are no more than fools who cannot see the light and are stumbling in darkness. This is obvious to us who are walking in the light and know the truth. This is not a time to fret or to panic if you are among the chosen. This is the time to trust the Lord as so many confess to doing. The hour of trial that is coming upon the world is revealing the truth about who really does trust the Lord and who doesn't.

We are still in the age where *we can make our calling and election sure,* but there is a limit to the time allotted to the Gentiles to leave off the trampling of the outer court and enter the holy place where the Almighty dwells. This is the place of shelter and safety, and there are few who actually enter. The forfeiture of our self-life for Jesus is the key into the land where righteousness dwells, where the Lord has gone before us and prepared a place for us.

Most of the religious leaders remain outside the gates trying to convince those who are called to follow them, even though they have not found the entrance themselves.

When the shadow gives way to total darkness, every person will find themselves either in the kingdom of God or outside its gates. There will be no further chance of escape.

MATTHEW 7:21-23
2 CORINTHIANS 13:5-7
REVELATION 16:10-11
MATTHEW 24:37-39

588 THE EAST WIND

By the east wind you shatter the ships of Tarshish. The place of contemplation and trading, *Tyre is among your partners. The east wind has wrecked you (Tyre). O, Tyre you have said, "I am perfect in beauty". Your borders are in the heart of the seas; your builders have made perfect your beauty. . . Tarshish did business with you because of your great wealth of every kind . . . Javan, Tubal, and Meschech traded with you; they exchanged human beings and vessels of bronze for your merchandise.* The prophesies and the records of Tarshish and Tyre are parables of the day in which we live.

The east wind is blowing and the pride of nations is being brought to the shame of the many nations who have made their governments their god. They all have failed and yet the educated fools who have gained power believe they can make the failure of all the other nations work in their favor. While they traffic in human souls and lives, they think they know what they are doing, while they are no more than pawns in the grand conspiracy to enslave the world and all of humanity.

Those who know the God of Jacob will not be enslaved, even though they may be murdered. The death of the body is an escape from the tyranny overtaking the earth and should not be feared. The pride of the rich and powerful of the world will be their undoing and their own destruction. The Lord's chosen will see the end of the wicked traders who serve their flesh and their carnal endeavors. Those who have joined the thieves and murderers will share their fate.

Is this not a call to take a stand for truth and justice regardless of the cost?

EZEKIEL 27:1-36; 14:1-5
REVELATION 7:9-17
JEREMIAH 25:15-38
PSALM 37:1-2

589 A CLEAN HEART

What does the Lord require of the person who would dwell in His presence? If He has created a new heart in the one who is born of His Spirit, whose responsibility is it to maintain its purity? The saint who walks in the light is the one who abides in Christ. The sinner who regards and defends the nature of the heart that has been replaced by God does not believe what He has done. A clean heart is a pure heart void of offense to its maker. Does the person who yields to temptation really love the Lord and obey the truth? The heart that speaks the truth to itself knows that it must remain blameless in the sight of God in order to please Him.

If we do not walk in His way by following His Spirit, how can we expect to please Him and walk free from sin. A saint is not the one who continues to follow the nature with which he was first born, but the nature that replaced it when that one was born of God. This is the nature that is free from sin and does not need to justify itself because it cannot obey the commandments and the voice of God.

To stand blameless before the Lord does not require a constant confession of sins but a true repentance and a contrite heart. The enemy of our souls knows that if he can convince us that we remain subject to our flesh and the nature with which we were first born, he is able to keep us separated from true fellowship with our Savior for all eternity and share Satan's fate. This truth is what separates the true "Body of Christ" from the false church that uses His name in vain.

If any person can understand what has been said here, they can indeed stand blameless before the throne of God with a clean heart.

2 CORINTHIANS 5:16-18
GALATIANS 6:14-16

P.S. The better the gospel is understood, the simpler it gets.

590 FAVOR

While waiting on the Lord, He began to speak of His favor. Among the millions and billions of human beings who inhabit the earth, how does the Creator decide who He will favor? He has told us that though humankind looks on the outward appearance, God looks on the heart. He has also told us that many are called, but few are chosen. How does God choose and why?

Throughout the Bible, we see many who are chosen by the Lord to fulfill His purpose for all mankind. They are often, if not always, symbolic types of the most favored Man of all time. The nation He has chosen, and shown favor also is symbolic of His Spiritual Body. The Almighty shows favor to individuals as well as nations that fear Him and obey Him. There is no substitute for higher sacrifice that can be made to earn God's favor than obedience.

Talent, beauty, physical strength, and intellect do not impress the Creator, but the person who fears Him does. Righteousness is the thing He counts valuable. A pure heart is of value to Him, along with faithfulness and a love of truth.

Among the host of characters the Lord has made a note of and favored throughout the history of mankind, it is easy to see that the ones who hear Him, believe Him, and obey Him are they who gain favor and approval. This is the substance of faith, without which no one can please God. The mystery regarding the blessing and favor of God is not as perplexing as the process by which a person becomes chosen by Him. But the answer lies in Jesus Christ, who incorporates the whole purpose of God in the entirety of everything He has created.

The persons who look at themselves as the center of creation need only to humble themselves and expand their understanding to realize and acknowledge that to receive God's favor, God must be the center and focal point of everything a person thinks and does. This is the significance of the mark of God on the forehead and hand.

It is here for all to see.

591 THE CALL

The call is going out and always has. The sound is seen and heard by every rationally minded person. Anyone who responds becomes called. This is the beginning of what may be interpreted as a series of choices and responses that an individual may eventually come to realize is the Spirit of the Creator calling that person to Himself. When the person being called finally acknowledges that it is God who is calling and submits to the call, he or she is born again. That person becomes one of the many who hear and respond to the call of God.

This is the beginning of a spiritual journey that may or may not end in being chosen. The one who follows and obeys the voice of the Holy Spirit and actually becomes one Spirit with Him is joined to Jesus and becomes chosen in Him. Jesus is the Chosen One, and God's chosen people are they who abide in Christ. There is no salvation apart from Him.

Even the elect retain their free will and the ability to turn back to where they have come from, thus denying the truth that has saved them. This is where the lust of the flesh, the lust of the eyes, and the pride of life present a person with the temptation and the deceptiveness of sin to turn back to the world from which they have come.

The call can be silenced by sin, the love of money and things, and even other people who are given a higher place than the Lord in a person's life. The voice of God can be reduced to just another of many voices trying to draw a person away from the truth. I have seen this phenomenon in people who have responded to the call of God and seemed to love Him, only to turn away and deny Him.

It is the overcomers who will remain chosen and those who are faithful to the end who are saved.

1 CORINTHIANS 15:1-2
MATTHEW 24:12-13; 10:22
1 PETER 2:1-5
PSALM 19:1-4
PROVERBS 8:1-4; 1:24-33

592 MADE ALIVE

Being alive to God is more than not being dead. Here on earth, we are all among the walking dead whose lives are being spent on vanity and consumed in self-preservation. Surely God has a higher way for those who have been made alive in Christ. The person who abides in Him is no longer subject to an endless existence of uncertainty and fear. We who have been made alive in Him are set free from sin and death.

Who would benefit from keeping those who have been made alive to God and his righteousness in bondage to the lust of the flesh, the eyes and the pride of a vain existence? The answer, of course, is the enemies of our soul and of the Lord. They are the ones who crucified Jesus thinking that they were defeating the purpose of God. We who have died with Him and risen from the grave with Him are the ones who are made alive in Him.

Now that we have been raised with Christ to newness of life, our heavenly Father would have us present ourselves as obedient slaves to righteousness and no longer to sin. *Do you not know that if you present yourselves to anyone as obedient slaves you are slaves to the one whom you obey, either of sin which leads to death or of obedience which leads to righteousness?* Certainly no one can serve two masters. We either serve our flesh and the sin it produces or the Spirit and the life He produces.

This is a life or death conflict that began in the garden and is settled in every person's life here on earth while each of us remain free to choose.

If we have been made alive to God, it is up to each one of us to follow after that life or not!

JOSHUA 24:14-24
ROMANS 6:1-23; 8:1-14
JUDE 1-23

P.S. Are there more divisions anywhere than can be seen in the so-called Christian church?

593 RIVERS

Rivers are a source of great mystery, intrigue and adventure. Whether of earth, heaven or metaphor, rivers hold life, death and even salvation below the surface of their flowing. The river that flows from the throne of God is the greatest and most glorious of all. It is truly exciting to explore the many rivers the Lord has presented to us in His word. No river is without significance in understanding the ways of God, whether flowing peacefully or raging, water or blood coming from the fountain of life, the mouth or a dragon, or a spring of the earth, their power and influence are worthy of exploration.

This writer lives on a boat floating on a river.

The life of creatures small and great are supported along with all forms of vegetation by the waters of rivers. Their water gives life to the living things of the earth. Beyond the natural rivers of the biological creation, there are metaphorical and metaphysical rivers which feed the souls and spirits of the wondrous spiritual creations of God. Even the monsters, leviathans and behemoths are fed by rivers. Beasts as well as humans are fed at every level of existence by rivers.

Floods produced by rivers destroy the works of mankind and nature and claim the lives of multitudes. They shape and reshape the earth by their power. Some of the great metaphorical floods that are able to cover earth destroy whole nations and people. When the Almighty turns rivers into blood, everything in them dies, and all who drink from them die, also. Such are the rivers of Babylon and Egypt. These are the rivers of the flesh merchants who promote the life of the flesh, which always ends in death.

Those who drink from the river that flows from the fountain of Israel are set on high, free from the rivers of blood and the water that flow from the institutions of the carnality of the natural, religious mind of mankind and the demons that inspire them. The river that flows from the throne of God is pure and healing and only inspires truth and prosperity. The water is crystal clear and pure and gives life to all who drink it. The muddy waters of the carnal mind and the desperately wicked heart of the natural human being are polluted with the contamination of lust and greed, envy and lies. Pure water only produces righteousness, love, peace and joy.

The confusion, division, violence and blasphemy that can be seen in the world of organized religion obviously has its source in the murky fountains of carnality that are mixed with the dust of the earth.

Point made!

REVELATION 22:1-5
EXODUS 7:14-25

594 THE FOUNTAIN OF ISRAEL

The Fountain of Israel has its origin in the depth of the heart of our loving Creator. The offspring of God Himself is the eternal generation of Christ of which Jacob came. The fountain has continued to flow from the beginning to the present day. There has been no lapse nor shall there be. The Fountain of Israel is the source of truth and life from which all who have walked the earth by faith have been nourished since the human race began.

All we who know the Lord have been grafted into the vine that sprouted from the fountain. We owe our spiritual forefathers a debt that can only be paid to God with our lives. All the saints of God are, and have been, members of the generation of Jacob and his Father. All those who have recorded the word of God for us were drinking from this fountain. So too are the ones who are speaking the truth today. There is only one truth and only one true Body of Christ, and it is the generation of those who walk in it.

Faith is the foundation and the rock from which the fountain flows, and Jesus Christ is the very essence of its origin. He is the way to it as well as the content of it; unless we are of His generation abiding in Him, we are not of the eternal generation that has proceeded from the Fountain of Israel. Its water is pure, and no impurity can be found in it. So too are its members.

The bride of Christ consists of those who obey Him and are the offspring of the fathers of the faith who always have. There are none able to stand blameless before God who do not have a pure heart. This is not positionally pure, but actually pure; and not positionally righteous but actually righteous. The Spirit of the Fountain only energizes those who actually love the truth.

REVELATION 22:12-17
PSALM 68:26; 73:1; 24:3-6
JOHN 4:7-14
GALATIANS 6:15-16
ACTS 8:29-33

595 UNEASINESS

Uneasiness deep in a person's heart and soul is the evidence of having not entered God's rest. If anyone has allowed themselves to be guided by another person who does not know where they are going, it is as though they are both wandering aimlessly in the wilderness. This is the reality of those who have believed and trusted in trained professionals who are paid to lead the great congregations of people who would rather follow popular instructors than to seek the Lord on their own.

I have heard one of the most prominent public teachers confess the uneasiness in her heart to her followers as though it was God's plan. Well, it is the Lord's plan for those who disregard truth in favor of dishonesty. The peace of God that silences uneasiness comes as a result of believing Him and obeying Him. The one who fails to do these two things is incapable of entering God's rest. This phenomenon is not new. Ancient Israel experienced the same thing while they wandered in the wilderness.

Uneasiness in a person's heart is a sign that all is not right with God. The remedy is to seek God with all your heart and turn from those who are willing to accept bribes to teach popular doctrines for the sake of personal gain and recognition.

There is no substitute for personal revelation of the truth of which every one of God's chosen are partakers.

HEBREWS 3:7 through 4:7
1 JOHN 2:26-28

596 BURNING FIRE

Fire is a force of nature and metaphor that will not relent while it has the fuel needed to sustain it. Our God, of course, is a consuming fire. The only ones who are able to dwell in His presence are they who have nothing that can be ignited. The everlasting flames of torment of hell are sustained by the fuel provided by guilt, regret and sin. The torment of such fire cannot be escaped or quenched, because it comes from within the one who cannot find forgiveness.

This is why it is critical to receive forgiveness while it can be found. The person whose heart is not right with God before their life on earth has ended is the one who will experience the torment of everlasting fire. The actual suffering of the soul that cannot escape the fire of regret for what could have been is the reality of being separated from our Creator.

Anyone who says they do not believe in hell is ignorant of the suffering incurred by not being able to secure forgiveness for their sins. This judgment is shockingly real and essential to understand. There is no one who is not in need of forgiveness, but there are only few who actually experience it and then abide in it.

For a person to continue sinning after being forgiven and cleansed demonstrates a lack of reverence and understanding of what it took for our Savior to secure the forgiveness required to dwell with Him. The idea or belief that we could dwell with Him in His kingdom without this understanding of what He has done is pathetic. Those who teach the forgiveness of future and ongoing sin have no knowledge of what it means to repent and have a contrite heart.

Just as real as a forest fire that can burn the whole landscape and living creatures is the metaphorical fire that burns the soul and spirit.

MARK 9:42-48
ISAIAH 33:10-17
REVELATION 20:11-15
EZEKIEL 28:14-19
DANIEL 3:19-30

597 THE FAR-OFF CITY

We who are on the highway to Zion remain in a battle where, in spite of having entered a place of rest, there are enemies who would displace us if they are able. They seek to penetrate the armor which the Lord has supplied, and we must remain vigilant. The end of the journey is, indeed, the end, and there is no place for complacency or apathy before our goal has been reached.

Although many of our enemies may have been defeated along the way, some of them are resilient and re-appear to defeat our onward progress. They may manifest in a host of forms, such as lust, pride, complacency, apathy and laziness. The subtlety and deceptiveness of sin does not rest while there remains any semblance of life in the fleshly body that has been put to death. Only we can revive its life. Unbelief is among the strongest of our enemies and is relentless to cause us to doubt what God has spoken.

The teaching and doctrine that can be heard from pulpits and telecasts seem endless, and the deception they contain also seems endless. These false prophets and teachers rise up from the ground and the sea. Their doctrines, which contain an element of truth, are nevertheless deceptive and destructive, giving heed to the carnality of the flesh and its lusts.

Does the Lord actually concur with this carnal understanding of Spiritual truth, or is it the delusion He has sent to those who have not received the love of the truth? He is the Judge who has separated those who really love Jesus from those who have taken His name in vain.

The Lord's soon appearing will reveal the truth and the reality of the saints who really serve Him.

2 THESSALONIANS 1:5 through 2:12

598 WILLFUL IGNORANCE

Those who remain ignorant due to their pride have willfully rejected the rebuke of the Almighty. They have deliberately chosen to be ignorant rather than to change the way of life with which they have become comfortable. This is the result of loving a lie more than truth and loving self more than God. *There is a way that seems right to a person but its end is death.* The Spirit of God is faithful to prick the hearts of these willfully ignorant souls until they have reached a point where they have hardened their hearts beyond being influenced by the truth.

There are countless souls who have chosen to be ignorant and deny the true gospel, because they have assumed an identity that conflicts with it, and their pride will not allow them to repent. SELAH! This phenomenon is evident within the denominational structure of every self-identified faction of Christianity. It is not possible to achieve unity without abandonment of these factions for the sake of the true "Body of Christ".

The Lord is surely calling to those who love Him and have received the love of the truth to come out of these factional denominations and organizations and become one in Jesus Christ.

There is but One true head of the Body of Christ, and there is no earthly headquarters for it. The head is Spiritual as are its true members, and all these individual parts have but one mind and one all-encompassing purpose on earth.

Ignorance is no longer a valid excuse for separatism and confusion but a willful act and the reason for the ignorance that is demonstrated by the carnal strife and division of all the worldly factions making up the so-called church on the earth and of the world.

EPHESIANS 4:1-16
1 CORINTHIANS 1:10-13

599 STARS

Beyond the bright lights seen at night that cannot be counted by humankind and the obvious skill of a master craftsperson who has placed them in such a way to be used for navigation as well as pictures and constellations, they are a testimony to the great Creator who is able to count them all and knows each one by name. They also represent spiritual and metaphorical beings that fill the pages of scripture.

While stars are the announcers of seasons, times, ages and events, they represent the foreknowledge of the Creator who has set everything in motion and has determined the beginning and the end of time. The stars are speaking to us today, and there are many among us trying to interpret what they are saying.

We know that stars are used by the Spirit of God metaphorically, because they cannot possibly fall to earth in their biological form. The angelic beings they symbolize are both good and evil and influence the course of history and the world. The saints of God who do His will are also symbolized as stars that are bright lights in the heavens. They, too, speak of the glory of God and of His wonderful works.

Without the testimony of stars and the magnitude of their symbolism and function in the plans of our Creator, we would be a much less prosperous people, whether just naturally or spiritually. While God's chosen are instructed not to worship the stars, we can surely worship the One who created them. Even those of Hollywood who are praised by many are but symbols of the finite works the Creator has given us.

How great is the One who is able to create and control even the stars?

DANIEL 12:1-3
REVELATION 8:12
ISAIAH 13:9-13

600 ABUNDANCE OF THE HEART

Out of the abundance of the heart, the mouth speaks. Each of us is being admonished to analyze the words that proceed from our mouth. Our words reveal the true condition of our heart as well as the path we trod. Our hearts are fountains from which we affect all those around us extending to the whole world. A heart full of love and wisdom speaks truth and life to all who hear its words. Do I need to explain what a heart full of bitterness and resentment proclaims?

We cannot escape our own hearts, and though a person may try to disguise its true contents with deceit, the truth will be made known. Even the wicked one disguised as an angel of light is revealed to the saint who is gifted with discernment. The slanderous words we hear from politicians, news broadcasters, and even ministers of religion only reveal the true condition of their hearts. Those who love the Lord and the truth speak healing and reconciliation to all who can hear them.

If we can speak the truth in our own hearts, we know what our Lord expects of us and how to reveal His heart to the world. Even when the Lord pronounces judgment and wrath on evildoers, His words and actions come from a heart filled with love. To understand His ways allows a person's heart to remain holy and pure and able to speak words of love and forgiveness.

How we measure up to the standards set by Jesus is the scale on which the abundance of our hearts is made known. Without specific accusation or condemnation, the reality of the content of the hearts of many who consider themselves Christians do not reach the plumb line or balance the scale,

We are all given the opportunity to judge ourselves, and if we are able to speak the truth in our own hearts, we also have an ability to fill our hearts with content that pleases our Savior.

Love is what matters!

1 PETER 3:8-12
MATTHEW 12:33-37
1 SAMUEL 16:7
PROVERBS 26:23-28

601 SEEING AND HEARING

What does the Spirit speak of? Can we really see the face of God and live? Is the voice of the Spirit heard with biological ears? *That which is born of Spirit is spirit and that which is born of flesh is flesh. . . The seeing eye and the hearing ear are created by God . . . The words I speak to you are Spirit and they are life . . . And Moses summoned all Israel and said to them, "You have seen all that the Lord did before your eyes in the land of Egypt to Pharaoh and to all his servants and to all his land, the great trials that your eyes saw, the signs and those great wonders. But to this day the Lord has not given you a heart to understand or eyes to see or ears to hear.*

Unless a person has passed through the veil into the realm of spirit where the Creator dwells he cannot see beyond the natural dimension of his biological eyes or hear outside of that place of existence. The one who insists on material facts in order to believe what God has said shuts himself out of the place of eternal life.

We are called to inhabit the land of the living where the Creator dwells and become citizens of heaven now. Do you think that being born of the Spirit leaves us subject to our carnal, fleshly understanding and perception of reality? Is that all being a new creation consists of? The gates of righteousness have been opened, but we can only pass through them by faith.

We are left with a choice to believe what God has written down for us and pass into the heavenly realm or to stand outside with those who have chosen to embrace their carnal understanding of spiritual things.

The written letter kills, but the Spirit gives life.

JOHN 6:63-65
1 CORINTHIANS 2:14-16

602 ONE

The revelation of the oneness of a created being with his Creator is one of the greatest any person can experience. Jesus often spoke of being One with His Father. He also spoke of the oneness of His followers with Himself and one another. The reality of this oneness is more than a metaphor or an enigma. It is a Spiritual idiom spoken of an absolute truth. *There is one body and one Spirit just as you were called to the one hope that belongs to your call – one body, one faith, one baptism, one God and Father of us all who is over all and through all and in all . . . . But he who is joined to the Lord is One Spirit with Him . . . I do not ask that You take them out of the world but that You keep them from the evil one. They are not of the world just as I am not of the world. Sanctify them in the truth; Your word is truth. As You sent Me into the world so I have sent them into the world. And for their sake I consecrate Myself that they also may be sanctified in truth. I do not ask for these only but also for those who will believe in Me through their word that they all may be one just as You, Father, are in Me and I in You that they also may be one in Us so that the world may believe that You have sent Me.*

Surely, we need no further Biblical evidence of the oneness of Jesus' followers with their Creator, if indeed they abide in Christ. We who have received His Holy Spirit are endowed with His nature, even while we inhabit these mortal, fleshly bodies here on earth. When time ends here on earth, all that will really change is our mortal body made of dust.

What kind of people ought we to be? SELAH!

JOHN 17:1-26

P.S. Have we gone too far east? Is God from Asia or heaven?

603 IDENTITY

Deep in the recesses of our being lies our true identity. We can get a glimpse of the awesomeness of our Creator through understanding his ability to not only know and identify every person He has created, but also to know the condition of their hearts. Many of us have deceived ourselves and are not aware of who we really are. Human beings are actually the books in God's library. He is the One who reads them and understands every detail in them. Though people can be deceived, the Spirit of God cannot. All things are open and discernible before Him.

Ultimately in every person's life, an image of who they are and what they believe is declared in what is written in the book and established by the works and deeds recorded therein. Every rationally-minded person who has come to an age of accountability has chosen an identifying mark that reveals who they have served and the works they have done. The books do not lie, and there can be no disputing them.

God alone can change a person's identity by creating a new person with a new heart and a restart of what is written in the book. This is as miracle greater than any other and allows the one who has sinned against God and served himself to reestablish both the image and the identifying mark on his forehead and hand, which are the symbols of what he believes and who he has served.

Are the ways of God not simple while being exceedingly deep? I hope everyone is able to see by what the Lord judges every person in spite of what we may have been taught on Sundays.

REVELATION 20:11-15
JAMES 2:17-26

604 TIME

Everything that is part of the natural creation is subject to the limits and boundaries of time. When Jesus spoke of eternal life, He was speaking of life beyond the confines of time. The dimension of the creation that exists outside of nature is where the Creator Himself dwells. He is constantly calling to us to join Him in the place where the boundaries of time do not exist. What you are hearing is such a call. In the realm of eternity, we are free from the limits that cause the distress and affliction of our fleshly bodies and our carnal minds.

In the heavenly realm we are free to access all the spiritual things that are beyond the grasp of our biological senses and desires. Outside of time, the Spirit of God reveals things that the carnal human being has no knowledge of that God has prepared for those who love Him. This is certainly a better place than the one into which the offspring of Adam and Eve have been born.

In order to pass from the land of time where everything comes to an end and death is a certainty, a person must become willing to forfeit his/her natural self-life in favor of the everlasting life of Christ. This is where we voluntarily sacrifice our personal self-life for the life being offered to us by our Creator. This absolutely requires faith. The one who can hear this call and believes Him who is calling only needs to obey what the Holy Spirit is saying.

The shackles of time that hold our biological bodies are only temporary just as our mortal existence.

Isn't God wonderful?!!

JOHN 17:3
MATTHEW 10:38-39
1 CORINTHIANS 2:9-16
2 CORINTHIANS 4:16-18
REVELATION 21:1-6

605 KEEPING WATCH

The Lord's watchmen are doing the Lord's bidding. Their spiritual senses are always alert to the enemy of the Lord's people. A watchman measures all threats of danger by the plumb line of truth. Lies are weapons used by the enemies of our souls that, if not detected and exposed, can cause God's people to reach out their hands to the evil desires of those who would destroy their souls. The pen in my hand is the trumpet and the voice by which this watchman is giving warning to those to whom the Lord has sent him.

There has never been a greater danger to those called by God than the threat we now face. The end is near, and the forces of darkness have nearly reached the pinnacle of the deception that the Lord will allow. The destructive doctrine of the harlot and her flesh merchants has reached the point where sin and endless confession is presented as virtue. Scripture has been twisted and perverted to portray sinners as humble victims of another person's transgressions.

To what can we liken this generation if not that of Noah. If you have been listening, the trumpet has been sounding loud and clear. The Lord has not left us who love the truth without warning. The signs of His soon return are everywhere, and his watchmen are giving an unmistakable signal to prepare for what is coming. The urgency of the hour is greater with each passing day for those who dwell on the earth.

Those who will not give heed to the watchmen keeping watch over the city have only themselves to blame for the suffering they will incur.

The trumpet has sounded!

2 TIMOTHY 3:1-17
MATTHEW 24:23-26, 36-39
EZEKIEL 18: 1-32

606 THE CAMP OF THE SAINTS

The camp of the saints and the Holy City are surrounded by the foes of truth. These foes are as the sand of the sea and as a flood that would wash away the righteous who remain on the earth. Although the true saints of God are not as readily seen and identified as the multitudes of false believers who claim to know the God of Jacob, the real believers are being revealed to one another by the Spirit of God and are being gathered from all the nations in a way the natural eye is incapable of observing.

The prophecy regarding the true "Body of Christ" and the true "Israel of God" is being fulfilled as you read these words. The time is at hand when we should be looking up; for our redemption is drawing near and the fire from God is also proceeding as these words are written. This is an exciting time to be alive on earth, to observe what the Lord is bringing to pass. If ever there was a time to be ready and waiting this is it.

Satan and his forces of darkness have shown themselves and never been more obvious to those who have been given eyes to see. If you have done all to stand, then stand and see what the Lord will do on behalf of those who fear, love and obey Him.

When He appears, our hope and joy will be fulfilled and complete. Wickedness and hate shall be no more, and only righteousness and love shall surround the saints of God. The book has been written, and we who remain on earth when He appears will experience something that all the saints who preceded us have hoped for, and we will be joined with them.

It is truly a joy to see and know what our great God and Savior is doing.

References are contained herein, as is the endorsement of the Holy Spirit. Amen.

607 LISTENING

Today the Lord is directing me to speak about listening. Those who are able to hear the voice of the Spirit of God and willfully obey it are His chosen ones. The voices trying to acquire our attention are endless, but there are few worthy of our consideration. We are all given choices as to what and whom we allow into our consciousness and give heed to. The discernment and the discipline to regulate what we listen to is the subject at hand.

If a person begins their conscious, awake day seeking the Lord and His voice, the chances of being influenced or led astray by the voices intent on doing so are greatly diminished. God's word is His voice given to us in writing. It is sure and true and is the one thing by which all other voices can be measured and evaluated. By abiding in Christ and taking everything we hear and listen to into subjection to obeying His voice, we are assured of walking in the light with Him.

The voices of religion, politics, current events, and all-natural occurrences are but distractions capable of interfering with the more worthy use of the time the Lord has allotted to each of us. This is not to say that the world has nothing worth listening to but only that it should not be given priority in our lives. The cares of the world will dominate our lives if we let them, and at the end of any day, we may have missed what God was trying to tell us.

The conclusion of the listening lesson is to put the Lord first in everything we listen to and respond to. This will please our heavenly Father.

1 JOHN 2:26-27
2 CORINTHIANS 10:3-6
PROVERBS 1: 23-33
HEBREWS 3:7-11
JOHN 10:14-16

608 RESPONSE

A person's response to events of life gives an indication and insight into their character. The ear that hears the rebukes of life will abide among the wise . . . Whoever loves instruction loves knowledge, but the one who hates correction is stupid.

The person who trusts the Lord understands that all the events of life, whether good or bad are the results of the Lord's love for us and are working together for our good. He/she responds to everything with thanksgiving, while the one without such knowledge responds with complaints and bitterness.

The expectation of the one who has lost his/her own life for Jesus' sake is the one who realizes that everything they experience is transforming them into the image of Jesus. The person living for self is void of such understanding and becomes bitter at things that cause him/her suffering and grief. The differences in response are dramatic and revealing.

The hand of God in our lives demonstrates His love for us even when we are chastised and afflicted. Before I was afflicted, I went astray, but now I keep Your word . . . Even Jesus learned obedience through the things that He suffered. A submissive response to chastisement produces the fruit of righteousness, while a rebellious reaction to the Lord's rebuke produces eventual death. Whom the Lord loves, He corrects just as a father the son in whom he delights.

The Lord is surely warning us about stubbornness and a negative response to a loving Father who has our well-being and eternal life as His motivation. Our response to all of life's trials, whether good or bad, are events that give us a choice to respond positively or negatively.

Let's go God's way!

ROMANS 8:18-30

609 SEDUCTION

The soul of a person is a treasure possessed by every human being. This precious possession can be what its Creator intended it to be or can be lost forever. Seduction is the sister of temptation and the partner of the deceptiveness of sin. The person who is vulnerable to seduction is the one who trusts in their biological senses and their carnal mind. The enemies of our souls can only seduce a person by appealing to the lust and pride of the person who is given to self-satisfaction.

If allegiance to self is greater than to God, the soul is in peril of being separated from God for eternity. This truth should put fear into the heart of anyone who has not lost their own life for Jesus' sake. The careless persons who believe that God does not hold them accountable for what they think and do have not understood the truth of the gospel and the salvation of God.

The seductive techniques used by the peddlers of the gospel dominate the airwaves, pulpits, and institutions of higher learning throughout the world. These ministers have yielded to the seduction of the same serpent who deceived Eve in Eden. Death and separation from God are the inevitable consequences of ongoing disobedience and yielding to the seduction of our fleshly, carnal desires.

The Lord God has given us everything required to overcome temptation and the seduction of our soul, but it requires a belief in the truth and obedience to it through faith. Yielding to the deceptiveness of sin and the seductiveness of self-gratification is the pathway to death and destruction so often warned about in scripture.

If any person wakes up to find him/herself separated from God because of his/her own choices, who is to blame?

PROVERBS 7:21-27; 9:13-18
REVELATION 17:1-6

610 A BETTER PLACE

At funerals it is not uncommon to hear someone say that the deceased is in a better place. It sounds spiritual, but the truth is that where the soul of the departed actually resides is usually unknown. It makes us feel good to think that a loved one is with the Lord in heaven, but the truth is that the souls who have not abided in the Lord while walking the earth does not abide with him after they leave the earthly body.

Truly I tell you with no one in Israel have I found such faith. I tell you many will come from the east and west and recline at the table with Abraham, Isaac and Jacob in the kingdom of heaven while the sons of the kingdom will be thrown into outer darkness. In that place there will be weeping and gnashing of teeth . . .And Jesus said to him, "Follow me and leave the dead to bury their own dead."

The idea that we can have any power over the soul of one who has departed, or as though optimistic hope influences their eternal destiny, are "pie in the sky" wishes without any foundation in reality.

The time to be serious and prepare for the inevitable departure from our physical bodies is while we inhabit them. The reality of going to be with the Lord when we die can be established while we are still in our fleshly bodies. The Holy Spirit is the One who bears witness that a person has, or has not, become one Spirit with Christ while walking the earth. The assurance of our souls going to a better place when we depart is given to us in advance of the death of the natural body.

It is the person who has forfeited his/her self-life in advance who has already taken on the eternal life that he/she ascends to when the natural body expires.

The hope of being in a better place when we die can only be confirmed by experiencing it ahead of that time.

MATTHEW 25:14-30
PHILIPPIANS 1:20-23
LUKE 12:1-3

611 OMNISCIENCE

Does our Creator know everything absolutely? Or has He limited His knowledge by allowing variables within the scope of what He has determined to be? The volition He has given to mankind is the variable which allows us to determine our own destiny within the boundaries the Lord has established. *Whosoever will, let him come.*

The greatness of God does not depend on absolute predestination of everything but allows for His created beings to choose the path they will follow. Choices made by human beings are reported in the Bible constantly. And in our own lives the Almighty allows us to make decisions that determine our ultimate destiny. The Lord has been surprised, and even brokenhearted, over choices made by mankind throughout their history.

Our Creator has, and always had, a plan and a purpose for His creation; and in the end He will bring it about. But in the meantime, the free will given to mankind and angels is unfolding, and hearts are being tried and tested that the Lord may know those who really love Him. The predestination of individuals is somewhat mysterious, although for most of us *God is not willing that any perish. . .* But it is obvious that many do.

While the end of all things is set and determined, the Lord is involved and active in bringing about that outcome. He is interacting with every one of His created beings and His call is going out throughout the earth as these words are written. The Lord is not playing a game. He has invested His own life that *whoever will* might find His salvation and become one of His chosen people.

Ultimately, it is Jesus who was and is predestined and chosen, and we also enter that predestination and chosen-ness in Him.

There are no active sinners in Him!

REVELATION 22:17
2 PETER 3:9-13
GENESIS 6:5-8

612 A STIFF NECK

The Lord is speaking of those who stiffens their neck, representing a stubborn and unyielding heart. The person who stiffens his/her neck in the face of reproof from God is very offensive to Him. *The person who is often reproved yet stiffens his/her neck will suddenly be broken beyond healing.* This is a stern warning to the ones who know they are being rebuked yet allow their pride to keep them from submission.

The record of ancient Israel's journey through the wilderness gives us many examples of what it means in God's eyes to have a stiff neck. *And the Lord said to Moses, "I have seen this people and, behold, it is a stiff-necked people. Now therefore, let me alone that my wrath may burn hot against them, and I may consume them in order that I may make a great nation of you.* Was Moses not a type and forerunner of Christ? Jesus is the firstborn of many brethren and the beginning of a new nation that have God as their Father. Do you have ears to hear? This new nation is the true Israel of God which has taken on the image of Christ and the nature of God. It is a people gathered from the four corners of earth who have learned to follow the Spirit of Life in Christ Jesus and has been set free from the law of sin and death (a stiff neck). Read Romans 8:1-17.

There are no stiff-necked rebels in this new spiritual nation of Israel, which has Christ as its firstborn and head and has entered God's holy land and His rest. Can you hear me, says the Lord? The ability to fulfill the law and walk as Jesus walked is achieved by abiding in Christ. A stiff neck is no longer an issue for the one who has lost his/her life in Christ and submitted to the Holy Spirit.

There is no alternate path that leads to the promised land and the kingdom of God!

HEBREWS 3:1 through 4:16
ROMANS 8:1-17

613 SERVICE

Eye service and lip service are marks of a hireling. Many hirelings are trained by their employers to believe what they are trained to do is equivalent to serving God. They learn to teach and preach about things which they have not actually learned from God but have been told that God is the source. In many cases, these hirelings believe they are serving the Lord, while others actually come to understand that they are serving an ecumenical organization that is its own kingdom and not God's. Some continue to collect a paycheck while others break away but continue to propagate what they were taught. Many of these hirelings realize the lucrativeness of preaching the gospel and use popular doctrines and some of their own deviations of the truth to prosper themselves monetarily, economically and socially.

How many of those we have learned to trust and allowed to lead us spiritually are actually servants of the Lord and not just disingenuous hirelings and peddlers of the gospel? What you are hearing is a revelation of truth that the Holy Spirit is presenting to those who love the truth.

The tax-exempt organizations that claim to be the church are the ones building their own kingdoms and hiring those who are willing to join in their façade for the purpose of financial and social security and recognition.

The only real servants of the Lord are those who have lost their own lives for Him and serve Him with their whole hearts.

Does this revelation matter to you?

JOHN 10:1-18
ROMANS 12:1-2
EPHESIANS 6:5-8
MATTHEW 15:8-9
MATTHEW 6:1-4

614 POLARIZATION

There is a polarization taking place throughout the world. *The wicked prowl on every side when vileness is exalted among the sons of men.* The scale is near the point where righteousness is about to give way to the wickedness that has taken root in so many places. We will soon know if the scale has tipped in favor of anarchy and destruction. The hand of God will be revealed to those who are able to see it. The civil strife taking place in the USA is indicative of the condition of the world. If the wicked are able to prevail, the whole earth will give way to those who would enslave the human race. The conflict of races and the nations will give way not to peace, but to anarchy and total enslavement.

What you are hearing has been prophesied, but the actual timing remains uncertain. Nevertheless, many signs have appeared, and the vile have surely raised their heads. The remnant who actually honor the principles of God have been put on defense against the ones who want to totally cast off the restraints of decency and reason.

We are nearing a crossroad to which there is no turning back. Unless those who prefer law and order make a valiant stand, the scale of justice will tip toward those who would totally discard it.

This is an alert given by one who loves righteousness and truth and is praying for justice to prevail.

2 CHRONICLES 7:14
ISAIAH 59:19 KJV
PSALM 11:1-7
1 TIMOTHY 2:1-4

615 A SPIRITUAL PEOPLE

When the scriptures speak of the offspring of Israel and the descendants of David, they are commonly making reference to a people who make up the eternal generation who have become the chosen of God. They are the saints and the special ones *who may ascend into the hill of the Lord or may stand in His holy place. They have clean hands and a pure heart. They have not lifted their souls to an idol nor sworn deceitfully. They are the ones who have received blessing from the Lord and righteousness from the God of their salvation. They are the eternal generation of Jacob, those who seek God, who seek His face.*

How many can truthfully make such a confession? Many of us are called to such a position and status, but only few who fulfill its requirements. Those who achieve the spiritual recognition of the Lord are the ones who have become one Spirit with Him and abide in Christ. They no longer sin, just as the apostle John has told us. The person who would dispute this proclamation is the same one who has not entered this holy place where only the righteous have entered. Because they have not experientially become one of the eternal generation of Christ, they create doctrines of dispensation, positionalism, unconditional eternal security, and future deliverance from the lust of the flesh, the eyes, and the pride of life.

Jesus has done it all and given the victory to those who actually believe Him and obey Him. These are the spiritual people who are no longer of the world and have learned to live according to the Spirit, not the flesh.

If you can hear my voice, says the Lord, you are being called to the spiritual land where I dwell. Amen!

616 WORKS OF GOD

God is at work. He is faithfully performing all He has prophesied and all He has promised. His blessings, curses, judgments and signs are all taking place before our eyes. Though there are few who recognize the hand of God working in our midst, He is nevertheless bringing His will to pass. Those of us who can see what He is doing are certainly blessed and secure in His love. Those who do not know Him and have not put their trust in Him are left to their own devices and the fear of uncertainty that society is producing.

The Lord is not only the hope of His people but the security that gives us peace and assurance in the midst of the turmoil and anarchy in the culture of hatred and conflict that has shown itself in a one-time harmonious society. Respect for authority lies in the ashes and rubble and dead bodies of those murdered and destroyed by ignorant and rebellious mobs of greedy, hateful bigots who would defile all that is righteous, good and just.

Could all this anarchy we see be God's judgment on a culture that has turned its back on truth and justice? We have an entire major political party willing and complicit in calling good evil and evil good. If these murderers are able to prevail against those who are upright in conduct and belief, we will see the darkness that is being seen in many large cities throughout this land and the world overtake the entire earth.

The antichrist may have his day, but the Almighty will also have His day, and we who love Him and have put our trust in Him will see the end of the wicked and wickedness itself.

Blessed are they who are given eyes to see and ears to hear the wonderful works of God.

PSALM 46:8-11; 98:7-9; 111:1-10
PROVERBS 29:26-27; 15:3
ISAIAH 5:18-23

617 A SOUND MIND

For God has not given us a spirit of fear but of power and love and of a sound mind. What is the Lord's standard of soundness of mind? Did Jesus Christ, the man, have a sound mind? This may seem like a silly question, but many things Jesus spoke caused large numbers of His followers to turn away from Him, and the religious leaders accused Him of having a demon. It is no different today.

While searching the mind of Christ, it became evident that God's standard of soundness is far different than the carnal understanding of the soundness of the mind. The carnal mind of a human being is actually at enmity against God. *But to be carnally minded is death, but to be Spiritually minded is life and peace because the carnal (natural) mind is enmity against God; for it is not subject to the law of God nor indeed can be. So then, those who are in the flesh cannot please God . . . But this mind be in you which was also in Christ Jesus who, being in the form of God did not consider it robbery to be equal with God but made Himself of no reputation taking the form of a bondservant and coming in the likeness of men. And being found in appearance as a man He humbled Himself and became obedient to the point of death, even the death of the cross . . . But the natural person does not receive the things of the Spirit of God for they are foolishness to him, nor can he/she know them because they are spiritually discerned. But the one who is spiritual judges all things yet him/herself is rightly judged by no one. For who has known the mind of the Lord that he/she may instruct Him? But we have the mind of Christ.*

The main point being, the standards set for evaluating soundness of mind are intrinsically different for the person living according to the flesh and the one living according to the Spirit.

ROMANS 8:9-14
COLOSSIANS 3:1-6

618 IDEOLOGY

We are in the midst of a war that has plagued humanity throughout the record of history. The lust for power is the simplified explanation for the conflict against those who desire peace and liberty. Those who want control over others would have us believe that the war in which we are engaged is about race and victimization, but that is a lie. The real conflict is ideological, and the standoff is about which ideology will prevail.

Those who love freedom and peaceful co-existence have created a structure of laws and rules that, if held in mutual respect and compliance, allow for a peaceful society where almost every individual has the opportunity to seek and achieve their desired goals. The nation, USA, in which we live was founded on and prospered under these principles.

The rule of law and personal responsibility have predominated up to this point, but the corrupt forces that desire absolute control over human destiny have multiplied and taken control of many of the nation's fundamental institutions and governing establishments. If these enemies of free enterprise and self-determination are able to prevail, the freedom we have known and experienced will end. The hopes and dreams of those who are ambitious and self-disciplined will give way to those who believe they will be given a free ride to prosperity.

The struggle is more desperate than the average citizen is aware of, and unless these well-organized foes of the republic are exposed and defeated, there will be no place left on earth to re-establish the freedoms we have known.

619 CONVERSION

The Lord is asking the religious community: If a sinner is converted, is he/she still a sinner? If so, to what have they been converted? *Because they do not change, therefore they do not fear God.* Are these questions and their answers not simple? Why, then, is there a worldwide movement that has produced doctrines that tell those who claim to be born again and converted to Christianity that they remain sinners after their conversion? Something is wrong! Can truth somehow be converted to a lie and remain truth? Does a sinner suddenly become a saint because they make a disingenuous confession of belief and ask Jesus into their heart?

The proof of a genuine conversion is accompanied by an absolute change in direction and focus. Anything less is deception and insincerity. For a religious leader to tell a person that their salvation is secure while that person is unable to cease from sin is an unparalleled travesty that ends in death. True conversion, without exception, results in a changed life that glorifies the Savior. Ongoing sin does not glorify Jesus and only brings reproach to His name. If a person confesses that Jesus has saved him/her, and then confesses that they remain a sinner, from what were they saved? This is no small issue in the eyes of God!

In summary, conversion means that something or someone has been changed from one thing to another. If something is converted but has not changed, the conversion is counterfeit and not genuine.

2 CORINTHIANS 5:17-21

620 THE GROUND

When the Lord speaks of the ground, He is often referring to the natural realm. His words do not come from the ground, and His prophets do not speak from the dimension of the carnal mind. Thus, interpretations of what God says by the natural person are often mistaken and misunderstood. The carnal, human mind is actually enmity against the Spirit of God and is unable to please Him. This truth does not fare well for the institutions of higher learning built and controlled by those who are void of spiritual revelation. *Spiritual things must be spiritually discerned.*

The person whose breath is in his nostrils and who speaks from the ground is the same one who casts the words of the Lord behind him/her, because they are misunderstood or offensive to the natural reasoning process. The one who loves the truth is the same one who loves the Lord and His ways. Such a person is one who has lost his own life and taken on the Spiritual life of Christ and become one Spirit with Him. Whether a person has heard this truth before or not, it only remains theory if it has not been experienced.

The Lord has made His promises and His declarations to be experienced and lived. We have entered an age where counterfeit faith and the perversion of truth are taught and preached far more commonly than the true gospel of Christ. The ground and evil spirits are the source of this perversion of Christianity and its propagators. Those who are following and subscribing to this carnal interpretation are the same as those who deny that Jesus Christ has come in the flesh. SELAH!

And Samuel grew and the Lord was with him and let none of his words fall to the ground. Anyone who is taking heed to words that proceed from the ground will reap the harvest of the ground.

GENESIS 3:14-19; 4:1-12
ISAIAH 29:4-16

621 PROOF

The fool demands proof and facts that he/she is standing in the midst of. Proof is only hidden from the person who is too ignorant to be able to identify it. Intellect is no help to the person who has embraced falsehood and lies in the name of science. The great Creator has hidden Himself in the clouds and the unseen realm of spirits just beyond the carnal person's ability to understand. It is truly amazing to observe the lengths to which a fool will go in an attempt to disprove the existence of an intelligent Creator.

The religious fool is different than the atheist fool. While believing in a Creator, he/she (the religious fool) refuses to obey Him. The destiny of both is the same. It is separation from God for eternity. The Creator has made a way for everyone to escape the separation from Himself as result of their sin. But rather than truly humbling themselves and being remorseful for their sins and turning away from them; they devise doctrines contrary to what God has said about the salvation from sin He has provided in order that they may continue to sin and maintain a false hope of sharing eternity with the Lord

Multitudes who have rebelled against the truth of God's word have filled auditoriums and universities to comfort one another in an attempt to establish their false belief that the sheer number of participants somehow confirms the legitimacy of the lie being propagated by the conspirators who have agreed together and schemed to take the pastures of the Lord to satisfy their own greed and lust for money and power. This conspiracy against truth has been going on since the beginning of historical records.

The fools who deny the existence of God and those who refuse to submit to Him are all of the same worldly population that is passing away and will perish when the revelation of the mystery of God is revealed before the whole creation.

ROMANS 8:18-25
REVELATION 10:1-7
HEBREWS 11:1-3
PSALM 19:1-4; 53:1-4

622 CONSERVATISM

Conservatism is not synonymous with righteousness, justice and integrity--neither in the socio-political realm or the religious. The same pseudo conservative politicians who would rather embrace the leftist baby murderers rather than a true conservative politically are of the same mindset as the hypocritical religious leaders of Jesus' day who crucified the Holy One. This is a strong indictment but is happening before our eyes. To be conservative can be a virtue if it is founded upon objective truth and integrity, but if a conservative person is greedy and envious and is subject to bribery, that person is no better than the leftist who wants to destroy the foundation of liberty and freedom.

Because of greed, envy and prejudice the conservative caucus has become divided and vulnerable to defeat. While politics is a drag to this watchman, I am compelled to make commentary because of the severity of what is at stake for those who truly love the Lord. While He will surely be a shield for us who love Him, the whole nation will experience the judgment coming upon it if the forces of anarchy prevail politically. We will be forced underground and punished for the sake of righteousness.

The realization of honest, conservative values should cause the person who believes in them to set aside pride and prejudice for the greater good of the unique nation the Lord has given us. Will God not judge any nation which forgets Him and gives way to wickedness? SELAH!

Just look at the history of the physical nation of Israel, and the ways of God can be clearly seen.

623 HE IS COMING

The day of the Lord will be a dreadful day for all who dwell on the earth and have made themselves enemies of God. The tumult we are witnessing throughout the world is but the beginning of the sorrows that are to come. Manmade disaster along with natural disasters are signs and omens of the climax of the world we have known. The limits and the boundaries of humankind have drawn near to what the Lord can tolerate.

If anyone reading this little expose doubts what is being proclaimed, that person has only him/herself to blame if they come to that day unprepared. When the whirlwind arrives, there will be no more time to get ready, and those who have not established a relationship with the Savior will not be able to find Him. The enemies of God will seek Him, but their fate will be sealed, and no further opportunity to repent will be found.

This is a strong word, but no more so than the multitude of prophecies and warnings given to mankind throughout the scriptures.

How bad must the human condition get before those who profess to trust God actually do it?

Seek Him with all your heart while He may still be found.

PSALM 32:6-11

624 THE HUMAN SOUL

The soul is the essence and the unique identity every person possesses. The soul's worth is immeasurable and must be protected with all diligence. Being willing to sell one's soul for anything the world can offer is a tragic and lamentable choice made by the person who is shortsighted and ignorant. The soul that has been lost can be redeemed, but more often than not, it isn't. The cost of redemption is death to the life for which the soul has been sold to obtain. SELAH!

What is being said here may be a little deep for the person who has studied the easy "beliefism" of modern theology. Any intervention of the Creator is able to revive the soul that has been separated from Him and died as a result. There are countless masses of people who have forfeited their eternal soul for temporary gain in the world. A list of all the things for which people have been willing to exchange their souls would be prohibitively long.

Every child of Adam knows what they have done, because *all have sinned (by choice) and fallen short of the glory of God.* How accurate is the "Book of Life"? The names written there are those of the souls of the faithful who have realized the value God has placed on their soul.

If anyone would come after Me, let him deny himself and take up his cross and follow Me. For whoever would save his life will lose it, but whoever loses his life for My sake and the gospel's will save it. For what does it profit a person to gain the whole world and forfeit his/her soul? For what can a person give in return for his soul?

Jesus not only shed His blood and gave His life for our souls; he also gave His own soul for ours.

It certainly makes no sense for any person to lift up his soul to an idol.

ISAIAH 53:1-12

625 CHANGES

The world in which we live and the planet on which we live are subject to change. Nature itself is in constant upheaval and perpetual evolution. The very foundations of the earth are unstable. Everything around us is in a constant state of change. There is nothing in the natural dimension which a human being can count on not changing.

Nevertheless, there are things unseen to which our souls can anchor that will hold fast and not be shaken or moved. The Creator Himself *is the same yesterday, today and forever.* His word that He has given to mankind is immutable and steadfast and can be relied on no matter what transpires in the natural realm.

The land of the living where God dwells is the land of the Spirit where we who have come to know the Lord have been given access and allowed to enter and dwell. In this place our souls can find rest and security from the storms and the changes going on all around us. Praise God! He is real, and He cannot lie, and He never changes. This is the assurance we have if we love Him and obey Him. If we abide in Christ, sin and the turmoil and tumult of the world around us have no power over our souls. SELAH!

There is assuredly a place of refuge and shelter for the person who has the faith to enter into the loving arms of the One who gave His life that we might know Him and be free from the sin that separated us from Him.

The flesh merchants of the earth would have us keep our eyes on the earth and our natural bodies from which the carnal human cannot escape, but they lie and have not found the place behind the veil where only the sinless soul can enter. They would rather feed on the flesh and the changeable nature of the natural realm to satisfy their own lust for wealth, recognition and worldly power than that of the Spirit. While they give lip service to the supernatural, they remain bound to the lust of their flesh as do those who follow them.

Can you see the reality of the realm where things do not change and there is no more fear or insecurity? It all lies in faith in the unchangeable God and His word.

Even a hurricane cannot move the soul of the one who is firmly anchored in the immutable word of God and His Spirit.

The upheaval is coming! Are you ready?

626 PREPARATION

The preparation of the heart belongs to man. There are many voices admonishing us to prepare for hard times, and they are most likely right. If we store up the things that may be needed in a time of shortages and confinement, our survival may be extended. But contrary to the survivalists and the preacher who tells you that all your sin has been forgiven and covered for all time, Jesus has told us to be vigilant and ready to meet Him at all times. According to the words of scripture, our hearts must be blameless before the Lord in order to be ready.

There is surely a hereafter, and that is the inevitable destiny for which Jesus, the apostles, and the holy prophets have all warned mankind about. This little discourse is just an additional admonition at this moment to prepare and be ready to meet your God. Do not let another minute pass in which you regard unrepented sin to reside in your heart. Unless you obey the gospel, it cannot save you. The lying preachers will be nowhere to be found when the day of reckoning has come, and their false assurance of eternal security and right standing with God will have no validity with the Righteous Judge.

God has made provision for us to be accepted by Him and stand blameless before Him, but it is only for the one who has done so according to His terms. The person who has made his heart pure as the Lord has shown us and become holy as He is holy, and as the Bride has made her garments spotless, is the one who has nothing to fear. This is the one who can rejoice at the appearance of Jesus Christ, and the one who is like Him.

Anyone who is still breathing and hungers and thirsts for righteousness and truth still has time to prepare and be ready for that great day.

Those who remain sinners on that day will reap the reward of all sinners.

PSALM 1:1-6

627 NATIONS

There are people from every nation God has made who have known Him. And there will be representatives from every one when we who love the Lord meet in the holy City. But among all the nations on earth, there are none like Israel. She is a small nation, and many greater nations have attempted to destroy her and still are. During all of recorded history since Israel was created, many nations have come and gone, but that one chosen by God to bear His name and record His word has been sustained through every form of destruction and attempt at annihilation that her enemies could imagine.

There are actually two Israels. One is the nation that all the world can see and fret over. The other is a spiritual nation consisting of God's chosen people gathered from among all the nations He has made. The Lord watches over both, because they are both fulfilling His purpose on the earth and in heaven. The testimony of Israel to God's plan and purpose for mankind is unique, and there is no other nation that can carry it. Spiritual Israel is the true Israel of God and is made up of only those who love Him and obey Him. They do His will and dwell in His presence.

There are many who try to take this honor for themselves, but they have not received the key that allows them into the holy place. The multitude of religious ecclesiastical representatives of every nation have tried to find the gateway into the presence of the almighty God of Jacob, and even if they find it, they are powerless to enter because they cannot open the door. The passageway is not really hidden from the natural human being, but the only way to pass through is to forfeit the life of the flesh that was formed from the dust of the earth. Very simple, but not very easy.

The only way to become part of the Lord's chosen nation is the way He has shown those who actually seek Him with all their heart, soul, mind, and strength and speak only the truth in their hearts.

I hope the journey goes well for all the sojourners on the path to Jerusalem above.

JOHN 14:6
ROMANS 2:28-29

628 PEACE

Mercy and truth have met together; righteousness and peace have kissed. The companions of peace are all ways of Godliness and love. *The Lord will bless His people with peace. Come you children, listen to Me; I will teach you the fear of the Lord. Who is the one who desires life and loves many days that he/she may see good? Keep your tongue from evil and your lips from speaking deceit. Depart from evil and do good; seek peace and pursue it. But the meek shall inherit the land and delight themselves in the abundance of peace . . . Mark the blameless person and observe the upright; for the future of that person is peace. Great peace have those who love Your law and nothing causes them to stumble. The kingdom of God is righteousness, joy and peace in the Holy Spirit.* The gospel itself is *the gospel of peace.*

Scripture is laden with references of peace for the upright in heart, but for the wicked and the sinner, there is no peace. *There is no peace, says the Lord, for the wicked.* The prophet and the teacher who lead the people who call themselves sinners, telling them that they will have peace and safety, are those from whom the Lord has told us to turn away.

The kingdom of God is made up of those who have learned to live in peace already, not those who hope for it in the hereafter. Those who abide in Christ have discovered the peace of God that He has given to the people who obey Him in the present. The person who regards sin in his/her heart cannot have the peace of God in the same heart. We all have but one heart, one soul, one mind and one life in which to experience the peace of God, which is in Christ Jesus.

If the nagging of your flesh is robbing you of peace, serenity is in obedience to the truth of the gospel.

ISAIAH 59:1-20
JEREMIAH 23:16-22
PROVERBS 14:12

629 RAGE

Rage is the expression of uncontrolled anger produced by the foolishness of an emotionally driven will devoid of understanding. The rage of a fool generates strife and conflict. We can see the rage of discontented, misdirected rebels on the news any given day. The rage will be met with the overwhelming response of a power beyond the ability of the perpetrators to comprehend.

Wrath is not the same as rage, but will absolutely quash the one who believes their rage will give them victory over the target of their rage and hate. Wrath is God's response to tyranny and open rebellion. The raging fool has no hope of victory over his/her behavior without the help and mercy of God. The Lord is able to redeem even a raging fool, if that person can find a place of repentance.

It is distressing to see a person who confesses being a Christian in a rage they confuse with zeal put on an exhibition before unbelievers in an attempt to convert them. These self-appointed exhibitionists are bringing reproach to the name of Jesus. Without the anointing of the Holy Spirit, even the written word of God produces death. If you have seen what I am saying, you can say Amen. We who love the Lord are directed *to be gentle as doves but wary as serpents.* Though we are warriors, we do not engage our enemies with the rage displayed by those who do not have the knowledge of God or a love of the truth.

We are often left with a choice to trust the Lord and wait patiently for His judgment to appear, or to step out in our own strength to try and put an end to the raging we see before our eyes.

PSALM 37:1-20
PROVERBS 29:8-11

630 VICTORY

The mystery of victory over sin through sacrificial death has been the Lord's plan from the beginning. *Precious in the sight of the Lord is the death of His saints.* The man, Jesus Christ, has gained the victory over sin through total obedience to His Father, living a sacrificial life that ended in a sacrificial death. The person who is joined to Him and becomes one Spirit with Him is the one who is able to walk as He walked and do the things He did. Is this not what the gospel teaches?

Jesus has won the victory for us by showing us how it is done. We have the victory by abiding in Him. He overcame temptation, sin, the world, and even Satan, by always living according to the Spirit. Is that not what we are instructed to do? The victory that any person can achieve is through the victory that Jesus has already won as a man, whose Father was God. If we are born of God, is He not our Father? Has the Lord not told us that we who are born anew are His brethren and joint heirs with Him?

Who, then, are these teachers telling us that we remain sinners after being born again? And what gospel are they preaching? This is no small matter! To believe such a lie leaves the one who lives it out to disqualify him/herself from the victory that the Lord has placed within the grasp of those willing to believe Him and follow His Spirit by faith.

If you have ears to hear what the Holy Spirit is saying, you are on the path to victory.

1 CORINTHIANS 15:50-58
1 JOHN 5:1-5
ROMANS 6:1-23; 8:9-14; 12:1-2
REVELATION 14:12-13

631 THE SET TIME

The Lord God Almighty has set times and seasons, boundaries and limits which establish when nature and those who hate God will be consumed and wickedness will be extinguished. The set time is drawing near in which Gentiles who have ruled the world under the leadership of Satan will end. In that day, the true Israel of God will be revealed and glorified along with the God of Jacob.

Lest anyone thinks this writer is a Zionist in the carnal sense, understand that the revelation is a view from the heavenly realm of the Spirit where no flesh has a place. From where did the revelation shown to the Apostle John originate? And who can accurately discern the heavenly vision without the revelation of the Spirit? The metaphoric language and the symbolic images are intentionally meant to confound the carnal mind.

Time is measured by the signs and seasons of the natural realm, but these do not affect the sequence of events outside of the limited dimension in which they occur. The Lord rules over heaven and earth, for He created both. For a created being, whether human or angelic, to think they could usurp the power of the Creator or frustrate His purpose is the demonstration of pride that will be harshly dealt with.

While our Creator is loving and merciful, He is also just. Those who have rebelled against God beginning in heaven and continuing on earth, are near the end of the set time they will be allowed to try and overthrow the One who created them.

Submission to the Lord and obedience to His word is the way to be on the right side of the calamity that is about to come upon the natural creation.

There have been set times throughout recorded history. So, too, is there a set time for the end of it.

PSALM 102:12-15; 104:34-35; 37:9-15
REVELATION 4:1-2; 17:1-6; 21:1

632 PRESUMPTUOUS SIN

Isolation of selected Bible verses for the purpose of constructing doctrines that satisfy the desires of those who have selfish and covetous motives for their establishment is a presumptuous sin of great magnitude. This is the practice of most of the main line denominations and their offspring. The great institutions of higher learning have refined and perfected these empty doctrines without the whole counsel of God or the guidance of the Holy Spirit.

Any group or organization established and built upon an error or a lie certainly is not a representative of the truth. This, also, is a strong indictment that the Lord is exposing these sinners for what they are by their own admission. In these last days the Lord is exalting the truth of His gospel and exposing those who are perverting it to build their own kingdoms.

The presumptuous leaders and their followers are attempting to take the pastures of the Lord for their own carnal and fleshly satisfaction. While Jesus has most certainly shed His blood and given His life for the sins of the whole world once and for all time, His great sacrifice does not automatically apply to every person without meeting the requirements God has set forth to partake of His salvation.

While Jesus' sacrifice was a once for all time event, the salvation He has secured is only for those who obey Him and remain faithful to the end of their earthly journey. To presume that the Lord will exonerate and accept those who continue to sin and partake in the behavior from which He gave His life to save them is pure foolishness and deception. *Those who sin willfully after receiving the knowledge of the truth have only judgment to look forward to.*

The idea that God forgives the sin of the one who goes on sinning after being forgiven and cleansed for past sins goes against the message of the gospel, and even sound reasoning. Believing in a lie does not require faith but presumption. The Lord has made clear what He gave His life to accomplish as well as the requirement for any person to partake of the salvation He has provided. The presumption that a sinner can abide in Christ and spend eternity with Him is actually heresy and blasphemy.

What stronger condemnation of presumption and its erroneous doctrinal roots and motivation could be made?

1 JOHN 3:4-9
1 SAMUEL 15:22-23

633 CALMNESS

As there is often a calm before a storm, or as the great waters recede before a tsunami, so too is a false sense of well-being ahead of catastrophe. To have a calm spirit while everything is tranquil around us is a blessing that, even in ideal circumstances, not everyone shares. But to remain calm in the midst of calamity is a gift that comes from a deep trust in the providence of the Lord. He knows if a person has it, as does the individual who possesses it.

Anyone who does not have the assurance of a calm spirit is not without hope if they are able to seek the Lord with all their heart and are willing to obey what He says. A real, living relationship with the Lord is the bedrock of the assurance that produces calmness in the inner depths of the one who actually trusts the Lord. Without such faith in Him and confidence in His word, the hope of well-being is only frivolity.

The storm, the flood, and the whirlwind are coming, and now is the time to settle all the issues that prevent us from the calm assurance of well-being that comes from having our hearts right with God. When catastrophe strikes, it will be too late. This trumpet sound and warning has gone out over and over.

It is this watchman's hope that many are listening and taking the call to heart.

PSALM 107:23-31

634 LIARS

This is an extremely serious discourse. The Lord often speaks of liars and never in a positive way. Satan is the father of lies. Is he not also the father of those who follow him in persistent lying? The first place to look for lies in every person's life is in a mirror. Lies begin in the heart of the one who is not honest with him/herself. If we cannot speak the truth in our own heart, what proceeds from our mouth is but a reflection of what is in our heart.

The most grievous of lies is the lie spoken to God. Ananias and Sephira, his wife, agreed to lie to the New Testament apostle thinking that they were merely lying to men, but they were, in fact, lying to the Holy Spirit. God's judgment was severe and instantaneous. The serpent's lies to Eve in the garden caused the fall of humankind and the curse of death that came upon the whole natural creation.

Even lies that seem harmless have consequences that produce condemnation and death in the perpetrator and the recipient who receives them. There are no liars abiding in Christ or His kingdom. The person who has received and believed the lies of the religious leaders of Ecclesia remain in a state of delusion and separation from the life of God.

Any person who is able to justify his/her life as a means of bringing about a good result, in the end is the one who has yielded to the seduction of the harlot and the father of lies. The spirit of every human being is a lamp of the Lord by which He is able to determine the truth and motive for whatever we speak or even think. If we are found to be liars in the final analysis, what do you suppose will be our eternal destiny?

Is this not something to give serious thought to?

All liars shall have their part in the lake which burns with fire and brimstone, which is the second death.

PROVERB 6:16-19
PSALM 15:1-5
JOHN 8:39-47

635 OUR BEST

What does our best look like in the sight of God? What does the work of the carnal human being amount to? If we do the best we can without actually submitting to the Spirit of God, our works amount to wood, hay, and stubble void of eternal value or reward. The endless projects and business directed by pastors and religious leaders are no more than feel-good distractions to ease the guilt of the sin that they have allowed their followers to engage in through their fleshly lusts. The Lord's best is in Himself where there is no room for our own best. What this means is that self-consciousness and self-gratification have no place in the person who has lost his/her life in Christ. The person who is allowing the Lord to do His work through him has ceased his own best personal effort to please Him or any person and is totally yielded to the Spirit of God. This is the place where the deceptiveness of sin has lost its power, and human flesh has become subservient to the Holy Spirit. This is basic gospel truth and leaves no place for a person to labor in their own strength and effort to do their best. This is the place of rest where all work is of God and where the works that He performs through us are works that follow us into eternity.

Striving is not part of being yoked with Jesus, and our personal best is not the best we can do.

GALATIANS 2:20
HEBREWS 4:10

636 SELF

Most of us have a consciousness and awareness of self. Our Creator has made us that way and given us a choice in how we see self in relationship to Himself and the rest of creation. The concept each of us has of self and the position we give to self is a strong indicator of our character and all that we do.

All our works and deeds, whether good or evil, represent the place we have given to our "self". The Lord surely knows if it is He who sits on the throne of a person's heart or if said person has placed self in that place of value and honor. This fact is not too complicated to grasp or understand. The place self occupies in every individual's life will determine whether they are proud or humble.

God resists the proud but gives grace to the humble . . . The humble He will show His salvation. If a person sees him/herself as the center of the universe, there is no possibility of that person knowing God or His ways. He is the center of the creation and the One who holds it all together. For any person to think that everything they are a part of revolves around their desires and well-being is a delusion of prideful arrogance and a totally misplaced concept of self.

A correct and proper understanding of self and the place self occupies in the grand scheme of the creation is one of subservience, gratitude and love—not the love the world knows but the actual love the Lord has shown us. There is no place for selfishness in God's love and no place for the selfish person in His kingdom.

Can you see why we are judged by our works and have the mark on our forehead and hand of the one we worship and serve? The mark identifies a person and their god.

Who do you actually worship with your self-life?

GALATIANS 2:20
JOHN 12:25-26
LUKE 10:25-28

637 GIVING

The Lord desires that we understand what giving consists of. He does not ask anyone to give what they do not have. He has asked us to give our lives, which includes everything that we are and have. Is this not what He has shown us by doing it Himself? His will is revealed many times over throughout the Bible.

Most of the teachers who speak about giving talk about tithes and offerings as though that is all God expects. Usually, those gifts should be given to the person speaking or the organization they represent. They often appeal to greed and self-interest, telling us that we will receive God's blessing if we give to their cause. This may be true in a few cases, but it is an attempt to enrich their own kingdoms more often than not.

The person who knows the Lord and walks with Him is directed to give as he/she sees what the Father is doing. Giving to the poor and the needy directly is what we see Jesus do. The Holy Spirit rarely leads us to give our physical resources to enlarge a ministry or organization of paid professionals who claim to be doing the work of God that the Lord purposes every individual member of His Body to do.

If our lives truly belong to the Lord, we will not expect professionals to do what the Lord desires to do through each one of us. Giving to the spiritually or physically poor and needy is giving to the Lord, and He will both bless and repay for that effort. To give to the rich to make them more prosperous will bring a curse and leanness of soul.

When we have given all that we are to the Lord, He is truly able to use us individually and enlarge the kingdom of God, which has no earthly headquarters, no worldly representatives, and no tax-exempt status, nor do the laws of mankind apply to their activity.

PROVERBS 22:9, 16; 21:11; 19:17
ACTS 20:35; 3:1-8
2 CORINTHIANS 9:6-15
ROMANS 12:1-2
JOHN 3:16
EPHESIANS 4:7-16

638 STRONGHOLDS

Both good and evil forces have strongholds in which they find security. The Lord Himself and His truth is the stronghold in which the righteous trust and find refuge from their enemies. Sinners, the enemies of God, and all those who have not received a love of the truth have built their own strongholds out of fables, lies, false doctrines and deceit. *Through deceit, they refuse to know God.* The strongholds they have built are walls they hide behind within the towers to which they run from the light of the truth. What they don't seem to realize is there is no refuge for sinners and rebels who willingly try to hide from the Spirit of God.

This watchman is commissioned to scale the great walls of denominationalism and pull down the trusted towers of false doctrines and the fables that are holding so many of the people the Lord is calling to Himself. The spiritual hierarchy of Ecclesia try desperately to defend their own strongholds and their captives, but the Lord and the truth of the gospel have greater power than all of the deception of religion to those who love the Lord and the truth.

In spite of all the worldly battles that are taking place all around us, this spiritual battle between light and darkness, Spirit and flesh, is the big one for which the consequences are eternal. Anyone who is able to hear what is being said has been given a choice to follow Jesus and the Spirit of Truth or to let carnality continue to hide in the stronghold of the flesh and the multitudes of religious hiding places built by the hands of mankind.

One clue that can identify carnal strongholds is tax-exempt status and earthly headquarters.

We have all been given enough truth to move on to the heavenly stronghold and escape the worldly!

EPHESIANS 6:10-18
PSALM 9:9
PROVERBS 21:22
PROVERBS 24:11-12

639 ENEMIES OF GOD

No one in their right mind would choose to be an enemy of Almighty God, but most who are have done so by default. There comes a point in nearly every person's life when they reach a place where their carnal mind becomes aware of an obligation a created being has to honor the One who created them. This is the point where most humans just turn away and ignore the Spirit of the Creator and follow their own fleshly desires. For many, the awareness of that Spirit just fades into obscurity.

At this point the nature of carnality becomes the dominant and controlling force that causes the sons and daughters of Adam and Eve to follow the nature of their parents. Unless the Lord intervenes, these people become enemies of God and live their lives in that condition to the end.

Some humans actually make a conscious decision to become an enemy of God by openly rejecting Him and denying His rightful place in their life. Others, the ones who become religious, attempt to pacify and gain favor with God through their own efforts and carnal understanding. They, too, remain enemies of God because of the pride they demonstrate by trying to appease God's legitimate demand for submission and obedience.

The Lord, in His love and mercy, has made a way of redemption and reconciliation, but there are actually few who are willing to embrace God's way even when it appears to them. The life offered by the Spirit of God requires those who have rejected the Lord's ways in favor of their own to give up their carnal, human existence in favor of a spiritual life that can only be experienced through the death of the old person and rebirth of a new person. This new person is one who follows the Spirit of God and rejects the dominance and lust of their flesh and their carnal ways.

The point here is that the carnal person is an enemy of God by nature, and the spiritual person is a child of God because of the new nature, the very nature of Christ that they receive by total submission to Him.

All of the enemies of God will perish.

2 CORINTHIANS 5:16-21
ROMANS 8:1-14

640 SONS OF EDOM

Remember, O Lord, against the sons of Edom the day of Jerusalem who said, "Raze it, raze it, to its very foundation" . . . O daughters of Babylon who are to be destroyed, happy the one who repays you as you have served us.

The modern-day sons of Edom look much different than the ancient, but their mission is quite similar. The modern, spiritual Jerusalem is a heavenly city unseen by the natural eye. The sons of Edom persist in trying to bring it down to the ground where they are able to put it into the reach of carnal hands and understanding of those who are not able to ascend into the heavenlies where the Lord dwells. You can hear them and see them everywhere in pulpits as well as electronic media constantly appealing to the flesh and the natural appetite of carnality all under the guise of preaching and teaching the many perversions of the gospel.

If you can hear what the Spirit is saying, you are being put into a position to do something about it. This watchman is only unveiling the masquerade of the false church and the false gospel.

The impostors who attempt to reduce the Spiritual city to a place on the earth have been here from the beginning. So, too, has the Lord warned us about them from the time of Jacob and Esau. The firstborn son was of the earth, while the younger son was of heavenly descent. God loved Jacob, but hated Esau, though they were brothers. The Lord blesses only the younger Son, the last Adam, while His hand is against the older son, the first Adam. So it goes throughout the Bible. The firstborn is of the earth, while the younger son is of heaven.

If you are able to see and hear this message, you are being given a choice to follow after the Spirit or the flesh: the true Israel of God or the one that has been established on the earth. There are two Jerusalems as well as two Adams. One is of the earth, represented by Esau and his Edomite offspring. The other is Jacob (Israel), who is a type of Jesus Christ who is the heavenly Man.

Is this not the truth that has been given us by God?

PSALM 74:1-12; 137:1-9

641 TREASON

We have witnessed treason on a grand scale by our political and legislative leaders along with their legal cohorts. These things should be obvious to any rationally-minded, honest person. Less obvious is the treason of religion with regard to Christianity. *For unto us a child is born, unto us a Son is given; and the government shall be upon His shoulder and His name shall be called Wonderful Counselor, Mighty God, Everlasting Father, Prince of Peace. Of the increase of His government and peace there will be no end.*

The treasonous, religious thieves have hijacked the true Christian church in order to usurp the rightful headship of Jesus over His Body. The worst of these treasonous religions which I am aware of is the Roman Catholic Church. She has multitudes of illegitimate offspring. While they have all displaced the legitimate government of God with their own, they have lost the real power of the Spiritual government of Christ. The Lord's government has not actually been overthrown but is flourishing in the unseen realm of the Spirit where only His saints have access.

His chosen ones hear His voice and know their place in His body. The Lord is perfecting His true church as these words are being written. Those who are listening to and following the treasonous leaders of religion do not know their place or the way to the Spiritual kingdom. They are being told lies that lead them into earthly kingdoms and, in the end, hopelessness and despair.

Enter by the narrow gate; for wide is the gate and broad is the way that leads to destruction and there are many who go in by it, because narrow is the gate and difficult is the way which leads to life, and there are few who find it. . . . And He Himself gave some to be apostles, some prophets, some evangelists and some pastors and teachers for the equipping of the saints for the work of the ministry for the edifying of the Body of Christ till we all come to the unity of the faith and to the knowledge of the Son of God, to a perfect man, to the measure of the stature of the fullness of Christ; that we should no longer be children tossed to and fro and carried about with every wind of doctrine by the trickery of men and the cunning craftiness of deceitful plotting, but speaking the truth in love may grow up in all things in to Him who is the head—Christ—from whom the whole body join and knit together by what every joint supplies according to the effective workings by which every part does its share, causes growth of the body for the edifying of itself in love. . . . There is one mediator between God and man, the Man Jesus Christ.

Treason is one of the most treacherous forms of betrayal and denial of truth that a human being can commit. The treacherous behavior on the streets of cities run by treasonous and tyrannical demagogues in the seats of power and authority are destroying the foundations and the fabric of society. So, too, are the religious leaders and their organizations plundering and oppressing the poor and needy, along with all who come to them for spiritual guidance. The secular and the religious governments are connected by the world and their treasonous behavior.

The Lord sees and He knows that the end of all treason, treachery and tyranny is coming. In this the people of God can rejoice.

PSALM 37:7-10
1 KINGS 16:15-20
REVELATION 1:7

642 THE OUTCASTS OF ISRAEL

The outcasts of Israel are a people dear to God. He gathers them together from the ends of the earth. They come to Jerusalem from every nation. They are the saints of God who know their Savior and dwell in His presence. They are the spiritual offspring of Abraham, Isaac and Jacob who seek the Lord with all their hearts. These outcasts are the poor and needy, the afflicted and the downcast, the humble and the meek that have put their trust in God and given their lives to Him. The outcasts of Israel are rejected by the world and those who love the world system. They do not fit in the religious establishments or the standards set by the hierarchy of religious institutions. They are the sheep who hear the Good Shepherd's voice and follow Him wherever He goes. These outcasts love the truth and cannot be bribed and will not compromise with false doctrines, fables or dead traditions. Their color, heritage or race is of no significance, nor is the human language they speak. The Lord knows every one of his saints, and they are precious to Him. They are the ones in whom He delights. These true Israelites are the ones who will judge the nations and execute the Lord's judgment on all those who resist the righteousness of God. If you are one of this holy nation, you recognize your brethren by the Spirit of God who resides in each one. There are no practicing sinners in this assembly of saints and none who live according to the flesh.

If the Holy Spirit is not bearing witness in your heart to the reality of this exposition, you'd best re-examine your own relationship and faith.

God's truth is not subject to mankind's interpretation or commentary.

643 BLOOD

The Lord speaks often of blood. *Without the shedding of blood, there is no forgiveness of sin . . . The life of all flesh is in its blood.* The most precious blood this world has ever seen is that of the man, Jesus Christ. His shed blood was and is the most significant sacrifice mankind has ever seen. Though it was a physical sacrifice, its power and scope reach beyond the physical realm and into the eternal, heavenly realm.

The blood of the natural, created animal and human is the foundation of biological life. The blood of a person can be innocent or guilty. A person may be bloodthirsty or a defender. The person who sheds innocent blood has made him/herself an enemy of God. A land polluted with blood is cursed by God. So too are the hands that shed it. *A person burdened with bloodshed will flee into a pit; let no one help that person.*

Could any blood be more innocent than that of an unborn or a newborn baby? What mark do you suppose is on the forehead and hand of the person that sheds it? The blood being shed throughout the earth by the murderers of the innocent does not go unnoticed by God, and He does hold them accountable.

The blood of Jesus is able to make atonement for even the murderer of innocents, but that atonement and forgiveness requires absolute repentance and contrition. The same is true for all those who are shedding the blood of the blameless on the streets all over the world.

The blood of the innocent and the blameless is not that of sinners, and all those who are bloodthirsty are they who seek the life of the flesh. SELAH! These are the flesh merchants who do business in Babylon with the mother of harlots and all her illegitimate offspring. Can you hear the Spirit speaking? He is speaking of the vast number of religious institutions that make up the false, illegitimate church that the world knows as Christian. Have they not all taken His name in vain?

Those who are taught to plead the blood of Jesus without ceasing their sin are also doing so in vain.

JOHN 5:14

644 SIGHT

What can the natural eyes of humans see? Surely, there is more. *The hearing ear and the seeing eye, the Lord has made them both. . . . Now Moses called all Israel together and said to them, "You have seen all that the Lord did before your eyes in the land of Egypt to Pharaoh and all his servants and to all his land—the great trials your eyes have seen, the signs and those great wonders, yet the Lord has not given you a heart to perceive and eyes to see and ears to hear to this very day."*

Do we still see people as trees walking, or has the Lord given us the eyes to see each person clearly? There is a whole other dimension that God has created on the other side of the veil through which flesh cannot pass. It is the heavenly land where Jesus sits at the right hand of the Father, and His chosen sit with Him in the Spirit with whom the chosen have become one. All who have been called are invited just as the marriage supper. But who has actually come? No one will show up there without a wedding garment and a pure heart. There is no substitute for oneness with the Lord and abiding in Him. The person who actually has eyes to see Him and follow Him is the one who has eyes and sight to see the salvation of God. A salvation that does not include the sight to see it will not be able to walk in it.

After Jesus' resurrection and ascension, He spoke to his church telling them that: *These things says the Amen, The Faithful and True Witness, The Beginning of the Creation (new) of God. I know your works that you are neither cold nor hot. I could wish you were either cold or hot. So then, because you are lukewarm and neither cold not hot, I will vomit you out of my mouth. Because you say, "I am rich, have become wealthy and have need of nothing"—and do not know that you are wretched, miserable, poor, blind and naked—I counsel you to buy from Me gold refined in the fire that you may be rich; and white garments that you may be clothed that the shame of your nakedness may not be revealed; and anoint your eyes with eye salve that you may see.*

The Lord speaks of the spiritual vision which is able to discern spiritual things not of the earth.

Are the references not contained for the one who recognizes them?

645 PARENTS

The person who speaks the truth in his/her own heart knows that none of us have chosen their biological parents, race, gender, or place of birth. Nevertheless, every rationally minded person is given a choice with regard to who they are, who they serve and the path they walk. Our Creator tests every heart and knows its deepest secrets and motives. The choices a person makes determine what mark appears on their forehead and hand.

Our birth parents have incalculable influence on who we are and who we become as adults, but each rationally minded individual ultimately chooses his/her own destiny. I am speaking for the benefit of many who have believed the lies of those who are telling us that we have a choice as to the things God has determined and left each individual to deal with. The truth is that we are who we are, and to think otherwise is a grand delusion.

It is painful to see the youth on the streets and observe them on the news media destroying their lives, because they have believed the lies of those who have taught and instructed them to tear down and destroy the very foundations that have allowed them the free choices they are making.

Accountability is inevitable for both leaders and followers of the anarchists who are calling evil good and good evil, and trying to destroy all that is good. There is a way out for anyone who will stop and search for the truth that is in plain sight of every person who is willing to be honest with him/herself. No one needs to be a slave to their emotions or their delusions. The truth is able to overcome both. The truth is what actually sets a person free to be what the Creator has intended us to be.

JOHN 8:31-32
HEBREWS 10:26-27

646 BOASTING

What does any created being have to boast about? What do we have that has not been given to us? From where does pride originate? The answers all proceed from a source outside of the ability of a carnal human being to perceive. No one has anything to boast about other than the God who formed everything and has given us all that we are and have. This knowledge should cause any rational person to bow in humility and give thanks to the One who has created all things seen and unseen. Pride is the source of all boasting and is very offensive to the Creator who has made us able to accomplish anything. As created beings we are all subject to mortality and death. There are no exceptions even among the most prominent and exceptional among us. It is God who holds every person's destiny in His hands, and He is most gracious and merciful to allow us to do anything.

Those persons who somehow think they are independent of the Creator have fallen into the delusion that they themselves are the source of their own life. Life itself is a gift that no created being has the ability to produce on his own.

The boastful have shown themselves to be fools void of the understanding of who and what they are. The rich and powerful of the world are no more than empty vessels in the hands of the One who created them. The end of every person is to return to the dust and give account to the Creator who gave them life and everything they were able to accomplish during their short stay on earth.

Those who have become fully aware of their mortality and their absolute dependence on the Lord are the humble ones who know Him and are able to please Him. We have all been given the opportunity to acknowledge His rightful authority and place of domination over us as well as the behavior He expects of us. Those who choose independence and self-exaltation will receive His rejection and be separated from Him for eternity.

This journey on the earth is a test and a preparation for how we will spend eternity. The boastful and the proud may have their day of glory in the here and now, but the time is coming when their glory will be consumed in the grave.

The humble who recognize their actual place and position in the grand scheme of things will have a reward which surpasses the carnal mind's ability to comprehend.

The Almighty has spoken!

PSALM 73:1-28
JAMES 4:13-17

647 SHIELDS

The Lord is a shield for those who walk uprightly . . . The Lord is my strength and my shield . . . For the shields of the earth belong to God. The earth itself is protected by the Creator, and for that reason alone we are able to exist in this fragile environment. But more than that, the Lord's chosen people who walk in His ways are protected from evil and all the forces that would destroy them if they were able.

The ignorant who believe in nothing more than chance, along with the religious that believe their own effort preserves them, do not know that the loving hand of God is what holds humanity and the whole creation in existence. Preservation of all that we can see and know in the natural realm is on the verge of disintegration and annihilation. The Lord has warned us to get ready and be ready, for the day is coming.

The shield that protects the earth will be removed, but the shield that protects God's people will continue right into the unseen heavenly realm where all the saints of God have already established citizenship. Those who trust in the physical security of the world will be left with nothing but destruction. It is clearly time for all who are called to *make your calling and election sure* before the time to do so has passed. These are not idle words, but the words of the One who holds all the shields.

Have we not all been warned?

1 CORINTHIANS 15:20-28
2 PETER 3:1-13

648 GREED

Greed is closely associated with the love of money and covetousness. The person who spends his/her life and energy in the pursuit of lust for things will be slain by it. *But these people lie in wait for their own blood; they set an ambush for their own lives. So are the ways of everyone who is greedy for unjust gain; it takes away the life of its possessors.* Such a person is subject to bribery and all forms of betrayal and unfaithfulness. Temptation to sin cannot be overcome by the person who loves any form of self-gratification more than God.

The one who is controlled by his flesh and its lust is the one unable to cease from sin. If you live according to the flesh, you will die; but if by the Spirit you put to death the deeds of the body (flesh) you will live. For all who are led by the Spirit of God are sons and daughters of God. If you are afflicted by greed, love of money and covetousness, Jesus has provided the solution and the way of escape through His death, burial and resurrection. He has made a way by allowing us to share in that death and resurrection life by choosing to believe Him and forfeiting the sinful life for His life. This requires faith and an uncompromising hunger and thirst for righteousness and truth.

Greed is the sure evidence that a person does not abide in Christ and does not know Him. Greediness is not covered by the blood of Jesus, unless the greedy person turns from it permanently. And no one is forgiven in advance of true repentance. If your theology conflicts with this assessment, your theology is wrong. Only those who cease from their sinning will find forgiveness and redemption in the end.

There is no substitute for repentance for a person to avail himself of the salvation God has provided

1 PETER 3:10-12
LUKE 13:2-3
2 PETER 3:9-10

649 WANDERING

The Lord has often told us that He will lead, guide, and direct those who trust Him and diligently seek His face. Nevertheless, the majority of humanity is wandering in a wilderness with no real hope of reaching any favorable destination. The many religions of the world offer guidance and the hope of a good end to the human journey, but most are delusional and without substance.

The way of the God of Jacob is the true way that leads to the land of eternal life where the Creator dwells. He has given us not only a map but also a guide and a counselor to help us find our way. Even so, it is possible for a person who has begun their journey on the right path to wander from it, if they do not keep their eyes fixed and their heart set on the final goal. The distractions are numerous, and the temptations to wander from the narrow way are many.

Let your eyes look straight ahead and your eyelids look right before you; ponder the path of your feet and let your ways be established. Do not turn to the right or the left; remove your foot from evil . . . Brethren, if any one among you wanders from the truth and someone turns that one back, let that person know that the one who turns a sinner from the error of his/her ways will save a soul from death and cover a multitude of sins.

We who are abiding in Jesus are the ones on the straight and narrow way. This is not a boast but a fact. *The person who abides in Christ does not sin.* So much for the churches filled with the wandering devotees who call themselves sinners and the leaders they follow. Anyone who has joined him/herself to such a congregation has certainly placed him/herself in a place of danger and error.

What you are hearing is a call from the Savior to examine the path on which you are walking and return to the way of holiness if you have taken a wrong turn.

PROVERB 16:25

650 GOOD DOCTRINE

Listen, and I will give you good doctrine and tell you what it is. Good doctrine is pure and contains no deceit or lies. It is not mixed with the ways of the world or the wisdom of carnal minds. Good doctrine produces righteousness and the fear of the Lord without compromise and hypocrisy. This good doctrine cannot be found in any of the religious institutions that I am aware of. The pure gospel and the whole counsel of God make no provision for mankind's carnal interpretations and commentary.

When the Spirit of Truth teaches His doctrine, it may contain metaphors and anomalies the carnal mind can easily misunderstand and misinterpret, be He never lies or deceives the person who has spiritual discernment. Fables and mankind's traditions have no place in good doctrine.

Jesus answered them and said, "My doctrine is not mine but His who sent Me. If anyone wills to do His will, he shall know concerning the doctrine whether it is from God or whether I speak on My own authority. He who speaks from himself seeks his own glory, but he who seeks the glory of the One who sent him is true, and no unrighteousness is in him." Whoever transgresses and does not abide in the doctrine of Christ does not have God; he who abides in the doctrine of Christ has both the Father and the Son. You are of God, little children, and have overcome them (false teachers) because He who is in you is greater than he who is in the world. They are of the world. Therefore, they speak of the world and the world hears them. We are of God. The one who knows God hears us; the one who is not of God does not hear us. By this we know the Spirit of Truth and the spirit of error.

Again, we are given a choice.

1 JOHN 3:5-9
1 TIMOTHY 4:1-2, 6-7; 6:3-5
2 TIMOTHY 4:1-4

651 THE DEVIL

When Jesus spoke to the Devil or about him, he called him Satan. That has been his name since iniquity was found in him, and he lost his place in heaven and the glorious name of Lucifer. Those who pridefully and ignorantly refer to Satan as Lucifer apparently do not realize they are glorifying him. He is now the adversary of all that is good and has become grotesque and vile. In the attempt to exalt themselves, those who refer to Lucifer only demonstrate their lack of understanding.

When Satan lost his place in heaven and was cast to the earth, he not only lost his glorious name, but he also lost his eternal position and became subject to time and a deadline for his final judgment. He knows his time is short and is causing all the havoc he is allowed by the Almighty to do. We who have been chosen by the Lord will crush Satan under our feet shortly, and his final demise will be realized.

Satan has been described and called by many names, and they all depict a dark and sinister nature, and his desperate attempt to defeat the Creator and the creation that is loved by God. Though he is a fool, he has made his way into nearly every aspect of the world and has gained control over most of the earth's population. The exception, of course, are the saints chosen by God who know what is happening and have put their trust in the Lord.

If you know the "Bright and Morning Star", you will not be referring to the devil as Lucifer.

ISAIAH 14:12-15

652 ENGAGED

The one who is engaged to become the "Bride of Christ" is also engaged in the process of making him/herself ready for the wedding. There is no time to waste and no excuse for having anything in our life that takes precedence over being ready for the marriage. The gospels are laden with parables, metaphors and outright warnings about being ready for the great day.

We who love the Lord are living in a world filled with temptations that will try and cause us to be distracted and even deceived into taking our eyes off our final goal. There are many things and situations that are worthy of our time and attention, and our fleshly desires will dominate us if we do not have control over them. The enemies of our soul are very alluring and will take us captive if we allow them.

It is also obvious that we are all engaged in the battle between flesh and Spirit that has been going on throughout the history of mankind. The victory for each of us is through obedience to the voice of God. If we can be deceived into disobeying the voice of God, our engagement can be broken.

Regardless of what the trained theologians may say, the marriage is not consummated until the end. Faithfulness is absolutely required, and purity is an absolute prerequisite. Anything less is adultery and idolatry. The false church is the adulteress, and her false doctrines are her idols. Can you hear Me, says the Lord? You are being warned in real time, and your fate is in your own hands.

There are no adulterers or idolaters who have spotless wedding garments or pure hearts.

REVELATION 21:9-27

653 DELIVERANCE

Regardless of our own preparedness, preparation and forethought, our deliverance and safety are from the Lord. There is no place of refuge outside of Him, nor are there any forces on earth or in heaven that can defeat Him. This should be of great comfort to all those who know Him and trust Him.

The forces of wickedness arrayed against the righteous in this hour appear overwhelming, but just as the army that surrounded Elisha at Dothan, the army of the Lord that surrounds His people is greater than the evil forces that can be seen with the natural eyes. The battle is the Lord's, and if we have eyes to see, our deliverance and the victory over evil are the Lord's.

The book has been written, and the battle has been won. With our faith we see past the limits of carnality and what appears as the defeat of righteousness. Nevertheless, the word of the Lord stands and will certainly prevail. *Justice for mankind comes from the Lord . . . The salvation of the righteous is from the Lord. He is their stronghold in the time of trouble. The Lord helps them and delivers them; he delivers them from the wicked and saves them because they take refuge in Him.* Abiding in Christ is the way of salvation from every form of wickedness including sin itself.

The deliverance for which the soul of nearly every person yearns is not found in trusting anything that can be found in the world. Unless we can learn to believe God and obey His voice, the hope of deliverance is not based in faith and trust.

This is in reality a plea to take the word of the Lord seriously to heart and be in a place where deliverance will be experienced.

DEUTERONOMY 32:39-43
PSALM 35:9-10; 18:1-3

654 INTRIGUE

The Lord would have his people be wary of the secret temptations of intrigue. The enemy of our souls has laid snares that are subtle but nevertheless deadly. The smooth and flattering speech of a seductress is able to disarm even the person who has known the ways of God. The intrigue of the tree of the knowledge of good and evil is a lure into the forbidden depths of the one who would exalt himself above the stars of God and be like the most high God.

The throne of God in the temple of God is a throne in the heart of every person who has made the Lord his/her absolute ruler and king in their life. The temptation to displace Him and allow another to take His place is the conflict that started in heaven and has taken root on the earth. If and when we allow our carnality to dominate our innate sense of good and evil, the throne in God's temple is supplanted by a false god. Is this not the sin of our first parents in Eden?

Jesus Christ has made a way back to the beginning to start over by putting to death the false god sitting on the throne in our hearts. Once the true God is established there, the only thing needed for His ongoing lordship in our lives is obedience. The person who remains in absolute obedience to the Spirit of God will not yield to even the cleverest intrigue.

The Lord has cautioned us not to take part with those who have yielded to the harlot who has taken part with those who have cast God's word behind them and become a partaker with adulterers.

This is not too deep or mysterious for the one who has received the love of the truth.

655 WALKING

How, where, with whom we walk is the determining factor in where we end up. The way a person walks reflects the entire course of their journey on earth. *The one who walks uprightly will be saved . . . the one who walks with wise people will be wise . . . the person who walks with integrity walks securely but he who perverts his ways will become known . . . if we say that we have fellowship with Him (the Lord) and walk in darkness, we lie and do not practice the truth . . . the one who says he/she abides in Him (Christ) ought him/herself to walk just as He walked.*

Figuratively speaking, the way in which a person walks is the measure of the person. The path on which we walk either leads to eternal life or to death. This truth is firmly established throughout the scriptures. To walk aimlessly and without knowing where we are going will, in the end, lead to the grave without any hope of eternal fellowship with God.

Now is the time to determine and resolve where we are walking and what is our final goal. This may seem to be an impossible task, but *all things are possible with God.* And to know unequivocally where our feet are taking us is certainly worth the thought and effort required to secure the assurance that we are following the Holy Spirit and abiding in Christ. If our flesh is leading the way we are walking, the end is death. But if the Spirit is allowed to lead the way we walk, our salvation is secure, and there is no reason to be lost or confused.

The way a person walks really is a big deal, and everyone has a choice.

PSALM 32:6-11; 1:1-6
MICAH 6:8
ROMANS 6:1-4
2 CORINTHIANS 5:6
GALATIANS 5:16-18
EPHESIANS 4:1-6

656 MURDER

Taking a life is not necessarily murder. Murder begins in the heart. We are told to love even our enemies, and how much more to love our brethren. *The person who does not love his brother abides in death. Whoever hates his brother is a murderer, and you know that no murderer has eternal life abiding in him.* A person can obviously be a murderer in the Lord's sight without even committing the actual deed.

Where do wars and fights come from among you? Do they not come from your desires for pleasure that war in your members? You lust and do not have. You murder and covet and cannot obtain. You fight and war. Yet you do not have because you do not ask. You ask and do not receive because you ask amiss that you may spend it upon your pleasures.

There are many of the religious community whose hearts are filled with hate and homicidal thoughts and motives while calling themselves Christians. Is this not delusion? We who walk on this earth in these last days are faced with the challenge of maintaining our love in the midst of the evil that surrounds us. We have been told that the love of many will grow cold. But the one who is faithful to the end will be saved.

Even a murderer can find forgiveness and redemption by choosing to allow love into his/her heart, but the one who will not see the truth will perish with the rest of the world.

He who says he is in the light and hates his brother is in darkness until now; he who loves his brother abides in the light. There is no cause for stumbling in him, but he who hates his brother is in darkness and walks in darkness and does not know where he is going because the darkness has blinded his eyes.

Is the Lord not telling us to carefully examine our hearts and motives?

1 JOHN 2:3-9

657 INTERCESSION

Have we all not been called to intercede for truth and justice, righteousness and peace? This is a rhetorical question asked to invoke a response of action. There has never been a more widespread need of intercessors around the world. Scripture has revealed that the hand of God can be moved by the intercessory prayers of His people. The hour in which we live has seen the rise of evil and wickedness on a worldwide scale that has never occurred in the recorded history of mankind.

The Lord is calling his chosen to stand up and intercede for all of humanity that many would come to know the truth and find mercy. This is a high calling that will not receive notoriety from the world or the governments of the world. The Spirit of God is the organizer and the inspirer of this worldwide movement that has the power to deliver many who have been deceived and are lost.

Our prayers and our testimonies can change the course of many people's lives and destinies. Intercession is the work of God that will follow us into eternity. To be silent in this time of worldwide anarchy is a transgression for which those who can hear the voice of God will have to give account. The voice of truth and justice, righteousness and peace can be spoken only by those who know it. When we intercede for one another and for the lost, our prayers delight the heart of the Lord, and He hears us. This is the communication that pleases the One who gave His own life for the world.

If you require scriptural references for what is being said, it is time to read your Bible.

658 THE FOUNDATIONS OF THE EARTH

The foundations of the earth are unstable. The earth is the ground on which the natural man walks. It is ever changing. The boundaries, the climate, and even north and south are subject to change. The instability of the earth and the world extends to all the cultures, laws and governments, and nations. If we have learned to trust in the ways of earth, our security is no more stable than the ever-changing current of the wind and water, and the whims of society.

Every human being is born into the instability of nature and the environment of change. Though mankind tries endlessly to secure his environment, he is fighting against the Creator's design. *The foundations of God are in the holy mountains.* These are the heavenly land that is eternal and not subject to change. This is the land where the Creator dwells with His chosen who have put their trust in Him. This is the land where those who have transcended the mortality of their flesh and put it into subjection of the Spirit of God are able to see the purpose for which the biological was created. There is true stability in this Spiritual realm we are called to inhabit.

Jesus Christ is the way into this land where life never ends and is not subject to change. Only those who have entered His chosen-ness and resurrection life are seated with Him in this heavenly land. The person who lives according to his/her flesh has no hope of escaping the instability of the foundations of the earth of which the flesh has originated. The Creator Himself has taken on this biological flesh that is captive to the earth and has revealed the way of escape from its dust.

He has shown the captive the way and the life for which we were designed. It is up to every individual to follow His lead or not.

659 HIS FOOTSTEPS

Though the Lord's footsteps are not seen by the natural eye, they are none the less set before the one who has eyes to see them. *Righteousness will go before Him and shall make His footsteps our pathway. . . . Your way was in the sea, Your path in the great waters, and Your footsteps were not known. . . . But whoever keeps His word truly the love of God is perfected in him; by this we know we are in Him. He who says he abides in Him ought to walk just as He walked . . . Whoever abides in Him does not sin; whoever sins has neither seen Him nor known Him.*

Who are you going to believe? The way, the truth, and the life have been set before us. The choice to follow them is up to us. The natural person who is living according to his/her flesh cannot see the footsteps which have been spoken of and the path of righteousness, which they believe to be unattainable. Consequently, these earth dwellers and flesh merchants have devised doctrines that justify and even excuse ongoing disobedience and sin. Their doctrines have their roots and their foundations in the ground. They speak from the ground, and those who hear them have their breath in their nostrils.

If we are to follow the Spirit of God, our eyes and ears must be open to His voice, and we must understand His ways. This is the only way through the gates of righteousness into the "Land of the Living". This is how we please and honor our heavenly Father. The way of religion, for the most part, only mocks the true salvation the Lord has provided.

Take it or leave it, says the Lord, but don't try to alter it.

660 THE THRONE OF INIQUITY

Shall the throne of iniquity which devises evil by law have fellowship with You; they gather together against the life of the righteous and condemn innocent blood. Both secular and religious governments have set themselves up as gods and established thrones which devise evil by their laws. *The wicked prowl on every side when vileness is exalted among the sons of men.* Has vileness not been exalted at every level of human governments? *These things says He who has the sharp, two-edged sword: I know your works and where you dwell, where Satan's throne is.*

The throne of iniquity is wherever iniquity and sin have been established as legitimate forms of behavior and conduct by those in authority who make law. Satan's throne is wherever mankind has compromised righteousness and truth in favor of expediency and pressure from the wicked and those willing to sacrifice justice for a bribe. Can you see it? These thrones have been set up at every place of power and authority in the world.

Unless we are citizens of a higher nation and have a higher form of government, we have, by default, become subjects of tyranny against God. This is no small revelation! Every person bears the mark and the image of the one he/she serves. The idea that we will, at some point in the future, take a mark on our forehead or hand is no more than a distraction from the reality of what has been happening since Adam and Eve were expelled from Eden when they let the serpent take the place of God on the throne of their hearts.

We have the power and ability to choose who sits on the throne of our hearts.

661 WHAT IS MAN?

When I consider Your heavens, the work of Your fingers, the moon and the stars which You have ordained; what is man that You are mindful of him and the son of man that You visit him? Blessed is the man You choose and cause to approach You that he may dwell in Your court . . . A man who is in honor but does not understand is like the beasts that perish . . . As for man, his days are like grass; as a flower of the field so he flourishes, for the wind passes over it and it is gone and its place remembers it no more.

Man's worth to God is so significant that He was willing to give His only begotten Son as a sacrifice for the souls of mankind that had rejected His truth and His commands and chosen to follow their own desires and the lies of a fallen angel. The sacrifice of Jesus has made a way of escape from the death and the separation from God that has left man as no more than a beast of the earth.

The person who lives according to his flesh is indeed as a beast of the earth, and his end is similar. Once a person gains access to the Spiritual realm where God dwells, the only way to remain and prosper there is to obey Him. The knowledge of God and His ways is but the beginning of the journey that leads to eternal life and eternal fellowship with our Creator. Believing a lie or following the desires of our sinful flesh will lead right back to where we were before we came to the knowledge of the truth. Satan knows this and has done all he can to make us believe the lie that a person can continue to sin but remain in a place of blamelessness in the sight of God.

Every person is of great value to the Lord, but only those who believe Him and obey Him are the ones who are chosen in the end.

662 THE BACKSLIDER

The backslider in heart will be filled with his own ways. . . . There is a way that seems right to a man but it ends in death . . . As a dog returns to its own vomit so a fool returns to his folly. To what can a backslider be likened? And what is his end? There are some among the religious professionals and their followers who believe that even the backslider will be saved. But from what is the backslider saved if he has turned back to sin and no longer abides in Christ? The backslider obviously does not fear the Lord and does not hate evil.

The argument of those who believe that once a person is saved his/her salvation cannot be lost do not seem to understand that sin is what separates a person from God, and it is sin that Jesus came to save mankind from. *If a person sins willfully after receiving a knowledge of the truth there remains no further sacrifice for sin but a fearful expectation of judgment. . . . For if they have escaped the pollutions of the world through the knowledge of the Lord and Savior Jesus Christ, they are again entangled in them and overcome, the latter end is worse for them than the beginning. For it would have been better for them not to have known the way of righteousness than, having known it, to turn from the holy commandment delivered to them.*

If the truth is not given proper adherence and not loved by those using it, where can the endless dispute over salvation go? *The soul that sins will die.* What will be the end of all the churches and the people in them who are taught that they cannot cease from sin when the final judgment comes. Will their erroneous and false doctrines save them if they have lived their lives according to the flesh?

Backsliders and false teachers will not receive special treatment because they have called on the name of the Lord in vain at some point in their lives.

Repentance and contrition are the way back to righteousness for both the backslider and the false teacher.

663 REAL FOOD

The Lord has provided nourishment for our physical bodies, and He has offered us food for our souls as well. Blessed is the one who hungers and thirsts for the heavenly food that feeds the spirit. Without food from the earth, our bodies will die, and without food from heaven we experience leanness and lack of purpose in our lives.

Jesus answered them, "Truly, truly I say to you, you are seeking me not because you saw signs but because you ate your fill of the loaves. Do not work for the food that perishes, but for the food that endures to eternal life, which the Son of Man will give to you. For on him God the Father has set His seal. . . . Therefore, do not be anxious saying, "What shall we eat?" or "What shall we drink?" or "What shall we wear?" for the Gentiles seek after all these things, and your heavenly Father knows that you need them all, but keep first the kingdom of God and His righteousness and all these things will be added to you." . . . But He (Jesus) said to them, "I have food to eat you do not know about." . . . My food is to do the will of Him who sent Me and to accomplish His work.

All these things are elementary gospel principles, but how many who call themselves Christians actually understand and practice them? We are truly called to walk as Jesus walked and do the things He did. Who would tell me it is not so? Does a sinner do these things? Is an unbeliever able to walk as Jesus did and do the things He did? I think you know. The Lord has called His chosen ones to true righteousness and holiness, not some hypothetical, positional standing off in the heavens. The truth is here and now, as is the food from heaven of which Jesus ate and will give to us who hunger and thirst for it.

664 SIN UNTO DEATH

There is sin leading to death. There was a sin committed by our first parents in the garden that led to their death. There is also a sin referred to in the New Testament that results in the same consequence. There is a great deal of discussion and commentary about a sin or the sin leading to death, but the commentary of the Holy Spirit reduces it to a simple explanation, not of singular or particular sin but a way of life that ends in eternal life or eternal death.

The Lord gave Adam and Eve a simple command. They disobeyed the voice of God, which resulted in their death. The Lord has explicitly told all believers of the New Testament that *if you live according to the flesh you will die.* This warning is not specific to a particular sin of the flesh but to the flesh in its entirety. The way of life in the garden was obedience by faith in what the Lord had said. It is no different now. The way of life now is obedience to the Spirit of God by faith. *As many as are led by the Spirit of God are sons of God.* Was the first Adam not a son of God? Did he not forfeit his sonship and his inheritance through his disobedience? We of the church age face the same temptation and the same consequence.

The actual test is whether we put God first or self first. If the Lord is our God, we obey Him. If our flesh is our God, then we obey it. Is this truth not amazingly simple? Sin unto death is following after the natural desire of our flesh. Eternal life is the result of following after the Spirit of God. Is this not what Jesus has told us and shown us?

The mystery of Godliness is very deep, but not really so complicated that a simple person cannot understand it. The way of understanding is a result of a love of the truth, not a high IQ or theological indoctrination.

Obedience through faith is the way of escape from the second death.

665 THE UNDEFILED IN THE WAY

Blessed are the undefiled in the way who walk in the law of the Lord! Blessed are those who keep His testimonies who seek Him with the whole heart! They do no iniquity; they walk in His ways. . . . For what the law could not do in that it was weak through the flesh, God did by sending His own Son in the likeness of sinful flesh on account of sin: He condemned sin in the flesh that the righteous requirement of the law might be fulfilled in us who do not walk according to the flesh but according to the Spirit.

Does it weary you to hear the truth? Does it conflict with what you learned in Sunday school? Let God be true and every man a liar. The truth is that if we live according to the Spirit, there is no occasion for us to sin.

To say more seems unnecessary. The Spirit of Truth will lead you into all truth.

PSALM 119:1-176
ROMANS 8:1-39

666 THE LORD'S ANOINTED

Oil is a symbol of the anointing of the Holy Spirit. Speaking in tongues is a manifestation of the same, but the real evidence of God's anointing is holiness, righteousness, the gift, and the fruit of the Holy Spirit in a person's life. There are many impostors and fleshly impersonations of the Lord's anointing, but they lack the power and the Lord's substantiation and witness.

The Lord's truly anointed ones are of the eternal generation of Israel who have become spiritual offspring of the fathers of the faith and the holy prophets, kings, and princes of God's chosen people. Without this anointing and witness from the Holy Spirit, there is no reality in any form of religion and no genuine love of the truth. Many try to find God in the scriptures, but without His anointing, they search in vain. The actual presence of the Holy One in a person's life is the reality of the anointing He bestows.

Miracles are often attributed to the anointing of God. Still, even the supernatural can be counterfeited for the purpose of deception and the testing of peoples' hearts and their true love. The anointing of the Holy One will always glorify Jesus and confirm the word of God.

There is no anointing that can substitute for truth and actual relationship with Christ. Jesus has shown us the way, and His Spirit takes the things of God and makes them real to us. This is the anointing that leads God's chosen people on the path of righteousness and the ways of God.

Could anything be more wonderful than the ways of God and His anointing?

667 THE LAND OF UPRIGHTNESS

Teach me to do Your will, for You are my God; Your Spirit is good. Lead me in the land of uprightness. Is there such a land here on earth? Or should we be looking for it in another place? Will we be able to see it with our natural eyes and walk there in our fleshly bodies? There has to be a spiritual answer to these questions, and there is. The Lord is calling his chosen ones to the place where He dwells, a place where only the righteous dwell and there is no sin. Is this in the hereafter, or is it here now? The Lord desires to make it very clear and very accessible to those who love Him.

Do you think you will find it in the Sunday church service; or even in a Wednesday Bible study? The truth is that it can only be found and entered individually in the secret place of communion with God. It is the grace of God that initiates a relationship with Him, but the progression of it requires commitment and effort on the part of the one who abides in Christ. There is no disobedience or sin in this place and no self-indulgence. The life of the person who enters and abides in the land of uprightness must, of necessity, abandon the life that lives according to the flesh. This is where the Lord reveals His total salvation, and we are saved to the uttermost. This is where the whole counsel of God is revealed.

Who has a heart to know and experience such wonders? Let him/her come freely.

668 VENGEANCE

Vengeance is mine, says the Lord, I will repay. . . . Let the saints be joyful in glory; let them sing aloud on their beds. Let the high praises of God be in their mouths and the two-edged sword in their hand to execute vengeance on the nations and punishment on the peoples to bind their kings with chains and their nobles with fetters of iron; to execute on them the written judgment—this honor have all His saints.

What does the Lord's vengeance actually look like? And what has been written about His judgment? Humiliation, shame and dishonor are some of the things that have been pronounced against the proud and disobedient. The word of God and the revelation of truth are weapons the Lord has supplied to His saints. The exposure of the lies and the oppression of the rebellious are a form of vengeance used by God's chosen. *Whoever exalts himself will be humbled and whoever humbles himself will be exalted. The wise will inherit glory but shame shall be the legacy of fools. . . . The evil will bow before the good, the wicked at the gates of the righteous. . . . Behold, I (Jesus) will make those of the synagogue of Satan who say they are Jews and are not but lie—behold, I will make them come and bow down before your feet, and they will learn that I have loved you. Because you have kept my word about patient endurance, I will keep you from the hour of trial that is coming on the whole world to try those who dwell on the earth.*

Edom represents the flesh and those who are of the earth. Israel represents the people of God who dwell in heaven. *And I (the Lord) will lay my vengeance upon Edom by the hand of my people Israel. . . . And they shall do in Edom according to my anger and according to my wrath, and they shall know my vengeance, declares the Lord God.*

The hour is at hand!

669 THE FEAR OF MAN

The fear of man brings a snare, but whoever trusts in the Lord shall be safe. There are countless voices that would try to cause us to live in fear and bring us into subjection under the dominion of the false promises of security. The fear of the Lord is the only way to be secure and *the fear of the Lord is to hate evil.* To walk righteously and to love truth and justice is the way to overcome the fear of man.

The whole world operates under the fear of the unknown and the threat of disaster. But those who serve the Lord have no such fear, because they trust Him who they love and they have the assurance that He loves them. *Perfect love overcomes all fear.* The Almighty controls the entirety of nature as well as the unseen realm of the rest of creation. There is nothing that is not subject to His authority. What is man that we should fear him? *We know that all things work together for good for those who love the Lord.* So, if we really do love Him and trust Him, why would we live in fear of man or anything else?

You will know if you really believe the Lord and trust Him based on your reaction to all the things that confront you and try to cause you to indulge fear. This is not just theory or religious jargon. This is the reality of faith that is based on the character of our Creator and His word. This is the way we can walk on our journey here on earth free from sin and fear.

Who are you going to fear? Who are you going to trust?

670 AN ADULTEROUS WOMAN

I have heard the voice of the Lord. An adulterous woman is the church which has been unfaithful to the One to whom she has been betrothed, and she has increased the unfaithful among mankind. She has turned truth into fable and righteousness into a far-off hope without present reality. She has made sin the common denominator among her victims and carnality the plateau of human achievement. While speaking of spirituality, she puts the declaration of the gospel into a future event that will only be realized in an age to come.

An adulterous woman portrays the faithful "Bride of Christ" as a confused and delusional entity that has not understood what being freed from sin actually means for those who remain victims of Adam's transgression and separation from God. While the truth is clearly and unequivocally declared over and over in scripture, the lie of the adulteress prevails over the great congregation of those who have not received the love of the truth and believe they remain sinners after they have been freed from sin.

Have we not clearly been given a choice as to whom and what each of us will serve? Ongoing sin and unfaithfulness unmistakably lead to eternal separation from our Savior. An adulteress will tell us that once we have been saved, we are secure and God no longer holds us accountable for the consequence of disobedience and rejection of His lordship.

MYSTERY BABYLON THE GREAT THE MOTHER OF HARLOTS AND OF THE ABOMINATIONS OF THE EARTH is just what her title implies. If you have been mesmerized by her beauty and her worldly glory, the time has come to follow the Holy Spirit out of her sinners' prison into the glorious liberty of the true "Body of Christ", which is One with Him and is faithful to Him.

671 COALS OF FIRE

Grant not, O Lord, the desires of the wicked; do not further their evil plot or they will be exalted! As for the head of those who surround me, let the mischief of their lips overwhelm them! Let burning coals fall upon them! . . . If your enemy is hungry, give him bread to eat, and if he is thirsty, give him water to drink for in so doing you will heap burning coals on his head, and the Lord will reward you.

We have come to an age where our adversaries and enemies have exposed themselves, both physically and spiritually. The burning coals being poured out on them are easy to see if you are looking. The display is about to dramatically increase, as truth and justice are given the stage. We have had to endure the lies of politicians, bureaucrats, religious leaders, leftists, anarchists and educators for a painful stretch of time. I have seen the judgment of God on their treachery, and He has been faithful to His word and His promise.

No liar will escape, and though the coals of fire may be metaphorical, I have seen them, and there is ultimately real judgment and retribution to all those who call evil good and good evil. The penalty is the fear, and the shame of the perpetrators is everlasting.

There are many ignorant fools who follow the lies of those who hate righteousness and truth, but when these wicked ones are exposed, many of their followers will turn to the truth and glorify God. They will turn at His rebuke, and their eyes will be opened. It is up to us who know and love the truth to stand firm and lead the captives to freedom.

We are living in a decisive time in the history of mankind, and the task our Lord has given us is significant.

The Lord is in His holy temple; the Lord's throne is in heaven; His eyes behold, his eyelids test the sons of men. The Lord tests the righteous, but the wicked and the one who loves violence, His soul hates. Upon the wicked He will rain coals, fire and brimstone and a burning wind shall be the portion of their cup.

672 FULFILLMENT

What could be better or more appropriate for a created being than to fulfill that for which he was created? *He (the Lord) gave them (Israel) the lands of the Gentiles, and they inherited the labor of the nations that they might observe His statutes and keep His laws. . . . Do not think that I (Jesus) came to destroy the law or the prophets. I did not come to destroy but to fulfill. . . . For the law of the Spirit of Life in Christ Jesus has made me (us) free from the law of sin and death; for what the law could not do in that it was weak through the flesh, God did by sending His own Son in the likeness of sinful flesh on account of sin: He condemned sin in the flesh that the righteous requirement of the law might be fulfilled in us who do not walk according to the flesh but according to the Spirit. . . . Blessed are the undefiled in the way who walk in the law of the Lord! Blessed are those who keep His testimony who seek Him with their whole heart! They also do no iniquity. They walk in His ways.*

The fulfillment of the life of the person who names the name of Christ is to walk as He walked and always do the things that please His Father and ours.

Only a life that has been completely given over to the Lord is able to fulfill the purpose and will of God. His law is in no way diminished or void in Christ. It is only able to be fulfilled by the one who abides in Christ. The person who claims to know the Lord but does not abide in Him will have leanness of soul and an unfulfilled life.

673 CONSUMERS

Have you seen the person who never has enough? That is the consumer who always consumes all that he is given on himself and has nothing left to give to others in need. This person will never have true abundance, because his lust consumes everything he obtains. You can identify such a person; the mystery of endless neediness will be revealed. The consumer is the one who never has sufficiency, whether physically or spiritually. This person is not truly thankful and never filled to overflowing.

The only hope for consumers is for their self-centered nature to be replaced by the nature of God. The Lord has made provision for all of us including the consumer. Satan is never satisfied and has no peace. He is the epitome of the consumer. He will devour everything and everyone he is able, while never achieving contentment or rest. The consumer bears his mark and his image. A person cannot bear both the mark and image of God and Satan simultaneously. Here again is revealed the choice we are given by our Creator.

The consumer saves no seed for planting future crops and spends no time planning for times of famine that come in every person's life. We can see this phenomenon in the natural realm all around us, and it is also observable in the spiritual realm to those who have eyes to see. The principle is the same in both.

It is more blessed to give than to receive. The one who gives sparingly will also reap sparingly. There is one who makes himself poor but has great riches and one who makes himself rich but yet has nothing.

674 THE HOLY LAND

The land that the religions of the world and their followers know as "The Holy Land" where Jesus walked as a man is drenched with blood, and peace there is no more than an illusion. The nation of Israel is but a testimony to the God of Abraham, Isaac and Jacob. The Almighty God does not dwell in temples made by the hand of man, nor any of the church buildings the religious call "the house of God".

The Lord's true dwelling place is in the hearts (temples) of his chosen people who are actually holy. They are spread around the world. The land the Bible speaks of as holy, upright, of the living, and God's land cannot be seen by the natural eye nor inhabited by the carnal man. God's chosen people are not of flesh and blood and are not of the world. They come from every nation and race, and they know one another after the Spirit and not the flesh nor the creed to which they claim allegiance.

If you are able to receive what is being set forth and understand the ways of God, there is hope for a home in the holy land where only the righteous dwell. Those who can only see this dwelling place (holy land) as a place on earth and a people or nation on the earth have not yet passed from death to life. Life is in the Spirit, and so too, is the holy land. The real holy land and the true Israel of God is in the Spiritual realm where no flesh can enter.

This message could be expounded on indefinitely, but if anyone can see and hear the truth about Zion and the holy land that is eternal in the heavens—God bless you.

And their dead bodies will lie in the street of the great city that symbolically (Spiritually) is called Sodom and Egypt where their Lord was crucified.

675 CROSSING THE JORDAN

The entire generation of the men of war that went out of Egypt with Moses perished in the wilderness with the exception of Caleb and Joshua. Israel was led across the Jordan River by Joshua into the land promised to Abraham, Isaac and Jacob. The significance of the crossing goes beyond the mere entrance of Israel into the land promised to the fathers of the faith, but metaphorically represents Jesus (Joshua) going before His people into heaven itself.

Though every individual follower of Jesus may have struggled through the wilderness of the world, everyone who reaches the Jordan and crosses after Him before their earthly bodies die are the ones who the Holy Spirit leads to the final victory, if they continue to follow Him to the end. As it was with the nation of Israel, the modern church has a majority of people who do not know the Lord and do not obey His voice.

For he is not a Jew who is one outwardly nor is circumcision that which is outward in the flesh; but he is a Jew who is one inwardly; and circumcision is that of the heart and the Spirit. . . . Indeed, I (Jesus) will make those of the synagogue of Satan who say they are Jews and are not but lie—indeed, I will make them come and worship before your feet and know that I have loved you, because you have kept my command to persevere. I also will keep you from the hour of trial which shall come upon the whole world to test those who dwell on the earth.

The question arises: Are you really a Jew? Do you really dwell in the promised land? Or do you dwell on the earth? God knows whose mark and image each of us bears.

676 CORRUPTION

Corruption of the human race is on full display throughout the earth. The end is near. Truth, righteousness, and integrity have been sacrificed to the idols of greed, envy and self-exaltation. Wickedness has overshadowed all that is decent and upright. The Lord has not forsaken his saints, but they are no longer able to dominate the forces of darkness arrayed against them. Voices of deception have temporarily prevailed against those of truth. Perversion has temporarily overtaken virtue.

What we are witnessing is only the darkness that precedes the dawn. After the whirlwind has passed, only the righteous will be left standing. Corruption will be judged by the One who alone provides justice for mankind. His word declares it to be so. We who love the truth are the witnesses who will see the demise of corruption and all those who love lies rather than truth.

Now, therefore, listen to Me my children, for blessed are those who keep My ways. Hear instruction and be wise and do not disdain it. Blessed is the man who listens to Me watching daily at My gates, waiting at the posts of My doors. For whoever finds Me finds life and obtains favor from the Lord; but he who sins against Me wrongs his own soul; all those who hate Me love death.

Surely it is obvious to anyone who loves truth and justice that those who have chosen the way of wickedness must be the ones who love death.

677 INSPIRATION

What inspires a person significantly influences who they are and what they do. SELAH! We have the ability to choose by what we are inspired and what motivates us. *Commit your work to the Lord and your thoughts will be established. . . . If you sow to the flesh, you will of the flesh reap corruption; if you sow to the Spirit, you will of the Spirit reap everlasting life. . . . He does not delight in the strength of a horse; He takes no pleasure in the legs of a man. The Lord takes pleasure in those who fear Him and those who trust in His mercy.*

To be inspired by the works of God clearly pleases Him. To be inspired by the accomplishments of mankind without acknowledging the One who created all things displeases Him. What you are hearing has been inspired by the Spirit of God and his word. What He inspires is the very essence of man's existence and purpose for living. The most intelligent and the most physically exceptional are but manifestations of the works of God. The beauty and the awesomeness of nature are merely manifestations of the Creator's greatness.

If we are able to draw our inspiration from the things the Lord has done, we will be on the path that leads to the incomprehensible mind of the One who created us. The inspiration given by the Spirit of God endows the recipient with wisdom, knowledge, understanding, joy, peace and eternal life.

Is it not sensible and reasonable to draw our inspiration from the heavenly Source rather than the earthly?

679 ROOTS

Roots that go into the earth and the ground produce fruit to sustain the natural man. Roots that extend to the Spiritual land produce fruit that sustains the soul and spirit of the heavenly man. One is temporary in its function, while the other is eternal. We all have knowledge of the earthly, but far fewer of us understand the heavenly. *The root of the righteous cannot be moved . . . The root of the righteous yields fruit.*

The fruit yielded by the metaphorical roots is that of the Spirit of God and nourishes the life of God within the one who knows Him. He has called us to cultivate and tend the heavenly-rooted fruit even more diligently than that of the earth. The eternal promises of the Lord are nearly all connected to sowing of seed to the Spirit rather than the flesh (earth). *He who sows to the flesh will of the flesh reap corruption, but he who sows to the Spirit will reap life everlasting.* We are again offered a choice concerning our priorities.

This is not hypothetical or a suggestion but an actual opportunity to be part of the true Israel of God and His inheritance or the alternative of perishing with the physical creation. *That which is born of flesh is flesh. That which is born of Spirit is spirit. . . . Life is in the Spirit.*

We can flourish while being rooted in the natural realm and imagine being spiritual, but never actually establish roots in the heavenly land.

What you are hearing is a wake-up call to the prosperous of the world who believe they are blessed because of their earthly prosperity, even though they have no real roots in the "Land of the Living".

679 COMPROMISE

Can good compromise with evil? Can righteousness compromise with wickedness and remain righteous? Does God compromise with Satan? There are endless voices extolling the virtue of compromise and reaching an agreement that satisfies the desires of polar opposites. This is the fantasy of souls without conviction or knowledge of absolute truth. Truth has no room for compromise with lies or untruths.

The love of truth leaves no place for compromise with itself, and any compromise would only contaminate and nullify the purity of its content. We are constantly faced with the temptation to believe the half-truths and the diluted and humanized versions of the gospel delivered to us by the Holy Spirit. God's word is absolute and unchangeable in its original form. Those who try to subvert the truth and deceive us into believing a lie that closely resembles the truth are agents of the "father of lies".

Only truth can save our souls from an eternity separated from the God for whom it is impossible to lie. Our own reasoning in our own hearts can easily lead us on a path of compromise and destruction. *There is a way that seems right to a man but ends in death. . . . He who follows after his own heart is a fool, but whoever walks wisely will be delivered.*

To make concessions to those who reject the counsel of God is to compromise with His enemies and to lose a blameless standing in His sight. While we are called to be peacemakers, we are not called to compromise with the bloodthirsty, violent or liars.

The path of righteousness is narrow, as are the gates of heaven.

680 COMMUNICATION

There are many forms of communication, especially in this age of electronic innovation, but the words formed by our tongue, lips and mouth are still the way most of us actually communicate. Our Creator has chosen to communicate with us through words written on whatever words can be written on throughout our recorded history. In this way His words are standardized, and in their original form set the absolute behavior standards by which all humans are accountable.

We have been given reason, conscience, intuition and instincts. All these attributes will point the rationally minded person to an awareness of an intelligent Creator who actually has a plan for what He has made. When we stand before Him at the end of our individual journeys here on earth, we will be judged on the merits of what we have done while walking on the earth. Communication at that point will no longer be verbal but will be totally telepathic. All that we have done in our bodies is recorded in our minds. The Almighty is able to read it in every detail.

If we have been reborn and forgiven for our sins, that is also recorded. If we continue to sin after being forgiven, cleansed, and given the very nature of God and a knowledge of the truth, we put ourselves in a very desperate situation. The sacrifice of our Savior that redeemed us from our past transgressions will no longer cover the sins of ongoing disobedience and rebellion. *For if we sin willfully after having received a knowledge of the truth, there no longer remains a sacrifice for sins but a certain fearful expectation of judgment and fiery indignation which will devour the adversaries. . . . For if after they have escaped the pollutions of the world through the knowledge of the Lord and Savior, Jesus Christ, they are again entangled in them and overcome. the latter is worse for them than the beginning. For it would have been better for them not to have known the way of righteousness than, having known it, to turn from the holy commandment delivered to them.*

Those who would teach us that future sin is already forgiven and covered are the false teachers that have been overcome by the deceptiveness of sin.

681 THE WAY OF ALL THE EARTH

All the earth and everything on it is subject to death and change. The curse that has come upon the natural creation is the result of sin. Even those of us who are reborn of the Spirit are, nevertheless, subject to the death of our fleshly bodies.

The good news is that, though the outward, carnal body must die, we have been given the hope of eternal life by the One who subjected us to physical death on account of our sin. We are called by our Creator to walk on this earth without sinning. If we obey Him, we are given the ability to please Him and to dwell in the spiritual land where death no longer has dominion over us. This is the land we inhabit by faith, by hearing, believing and obeying the Lord.

There have been many who have shown us how to walk by faith and overcome the way of earth, Jesus Christ being the supreme example. His sacrifice and His demonstration of how to overcome our flesh is not that of Divinity but of His absolute faithfulness to His father. He has shown us what true righteousness consists of and has also empowered those who walk by faith to do the same.

Numerous scriptures have validated what you are hearing and confirmed the truth of a people who have walked the earth whom God calls saints. Sinners have no part in the land of the Spirit nor claim to the promises the Lord has made to His chosen ones. Anyone who remains a sinner has done so by choice and has also remained subject to the ways of earth.

To dispute the validity of what has been put forth is to join with the multitudes who have not received the love of the truth.

682 THE BOTTOM LINE

The book is written. The bottom line is established. The Lord, Jesus Christ, is coming to judge the living and the dead. Every person will be ready or not on that final day. The time for preparation is now, this very moment. Those in desperation are better off than those with false hope and erroneous belief. Truth is absolute, and no lie will save the one who has embraced it.

The woman who is drunk with the blood of the saints and the blood of the martyrs of Jesus, with whom the kings of the earth committed fornication and the inhabitants of the earth were made drunk with the wine of her fornication, is being judged as these words are written. Shame and disgrace are being poured out upon all who have taken the Lord's name in vain and used it in pretense.

The bottom line concerning the salvation God has provided is freedom from sin. Sin is what has separated every person from God and brought the curse of death upon the whole natural creation. The grand lie that man can continue to sin and be blameless before the Lord has become the standard of the orthodoxy. The time has come to flee for your life from those who preach and teach this blasphemous heresy.

Is the bottom line not simple and straightforward to those who love the truth? Truth will prevail.

683 DIVISION

Is Christ divided? Is His body not one body on the earth? How, then, do the many institutions calling themselves the church all speak different spiritual languages and embrace multitudes of diverse doctrines? What the Lord did in Babel, He has again done to the many entities calling themselves by His name. They are not His true body, and they speak for themselves rather than God. The Lord calls them Babylon. If you have eyes to see and ears to hear, this assessment is quite valid.

The true "Body of Christ" on the earth speaks with one voice and has but one Head. He is not chosen by any of the institutions of mankind, and is not of this world. He does not adjust His judgment according to the changes and diversity of cultures, societies, languages or the whims of human beings. While Satan and his army of demons and institutionally accredited and legally endorsed ministers lead the religious organizations calling themselves churches, the true "Body of Christ" does the will and work of God.

When the "Mother of Harlots" and her many illegitimate offspring are exposed to the world, will you be one of their tax-exempt donors and members? Will your name be among the membership rolls on earth or in heaven? Who hears the voice of the Spirit of God? And who loves the truth and is willing to obey? These are the chosen and the ones, who have lost their own lives, through whom the Lord lives.

Flattering words and praise do not impress the Lord, but obedience and faithfulness does.

The "Book of Life" will and does reflect the names of us who have truly given our lives to God and do His will. There are none written there who continue to sin after being born into the eternal generation of Christ!

684 PLEASURES

Our Creator has designed us to experience pleasure. It comes in many forms. At the natural level, pleasure has boundaries and limits that, if passed, may become sinful. Pleasure itself is a test that reveals the hearts and motives of man. What we choose to give ourselves, what we find pleasurable is an indicator of our individual values and passions. *He who loves pleasure will not be rich.* Wealth measured by spiritual standards is significant.

Righteous pleasure that proceeds from the right hand of God has no limits. *In Your presence is fullness of joy; at Your right hand are pleasures forevermore. . . . How precious is Your lovingkindness, O God! Therefore, the children of men put their trust under the shadow of Your wings. They are abundantly satisfied with the fullness of Your house, and You give them drink from the river of your pleasures.*

On the other hand, a person can also find pleasure in forbidden and wicked things that lead to death. There are more who fall into this category than the Godly. *The coming of the lawless one is according to the workings of Satan with all power, signs and wonder and with all unrighteous deception among those who perish because they did not receive the love of the truth that they might be saved. And for this reason, God will send them strong delusion that they should believe the lie that they all may be condemned who did not believe the truth but had pleasure in unrighteousness.*

These unbelievers can be seen in churches around the world as well as in the halls of politicians, schools and universities, and on the streets of the great cities. There are actually few among us who love the truth.

I hope that every reader falls into the category that does know how to regulate carnal pleasure and loves the truth.

685 SEVEN HEADS

On earth there is nothing like him which is made without fear. He beholds every high thing; he is king over all the children of pride. . . . You divided the sea by Your strength; You broke the heads of the sea serpents in the waters; You broke the heads of Leviathan in pieces and gave him as food to the people inhabiting the wilderness. Of whom does the Lord speak? *The fear of the Lord is the beginning of wisdom.* In the Book of Job, the Lord spends a whole chapter describing this great creature He has placed on earth. *There the ships sail about; there is that Leviathan You have made to play in it.*

Those with ears to hear metaphors of the Spirit will understand the sea and the serpents and all who do not fear the Lord. The mysteries of sevens and the fullness of all that the number represents is telling us that God's plans are coming to completion, and the Devil, the Serpent has an end of his reign on earth. He will be cast into the lake of fire along with the beast, the false prophet and all those whose names do not appear in "The Book of Life". It is by their works they all are judged, and for their deeds they will be rewarded.

It is clearly the will of God that His people not continue to sin, and also clearly, those who do His will who are His chosen. If the Lord Jesus is really our king, we are not giving heed to lies or any of the false prophets of our day who are proclaiming "peace and safety" to those who are unable to cease from sin. Such prophets, teachers, and those who follow them are giving heed to the high things which the children of pride observe.

686 A FRIEND

A person who has a friend must himself be a friend. *There is a friend that sticks closer than a brother (or sister).* There are different levels of friendship, but the one being addressed is the one that goes as deep as love itself. The depth of true friendship is relationship that values the friend as much as self. This is a relationship that cannot be bought, sold or broken. It goes beyond the natural realm and into the spiritual. Carnal friendships come and go, but those that reach to the spiritual level pass through the limits of carnality.

God Himself called Abraham His friend. SELAH! Could there be a higher honor than this? In order to be a friend at this level requires knowledge, wisdom and understanding that surpasses being in agreement with regard to worldly affairs or religious dogma. Trust and confidence are the foundation of a friendship that is able to endure the tribulation brought on by all the forces that come against it.

True friendship is not about what another person gives us or what benefit they are to us, but their actual value as an individual and fellow traveler here on earth. To be a friend in the highest sense as with the Lord, trust must be absolute and unwavering. God may be the only one capable of such friendship, but if we can believe Him, He has made us partakers of His divine nature and thus enabled us to do what He does.

The friendship of David and Jonathan gives us a biblical perspective of the friendship human beings are capable of if the Spirit of God establishes it. The value of a true friend goes beyond the value of worldly riches, wealth, and every other commitment a person may have, except to God. To betray real friendship is to destroy one's own soul.

Is it not time to re-evaluate our own friendships?

687 SEGREGATION

The segregation of which the Spirit is speaking is not according to race, ethnicity, religion, philosophy or identity. It is the segregation of those who know and fear the Lord God from those who don't. This is a separation that extends into the hereafter and all eternity. *As God has said: I will dwell among them and walk among them. I will be their God, and they shall be My people. Therefore, come out from among them and be separate, says the Lord. Do not touch what is unclean, and I will receive you. I will be a Father to you, and you shall be My sons and daughters, says the Lord Almighty. . . . What agreement has a believer with an unbeliever? . . . When the Son of Man comes in His glory and all the holy angels with Him, then He will sit on the throne of His glory. All nations will be gathered before Him, and He will separate them one from another as a shepherd divides His sheep from the goats. And He will set the sheep on His right hand, but the goats on the left. Then the King will say to those on His right hand, "Come, blessed of My Father. Inherit the kingdom prepared for you from the foundation of the world."*

There can be no doubt that the salvation of God is exclusive and not universal. We all have a choice to make and a path to follow. It is ironic that those on the King's left are, by default, leftists, and those on His right are righteous.

Segregation is the polarization we see throughout the world today. It is determined by those who love the truth and those who prefer lies. It is delusion that causes a person to prefer unrighteousness over righteousness, and evil over good; but it is what it is, whether we can comprehend it or not.

We are left with a conscious decision as to whom we will serve and obey and where we will spend eternity. None can say, "I did not hear," or "I did not know". The truth is before our eyes.

688 FOLLOW UP

This is a combination follow-up on the two previous discourses, A FRIEND and SEGREGATION. *The righteous should choose his friends carefully, for the way of the wicked leads them astray.* The reality of good and evil, right and wrong are not subjects of opinion if the God of truth and justice has already made his will on any matter known. He does not change, nor do His commandments. What the Lord has said is so, whether we can believe it or not. *Greater love has no one than this than to lay down one's life for his friends. You are My friends if you do whatever I command you. . . . Do you not know that friendship with the world is enmity with God? Whoever, therefore, wants to be a friend of the world makes himself an enemy of God. . . . These things I have spoken to you that in Me you may have peace. In the world you will have tribulation; but be of good cheer. I have overcome the world. . . . They are not of the world, just as I am not of the world. Sanctify them by Your truth. Your word is truth. As You sent Me into the world, I also have sent them into the world.*

The segregation of the Lord's followers could not be clearer than the words of Jesus have described. The separation of believers and unbelievers is not optional for the one who is actually a Christian.

Faithful are the wounds of a friend; but the kisses of an enemy are deceitful.

689 PERFECT HATRED

Can there be such a thing as perfect hatred in the eyes of the Lord? *The fear of the Lord is to hate evil. . . Do I not hate them, O Lord, who hate You? And do I not loathe those who rise up against You? I hate them with perfect hatred; I count them my enemies.* This is not a license to harbor hatred in our hearts nor to dwell on it. Perfect hatred is a spontaneous response to wickedness of any kind.

The Lord has told us to hate anything that has a higher place in our hearts than Him. All such devotion is idolatry and unfaithfulness. This notion is radical, but God is a radical Person. His first and greatest commandment is to love Him with all our heart, soul, mind and strength. This leaves no room for us to put anything before Him. Everything else is to be hated in comparison to our devotion to Him. What you are hearing is the proper perspective of our very existence and reason for living.

Those who know their right hand from their left surely know their place in the world and the ways of God. If we have such knowledge, anything that distracts us from the path of righteousness is sinful. The Lord is merciful and knows our frame, but He has given His chosen ones the ability to walk the earth as He did as a man. Those who teach otherwise are calling God a liar. They are defending the enemies of God. God's law is not void, and those who follow His Spirit are able to fulfill His law as Jesus did. *For the law of the Spirit of Life in Christ Jesus has made me free from the law of sin and death. For what the law could not do in that it was weak through the flesh, God did by sending His own Son in the likeness of sinful flesh on account of sin; He condemned sin in the flesh that the righteous requirement of the law might be fulfilled in us who do not walk according to the flesh but according to the Spirit. . . . But you are not in the flesh but in the Spirit if indeed the Spirit of God dwells in you. Now if anyone does not have the Spirit of Christ, he or she is not His.*

What and who do you hate? And what and who do you love? A truthful answer will reveal every person's relationship with love and faith.

690 COST

There is a cost for everything. Just as we are paid for actions, we are also paid for our thoughts. The law of sowing and reaping applies to everything we do and think. While a thought may be neutral when it enters our mind, what we do with it takes on consequence. The benefit of obeying the voice of God is enormous, but the cost of disobedience is inversely devastating. While the cost of disobedience may not be realized immediately, it will have both earthly and eternal consequences.

The cost of the redemption of the souls who have rebelled against the light that every person is given is beyond human understanding. Nevertheless, we can experience the light and live in it. Every person is in need of forgiveness and redemption. *The one who is forgiven much loves much.* Only by revelation is one able to begin to understand the cost that God paid for mankind to be reconciled to Him. The cost of our sin is the death of our soul, and the death that Jesus died for us was the sacrifice of His own soul. How can this sacrifice be measured by man?

If a person is willing and, in fact, does sacrifice his own life for Jesus' sake, it is the evidence that a person really loves Him. This is the way to His kingdom and eternal life. God's rest and peace have been paid for by Him, and by believing and obeying Him we are able to enter His dwelling by faith. The actual cost of receiving the life of God is the loss of our own life in submission to Him.

The same is true of every aspect of relationship with the Creator. The cost is abandonment of self-will to His will as well as the abandonment of our own kingdoms for His.

While salvation is a free gift, it will, nevertheless, cost us our life.

691 FRIEND OR FOE?

Friend or foe, how can we know? *A friend loves at all times.* The flattering words of a foe are meant to lay a trap for our soul. The rebuke and the counsel of the one who loves us is meant to sharpen our countenance and to increase our well-being. The counsel of the enemy is designed to put us at ease and disarm our defenses. *Fervent lips with a wicked heart are like earthenware covered with silver dross. He who hates disguises it with his lips and lays up deceit within himself; when he speaks kindly, do not believe him for there are seven abominations in his heart. . . . Faithful are the wounds of a friend, but the kisses of an enemy are deceitful. . . . Iron sharpens iron; so a man sharpens the countenance of his friend.*

The point being: those who are claiming peace, safety and well-being to those unable to cease from sin are revealing themselves as foes of our eternal soul. They are ministers of darkness disguised as ministers of light. Pulpits, stages, airways and media are filled with their perversions of the gospel. We have been warned of the craftiness and deceitfulness of those who would make merchandise of unwary, well-meaning followers of backsliders and false prophets and teachers who are trying to gain disciples for their own worldly gain and ambition.

Without holiness no one will see God. These foes of true righteousness will be judged, and the saints of God who love the truth will escape the snares of those who promote the ongoing life of the flesh and its lust. *Those who live according to the flesh will die. . . . Those who live according to the Spirit will live.* There is no in-between and *no lie is of the truth.* Only the faithful and blameless in the sight of God will escape the separation of sinners and saints at every person's final judgment.

The words of the enemies and foes that have perverted the truth of the gospel and the doctrine of Christ, along with all their followers, will share the fate of the adversary of our souls.

692 GLUTTONY

Integrity of the soul of a glutton can be compromised by the lust of his flesh. *A companion of gluttons shames his father. . . . To show partiality is not good because, for a piece of bread, a man will transgress.* Gluttony is evidence of a life that is lived according to the flesh. There is no excuse for gluttony more than any other sin. We live in a world of gluttons, but if we live according to the Spirit, we will not partake of their transgressions. The one who lives according to the Spirit is temperate in all things and rules over his fleshly desires. We are certainly directed to judge ourselves, and gluttony is not difficult to identify and make a judgment about.

The fruit of gluttony is usually obvious, and the gluttons preaching the gospel shame the One who died to free them from their sins. Have you seen them? This watchman's heart weeps for those who vainly proclaim that Jesus has saved them while their sin is on display. Obesity, while not exclusively limited to gluttony, is usually an indicator of indulgence of the flesh. Is such a person really qualified to preach the gospel, and can they be trusted to speak the truth? This observation is not intended to slander but to bring sinners to repentance.

If gluttony can be overlooked and disregarded, what other sins that are less obvious may be lurking out of sight? *He who covers his sins will not prosper, but whoever confesses and forsakes them will have mercy.* To confess without true repentance will not qualify to be covered by the blood, and to plead the blood without forsaking sin is futile.

Open rebuke is better than love carefully concealed. The root cause of many of the diseases that plague mankind is the result of gluttony! *They profess to know God, but in works they deny Him.*

693 A LOOK AT POLITICS

We are all affected by politics, whether directly or indirectly. Even those of us who have no interest in the political scene receive the consequences of elections and political appointments. The political bias of bureaucrats, news commentators, teachers, professors and agitators all have an influence on our well-being or lack of it. The list also includes lobbyists and business people as well as the military. Bribery, blackmail and extortion are also contributors to the confusion and corruption of politics and politicians.

If there is any integrity in politics, it is hard to find or identify. The politicians that actually speak the truth and keep their promises are few and far between. So it is with the representatives of the people who put the people first before their own interests. This also applies to the nation itself. Because of the lack of term limits, career politicians spend their lives accumulating bribes and payoffs that only serve to make them wealthy at taxpayer expense.

Among the corrupt politicians can be found treasonous acts that go undetected and unprosecuted. Party loyalty has priority over the sworn oath to uphold the country's Constitution and its laws. This can clearly be seen on display in the halls of Congress and in election polling stations. The foxes are guarding the henhouses, and the wolves are keeping watch over the sheep pastures.

While it seems little can be done, we can be comforted to know that *the kingdom of God rules over all. . . . The wicked will be cut off . . . And the righteous will see it . . . There is no plan formed against God that will succeed . . . And there is no counsel that can avail against the Lord.*

The politicians and princes of the economy will not prevail. and will be exposed and put to shame along with those who love violence, war and oppression.

We are facing political issues as these words are written that threaten the freedom and liberty we have taken for granted. And unless the hand of God preserves them, we could lose them. Is it not time to pray to do whatever the Lord leads us to do?

Politics do influence spiritual activity on earth.

694 HOW LONG?

The same Spirit that inspired the Psalmist is now leading those who love the Lord to pray for the end of the prosperity of the wicked and for the establishment of truth and justice in the nation where we live. Psalm 5 is a prayer that applies to this modern day much as it did in the days of David. God hears the prayers of the righteous and will act on their behalf. The struggles against the lies, wickedness, vileness, oppression, violence and anarchy do not go unnoticed by the Lord, and His ears are open to those who love righteousness and truth.

We who can agree with one mind in the Spirit can move the hand of the Lord to subdue the forces of darkness that are so desperate to cast off the bonds of righteousness and decency. These forces of darkness have formed a confederacy to abolish freedom and liberty and take control of every person's rights and volition. The government that claims to provide for us and give everyone a voice that will be heard is a diabolical confederation designed to make us slaves. The conspiracy of the elite is no more than a plot to bring the entire population under their control.

The polarization of the two sides in the conflict can easily be discerned as good or evil by those who love the truth. What is being described is an actual war of good against evil. We who know the truth know that good will prevail, but the question is when? How long will the Lord allow the wicked to have dominion? This is the time to stand in the gap to petition the Almighty to intervene in the affairs of man.

This is not merely a matter of political preference but of the life or death of liberty and freedom. Those who remain oblivious to the battle must have their eyes opened by those who are able to see. The government which offers everything for free will make slaves of everyone who accepts their lies and will attempt to silence all opposition.

Stand up!

695 KNOWING

To know love is the essence and the pinnacle of life. This is true not only for human beings but even our Creator. In this we are created in His image. To know and experience the love of God is the greatest thing we have the capacity to know. His greatest and first commandment is to love the Lord and second is to love one another. *Love never fails. . . Beloved if our heart does not condemn us, we have confidence toward God and whatever we ask we receive from Him because we keep His commandments and do the things that are pleasing in His sight and this is His commandment; that we should believe on the name of His Son Jesus Christ and love one another as He gave us commandment. Now he who keeps His commandments abides in Him, and by this we know that He abides in us by the Spirit whom He has given us.*

The particular individual out-working of love is unique to every person. Thus, the personal relationship to God is essential to enable us to walk with Him and abide in His love. How profound is this knowledge? Does it not demand that every person put forth the effort to understand and know for themselves the will of God for their lives? No one else can do it for us no matter how well-trained and educated they may be. Every one of us will stand before our Creator and give account of what the love He has given and shown us has produced in our lives as well as the lives of others. This revelation is not meant to condemn anyone but to encourage each of us to show and demonstrate the love and knowledge of God that we will not be ashamed before Him when He appears.

Beloved, now we are children of God and it has not yet been revealed what we shall be, but we know that when He is revealed we shall be like Him, for we shall see Him as He is. And everyone who has this hope in Him purifies himself just as He is pure. Is this not love? *God is love.*

696 THE MONEY BOX

But one of his disciples, Judas Iscariot, Simon's son who would betray him, said, "Why was this fragrant oil not sold for 300 denari and given to the poor?" This he said, not because he cared for the poor, but because he was a thief and had the money box; and he used to take what was put in it. . . Among the multitude of money boxes throughout the world today, there are many thieves who have betrayed Jesus and are stealing the resources that have been donated to care for the poor and further the gospel.

Have we all not seen it? The religious institutions, the preachers, teachers, missionaries and pastors are the modern-day Judases who are thieves, who are greedy for wealth, power, and their own kingdoms. They are using the name of Jesus and the gospel to further their own ambitions. Is there anyone who loves the Lord who is unable to see the absolute corruption in the modern-day church?

While the motive for giving may be pure for those who support these denominational organizations, cults and false ambassadors, what are they really accomplishing in the Spiritual realm? This is a painful subject to discuss, but the end of Judas was also an unpleasant climax.

We are called to be conscientious stewards of what the Lord has given us. The fact is that when we give to these self-seeking thieves and greedy entities, we are advancing the perversion of the gospel and the betrayal of Christ.

Who can say it is not so?

697 TOOT. . .TOOT

It seems as though every voice with a public platform is tooting their own horn, proclaiming their influence, giving, converts and how much they do for God. Does the Lord really acknowledge them as His representatives on earth? The world seems to hear them, but is what they are saying really from God? There is massive confusion in the messages being proclaimed, as well as disagreement and conflict amongst all those who claim to be "the church". The true "Body of Christ" is not divided nor does it toot its own horn. It is not of the world, and the world does not hear the message being put forth by the true followers of Jesus.

We who love the truth have a message that the world will not receive or give heed to. The honest message of the gospel does not make the best-sellers lists published by the merchandisers. Just as Jesus passed under the radar of the religious and political leaders of his day, so too is He doing now. When He appears in His glory, those who are tooting their horns now will be looking for a place to hide from His face.

This is a warning to those tooting their own horns, promoting their own ministries along with their devotees and contributors. This watchman is not concerned with winning a popularity contest or making worldly friends. Faithfulness to the Lord and the truth is his passion and his reward. If you can hear and receive what is being said, you are one of the few Jesus has made reference to and is calling to join the chosen ones who are willing to sacrifice their own lives to partake of His.

There is a choice to be made!

698 DESCENDANTS

Has the Lord not made clear who the descendants of His faithful servants are? They are spiritual offspring of those who are of the household and generation of faith. The generation of Christ is an eternal generation of all the righteous servants of the Lord that He has given witness of throughout the Bible. Never has He called anyone a saint, or chosen, who has persisted to sin or whose heart has turned away from Him. This truth is constant to this very day. The descendants of the forefathers of the faith are and always have been those who obey the voice of God. Their true offspring are the chosen ones who walk according to the Spirit and obey His voice.

As long as we have breath and a willing heart, we are able to become a part of the eternal generation who walk the path of righteousness as the Lord has shown us. There are none who remain sinners to the end of their earthly journey who will dwell with the Creator in "The Land of the Living". The salvation provided by the Lord is only revealed to those who fear Him and obey Him. They are the true descendants of those whom the Lord has declared holy and saints. The salvation revealed to the humble believers of the truth is the salvation from self and sin. Any other interpretation of salvation is delusion.

The true Israel of God and the real descendants of Jacob are those who seek God with all their hearts and give no confidence to the flesh or the wisdom of man. Human descendants are just that, and they are not of the eternal generation, but are of the many generations that have passed away.

We who are actually called by the Father are given opportunity to enter and be part of the eternal generation and the promise made by God to those who love Him. We who believe Him are the ones who share in the inheritance of Christ.

699 A JEW BY NATURE

The person who is a Jew by nature has been endowed with the nature of God. *But when I saw that they were not straightforward about the truth of the gospel, I said to Peter before them all, "If you being a Jew live in the manner of Gentiles and not as the Jews, why do you compel Gentiles to live as Jews? We who are Jews by nature and not sinners of the Gentiles knowing that a man is not justified by the works of the law but by faith in Jesus Christ, even we have believed in Christ Jesus that we might be justified by faith in Christ and not by the works of the law; for by the works of the law, no flesh shall be justified. But if while we seek to be justified by Christ we ourselves also are found sinners, is Christ therefore a minister of sin?" . . . I have been crucified with Christ. It is no longer I who live but Christ lives in me.*

If Christ lives in us, we do have the nature of a Jew, which is the nature of Christ, which is also the nature of God Himself. The logical truth is not fantasy, fable or delusion but the truth of the gospel. A true Jew is a true Israelite who is a true spiritual descendant of Abraham. While these things may be mysterious, they are, nevertheless, true and well-founded in scripture. *If we are Christ's, then we are Abraham's seed and heirs according to the promise of God.*

Indeed, I will make those of the Synagogue of Satan, who say they are Jews and are not but lie—indeed I (Jesus) will make them come and worship before your feet and to know that I have loved you because you have kept my command to persevere. I also will keep you from the hour of trial which shall come upon the whole world to test those who dwell on the earth.

The nature of a Jew is the nature of the one who is chosen in Christ, not by natural procreation but by Spiritual rebirth.

700 CORRECTNESS

Who decides correctness? On what is it based? How is it determined to actually be correct? Is there really someone other than God who has the understanding and wisdom to make a determination about what is or isn't correct behavior and truly righteous? Popular consensus has surely proven to be unreliable and even destructive.

There is no person or group of people who put self-interest before others who can be trusted to decide what is correct for others. Only those who love and honor our Creator and our fellow human beings can possibly determine correctness for the good of all, even unborn babies. If the self-consumed are allowed to make the decisions regarding correctness, there will be no justice for any of us.

Certainly, the heads of multi-national corporations, corrupt politicians along with special interest groups, such as unions and sexual deviants, are not going to do what is correct for people who have moral and ethical standards of decency. The whole issue of correctness will determine the well-being of society and culture. Cultures that have embraced incorrect practices, oppression and violence have not survived. Real correctness is based on love and respect of everyone.

We are entering a time when what is known as "political correctness" has reached the point where anyone who does not agree with the current measure of correctness is considered an irrelevant outcast. Those who embrace modern political correctness seem to have determined that anyone who disagrees with them are not worthy to have the rights of those in agreement. This form of correctness is robbing everyone of their freedom and liberty.

Absolutes have become nebulous, and standards of decency have descended into whatever the lawless mobs feel like doing.

Political correctness will soon be corrected. *He who hates correction is stupid.*

701 CANCEL CULTURE

Have the voices of reason, decency, truth and righteousness been cancelled out by the voices of mainstream media, special interest groups, educators, leftist politicians, globalists and social engineers? The answer is rhetorical and obvious. The power brokers and their cohorts have nearly extinguished and cancelled the voices that dissent from the forces of darkness that dominate the public arena. The culture of individual freedom, liberty and self-reliance is being cancelled by those who desire government control and domination over the affairs of every person. If they succeed, we will be their slaves and the subjects of their anarchy. The laws that were once passed by representatives of the people are gradually and subtly being replaced by treasonous bureaucrats and appointees of those who have fraudulently seized the control of government. The time for decent, freedom-loving people to wake up to what is happening and stand up is desperately near the point of no return. If the cancel culture is able to succeed in silencing the voice of truth and justice, where will we turn for reprieve and security? The whole world is watching to see if liberty and freedom will be able to withstand the cancel culture that seeks its demise.

Where can we turn if not to God and one another who are like minded and share our values?

The cancel culture will soon be cancelled along with the FU crowd.

702 MOVING ON

While affairs of this world must be dealt with, even by God's people, we cannot allow ourselves to be consumed by them. *You, therefore, must endure hardship as a good soldier of Jesus Christ. No one engaged in warfare entangles himself with the affairs of this life that he may please Him who enlisted him as a soldier.* Yes, the Lord's chosen have as their primary mission on earth to please their heavenly Father and walk as Jesus walked as He has and is showing us.

Our leaders and lawmakers do affect our ability and liberty to carry out what the Lord desires to do through us, but He does control the activity of even those who oppose His will. If we follow His Spirit and obey His voice, there is no power on earth that is able to stop us from carrying out His will. Satan himself is subject to the one abiding in Christ. Though we may be persecuted or even killed for the sake of obedience to the Lord, we will remain secure in His love. *Do not fear any of those things which you are about to suffer. Indeed, the devil is about to throw some of you into prison that you may be tested, and you will have tribulation ten days. Be faithful until death, and I will give you the crown of life.* These things have happened and are happening many places around the world to those who love the Lord.

We have come to a time where wickedness is established by law, and those who call evil good and good evil are prevailing even in this nation that was founded on Biblical principles. Nevertheless, the Lord is raising a standard against them, and we who know the Bible know the end of the story. Our citizenship is in heaven, and our hearts and souls are secure in the Lord.

Do not fear any of the things that may be coming. Only trust the Lord, and keep your eyes on Him.

703 THE ACTUAL RAPTURE

The catching away of the saints will not occur in secret, nor will it include sinners. When Jesus appears, the saints who remain on the earth will be changed, and mortality will put on immortality, which is the change of our mortal bodies taking on the form of immortal bodies. All of God's elect will have already been made participants in His kingdom. Abiding in Christ and becoming One Spirit with Him are things that happen here on earth in advance of His coming back.

There is no one who has remained a sinner who will be among those caught up to meet Him. They will remain to experience the wrath coming upon all those who dwell on the earth who have not believed the Lord or lost their own lives for His. Being ready to meet the Lord is something that every person must do, whether He comes for us individually or collectively. The end result will be the same. Anyone who is not abiding in Christ while walking on the earth can be ready to meet Him in either case. Those who have told you that you will be raptured out of your sinful nature and your sinful body have lied to you. They are false prophets and teachers who have misinterpreted the Bible and misunderstood the gospel. There is no more time for such foolishness! We are either ready to meet the Lord or not. Our hearts are either pure or not. We have either lost our own lives for Jesus sake or not. Do you see the pattern here? It goes on and on throughout the gospel and the entire Bible.

Anyone who can hear the Holy Spirit's voice should surely be getting ready to face the final judgment.

704 PATIENTLY WAITING

While our patience is being tested, so is our endurance. The Lord is coming in His timeline, and we who wait without losing heart will have great reward. His plan is not without revelation to those who have learned to trust Him and wait patiently for it to come. To anxiously seek answers from the multitude of prognosticators selling books, and preachers, prophets and teachers trying to gain followers will result in confusion and false hope.

Those who patiently wait on the Lord will not be caught unaware of what He is doing. *These things I have written to you concerning those who try to deceive you that the anointing which you (God's chosen) have received from Him abides in you and you do not need that anyone teach you; but as the same anointing teaches you concerning all things and is true and is not a lie, and just as it has taught you, you will abide in Him. . . . Wait on the Lord; be of good courage and He shall strengthen your heart. Wait, I say, on the Lord.*

What profit is there in heaping up teachers who only agree on things that are supported by popular consensus and are monetarily profitable at the book store and the box office? Their theoretical fables only lead to complacency and lackadaisical thinking. The person who realizes the urgency of the situation in which we find ourselves and also the need to be prepared will be making sure his/her heart is pure and blameless in the sight of God. He/she will certainly not be blaming his/her compulsion to sin on a sinful nature. *Those who live according to the flesh will die.* They will not be raptured out of their sin or their sinful nature.

Without holiness no one will see God. Without patiently waiting on the Lord, no one will achieve holiness.

705 BUYERS AND SELLERS

Buy the truth and do not sell it; also wisdom and instruction and understanding. To buy these things is to take possession of them and make them your own. They cannot be bought with money, but they can be sold for profit if they are not treasured above all worldly riches.

A fool may sell the truth in order to advance himself in the world or take a bribe to pervert justice. The one who is willing to sell truth to gain worldly treasure and influence has wandered from the truth and will pay a very high price for the exchange.

The person who treasures heavenly things above the earthly is willing to give all his earthly treasures and even his life to obtain the heavenly. *The kingdom of heaven is like a merchant in search of fine pearls who on finding one pearl of great value went and sold all that he had and bought it. . . . And the twelve gates were twelve pearls each made of a single pearl and the street of the city was pure gold like transparent glass. . . . Open to me the gates of righteousness that I may enter through them and give thanks to the Lord. This is the gate of the Lord; the righteous shall enter through it.*

He was despised and rejected by men, a man of sorrows and acquainted with grief; and as one from whom men hide their faces he was despised and we esteemed him not. . . . I (Jesus) am the way, the truth and the life. No one comes to the Father but through me. Are all the forementioned quotes from the Bible not connected? So, who is willing to buy them and not sell them for a lie or worldly gain?

706 A PERSON'S TRUE AND ONLY NATURE

Our earthly parents had a nature that they chose in the garden before they were evicted and died. They were the son and daughter of God before they disobeyed Him. Since then, they have taken on a sinful nature as a beast that is controlled by its flesh. God's nature is Spiritual, loving and holy. The two natures do not reside together in one body any more than do good and evil or light and darkness.

The colossal lie of the serpent who is Satan is that the nature of fallen man and the nature of God co-exist in the person that has been redeemed and born of the Spirit of God. The one who has received the Spirit of God has also received His nature and has become a new creation. The double nature fable that is popular in the modern church is a lie, just as the doctrine of the saved continuing to be sinners while possessing the nature of God.

The soul of the person who continues to sin has the mark of a beast of the earth on his forehead and hand signifying who he serves and the work he does. The person who embraces the nature of God and follows His Spirit has His mark on his forehead and hand signifying who that one worships and serves. This one is no longer a sinner or dominated by his flesh.

Is all this not simple and clearly in agreement with the gospel? You are either fleshly and have that nature or spiritual and have God's nature. This is the truth.

707 CROSSING OVER

The answer to the question, "Is it possible for a person dwelling on earth to pass over the boundaries of carnality and actually inhabit the Spiritual land where Jesus is and have victory over the flesh while still confined to it?," may seem simple and it actually is, and Jesus has demonstrated it for us. The first thing that any person aspiring to actually live and walk in the Spirit free from sin is to break away from those who are telling us that we cannot be free while inhabiting our fleshly bodies.

The footsteps of God that He has left for us to follow through the channels of the sea, the wilderness, and across the river are the pathways laid down for those who love the truth to find their way to the place of rest where God dwells. This is what real faith consists of. Believing the voice (word) of God and obeying it is the way to cross over the natural boundaries established by our Creator that carnal man cannot cross over. The person confined and dominated by his flesh and carnal understanding is its prisoner and slave.

The freedom Jesus has offered us is freedom from all that binds us to the earth and to sin. Once we are free, the boundaries of carnality no longer apply. *To be carnally minded is death; to be Spiritually minded is life and peace. . . The one who lives according to the flesh will die; the one who by the Spirit puts to death the deeds of the body will live. Those who live according to the Spirit are sons of God.* These sons of God are the chosen ones who have crossed over to the other side where no flesh is able to go. *Where I (Jesus) am, there will my servants be also. . . . You have been seated with Christ in heavenly places. . . . Let the dead bury their dead.*

You follow Me! Says the Lord.

708 THERE IS A CUP

The cup of which is being spoken has been passed from generation to generation. It is the delusion sent to those who have not received the love of the truth but have pleasure in unrighteousness. This cup may be seen and identified as the one sent by the Lord to all those who prefer a lie to the truth. Jeremiah speaks of this cup. *Babylon was a golden cup in the Lord's hands that made all the earth drunk; the nations drank her wine; therefore the nations are deranged.* John speaks of the same cup in the revelation of the end of time. *So he carried me away in the Spirit into the wilderness and I saw a woman sitting on a scarlet beast which was full of the names of blasphemy having seven heads and ten horns. The woman was arrayed in purple and scarlet and adorned with gold and precious stones and pearls having in her hand a golden cup full of abominations and the filthiness of her fornication. . . . I saw the woman drunk with the blood of the saints and with the blood of the martyrs of Jesus.*

Have you seen her grand cathedrals and the lavishness of her wealth built on the backs of the poor and those who are drinking of her cup? The day of reckoning has arrived. The delusion is exposed.

There is also a cup the Lord has revealed as the cup of salvation Jesus gives to His disciples. *Then He took the cup and gave thanks and gave it to them saying, "Drink from it all of you. For this is my blood of the new covenant which is shed for many for the remission of sins."*

There are clearly two cups given to mankind from the hand of the Lord. The one is a cup of judgment given to those who do not believe the truth, and the other to those who love and obey the truth.

Every person will know which cup they are drinking from by their deeds and their obedience to the voice of God.

709 OVERFLOW

The words being shared day by day are the overflow of what the Spirit of God gives every day to a man seeking the face of God. This is not unique, but it is unusual in a day when the people being called by the Spirit are trying to make connections with Him through electronic media. There is no room to boast in what the Lord shares, but there is a place of rejoicing and thanksgiving for the one who gives as well as the one who receives what is on the Lord's heart.

Overflow is the result of a vessel being filled beyond its own capacity, thus spilling over. What is being described is not beyond the capability of anyone who is seated with Jesus at the right hand of our Father in heaven, whose heart and mind are set on heavenly things.

To retreat to the heavenly realm is a choice and a commitment to seek the Lord with all our heart, mind, soul and strength. The result of such diligence is a great Spiritual reward and blessing from God. The casual enquirer and the one who in not whole-hearted has no part in the blessings being bestowed on those who give their all.

This is not an indictment but an invitation to join those who actually abide in Christ. The Bible and the words of Jesus certainly make it clear that total commitment and devotion to the Lord is the path and the way to please God and dwell in His presence. There is no other way! Jesus has told us and shown us how to please His Father. To do it is every person's individual responsibility. No one can do it for us.

If the overflow of the Spirit is not flowing from your life, look in the mirror, and you will see why. *Now the Lord is the Spirit, and where the Spirit of the Lord is, there is liberty, but we all with unveiled face beholding as in a mirror the glory of the Lord, are being transformed into the same image from glory to glory just as by the Spirit of the Lord.*

What do you see?

710 EMBARRASSMENT

Recently the politicians who support fraudulent elections and leftist causes are saying that the voices of truth and justice should be embarrassed by their stand for transparency and honesty. This sounds a lot like calling evil good and good evil. *An unjust man is an abomination to the righteous, and he who is upright in the way is an abomination to the wicked.* Things are turned around in a nation that once promoted truth, justice and liberty. The voices of tyranny and treason have become louder and more prevalent than the voices of truth and justice.

The voices screaming racist and oppressor are those who are actually the ones who are engaging in these things. When they speak, they accuse the upright of doing the things that they themselves are doing.

When the truth is finally exonerated, those telling the upright that they should be embarrassed will be put to shame. *A righteous man hates lying; a wicked man is loathsome and comes to shame. . . . Do not fret because of evildoers nor be envious of the workers of iniquity, for they shall soon be cut down like the grass and wither as green herbs.*

Those who are speaking of the righteous being embarrassed will experience real embarrassment when they are exposed for their hypocrisy. The voices of those attempting to silence and cancel the true patriots of our nation have aligned themselves with globalists who want to make slaves of the entire population of the earth. There can be no compromise with them and no surrender to their tyranny.

I am not embarrassed or ashamed of the truth.

711 THOUGHTS AND DREAMS

Our thoughts and our dreams can be a source of great comfort and pleasure or a source of torment and destruction. Spirits have the ability to influence both. The Lord is in control of even these things. He uses what we entertain both in our conscious and our unconscious states. The source of our thoughts and our dreams are the result of the will of God. He uses this method of communication to reveal himself as well as His purpose for our lives.

The record of dreams and visions are well-documented throughout the Bible, both Old and New Testaments. Our life on earth is like a dream once it has passed. All of our works and deeds are recorded and kept in the book of our mind. Everything is open and known by our Creator. Every person will spend eternity with the thoughts and dreams as well as what each of us has sown and done on earth.

The adversary of our eternal soul is attempting to capture and devour as many as he is able to deceive and lure into rebellion to the will of our Creator. This is why we are directed to *take every thought captive to the obedience of Christ* and to *abide in Christ.* The one who obeys these edicts is safe and secure from the forces of darkness that desire to have us share their destiny.

Surely, the Holy Spirit is speaking to many who have allowed their minds to wander without the guidance of the Spirit of God and the knowledge of His will. Every individual is responsible to God for his own thoughts, dreams and resulting deeds. What we do with what we are given will determine where we spend eternity.

Is this truth deep enough and profound enough to provoke a positive response?

Thoughts and dreams and our response to them are indicators of our destiny. Let's get it right!

712 DAILY AFFIRMATION

By means of daily consistent seeking the Lord's face and the instruction of the Holy Spirit, good habits are developed, and righteousness is the proof of what is sowed. *Blessed is the man who listens to Me watching daily at My gates waiting at the posts of My doors, for whoever finds Me finds life and obtains favor from the Lord. . . . So I will sing to your name forever that I may daily perform my vows. . . . I die daily. . . . It is no longer I who live but Christ lives in me.* The diligent and consistent development of good habits and daily affirmation of them is demonstrated by Daniel who *knelt down on his knees three times a day and prayed and gave thanks before his God as was his custom since early days.*

Daily affirmation of what the Lord has done in our lives and the consistent acknowledgement of His Lordship will produce His very image and nature in us. Once good habits are firmly established in the devotee, the chances of stumbling are greatly reduced. This daily affirmation becomes a moment-by-moment affirmation that leads to *praying without ceasing and taking every thought captive to the obedience of Christ.* This is how it becomes possible to *walk as He walked and do the things He did.*

When we affirm His word in our lives constantly, we become as He is and always please our heavenly Father just as Jesus did as a man. This is the gospel and the doctrine of Christ. Sinners have no part in this relationship and no part in the blessings that it brings. Those who truly seek the Lord unceasingly with all their hearts are His chosen and faithful. They are the ones who walk by faith.

What has been described is not just something to aspire to, but it is something to consciously enter into.

The Lord is waiting for you!

713 LOVED ONES

As my mind wandered through the annals of my life here on earth, and I gave thanks to my Father for all those whom I love, my heart was expanded, and I gave thanks for all those who have loved me. Then the expansion grew, and I realized the love that the Lord had put into my heart went beyond all those whom I was able to recall onto those He loved as well. This is the truth, and it is a miracle. To get a glimpse of the love of God reveals the purpose of life as well as who God really is. His love encompasses His whole creation.

Those of us who know His love have been given the greatest gift that anyone could receive. Those who do not know His love are to be pitied, reached out to. It is the love of God working through our mortal existence to reach those He is calling to Himself. This is an effort that exceeds carnal understanding and mankind's religion. Loved ones include our enemies and those who hate God and those of us who love Him. Thus, we are commanded to *love our enemies and do good to those who despitefully use us.* If you hear the voice of the Holy Spirit, you are being given the knowledge of the truth and the love that surpasses human understanding.

This whole exercise is about expanding our hearts and minds to experience the love of God and be joyful in it.

There is no greater love than for a man to lay down his life for his fellow human beings.

If you love the truth and lay down your life for the Lord, He will surely do His work through you.

We will all be judged according to our work, and our work will declare who we really love.

God loves those who love Him.

714 RECOGNITION

Recognition of the works of God begins with the knowledge of Him. Everything He has made and everything that exists is directly or indirectly attributed to the One to whom we must give account. Without the recognition of His hand in our lives, we are left without understanding of our purpose for living. In order to recognize truth every individual must respond to the light that has been given him/her. Those who respond negatively are the ones wandering through life without an anchor and have nothing absolute on which to grasp.

We who have recognized Jesus and who He really is have come to know our Creator and His ways. We have, in turn been made able to make use of the tools God has given us to maintain a secure journey here on earth without fear of disaster. The many temptations which are traps and pitfalls we all encounter are but tests to strengthen and confirm our faithfulness and resolve. All those the Lord has called who have recognized His sovereignty and His ways come to the realization that everything we encounter on our pilgrimage is working for our good and is conforming us to the image of Christ.

Once a person has embarked on this journey of faith and recognition of truth, the way to maintain a straight course is to abide in Christ. He will never fail and neither will anyone who abides in Him.

The value of recognizing who Jesus Christ really is is immeasurable. *He is the Way, the Truth and the Life. No one comes to the Father but through Him. Amen!*

715 THE GENERATION TO COME

Our hope for the generation to come, even though it may be brief, is that they will not be unbelieving, rebellious, and unfaithful as their fathers are. So, the gospel message is being left to the generation to come as a pure testimony, unlike the popular commentary being disseminated to the generation today that has embraced the flesh merchants' perversion of the gospel that binds those who believe it to the earth and their sinful nature.

The Holy Spirit is in charge, and his testimony is one of purity and holiness. We can but hope that the hearts of the next generation will come to love the truth and escape the delusion of their elders and become part of the eternal generation. Those who have chosen the sinner's version of the gospel are leaving a message of what not to do for the next generation. It is the hope and prayer of this watchman that the generation to come will be given the discernment and love of the truth, that their days will not be consumed in futility and their years in fear.

Our God is merciful, and He hears the prayers of us who love the truth with regard to His salvation. The end of earthly generations is near, but the eternal generation of Christ and His faithful servants will survive into eternity. This is the destiny of those of the generation to come who receive the love of the truth and the nature of the God of truth.

We of this generation are not left without the voices God has chosen to proclaim the true message of the gospel once delivered to the saints of the early church. Their voices are heard even in the midst of the peddlers of their own self-serving perversions of the modern gospel.

May the Lord's blessings be upon the generation to come and the true Israel of God.

716 CONSENTING

There is a host of consenting religious professionals who have partaken with thieves and adulterers. They have cast the words of the Lord behind them while still proclaiming His statutes. Their voices can be heard from every legal venue. While proclaiming freedom, they actually promote bondage in order to satisfy their own greed and covetousness. *The thief does not come except to steal and to kill and to destroy. . . . His ministers are disguised as ministers of righteousness.* Yet the fruit of their doctrine produces the sin that Jesus died to free his people from.

Is this message and this indictment too harsh? Or does the gospel actually teach that Jesus frees us from sin and the death that it produces? The paid professionals who proudly stand before masses of people and proclaim that they remain sinners after being saved clearly deny the reality of salvation; thus casting God's words behind them.

The notion that Jesus' blood covers and cleanses future and unrepented sin before the transgression occurs is the delusion of those who have pleasure in unrighteousness and deception.

The person who has truly been saved from sin and has received the nature of God will not continue in the practice of disobedience to the One who saved him. What is salvation if not deliverance from the act that causes the death of the soul of the one who continues in it? Let's get real! *The person who does not change does not fear God.* Such a person will not spend eternity with Him.

Following Jesus leaves no place for sin and *the one who abides in Him does not sin.* Let the sinners who remain dead in sin bury their own dead. You follow Me, says the Lord.

Do not give consent to those attempting to take the pasture of the Lord for themselves.

717 A WELLSPRING OF LIFE

The understanding of the ways of the Lord is, indeed, a wellspring of life to those who attain such knowledge. Simply put, the knowledge of God is the very thing that enables man to walk free from sin and the way of death. *Awake to righteousness and do not sin for some do not have the knowledge of God. I speak this to your shame.* Of whom does the Lord speak? How many different ways can the Holy Spirit make known the path of righteousness and salvation? Surely, He has presented the wellspring of life where the river that flows from the throne of God originates. He has called out to mankind from the highest places of the earth to make known the way of salvation.

Mercy and truth have met together, righteousness and peace have kissed. Surely the source of such revelation is the wellspring of life where the tree of life is rooted. Is there sin in this place? The person who possesses the knowledge of God and the understanding of His ways has discovered the source of truth and holiness. It cannot be found or accessed through the carnal mind or the halls of higher learning where the professional religious guides are trained. The Spirit of God and the wellspring of life does not flow from these institutions built by the hands and understanding of mankind out of hewn stone. What flows from these places of higher learning are the rivers of Babylon filled with the blood which is the *life of the flesh.* Their doctrines preserve the life of the carnal man and his habitation on earth.

The one who seeks to dwell where Jesus is will not be assisted by Babylon or any of her illegitimate offspring. If you are able to follow the path on which the Spirit of God is leading, you will find yourself moving far away from the religious institutions that have covered the earth and toward the wellspring of life of which Jesus Christ Himself is the source.

718 THE PROMISES OF GOD

The promises of God that manifest themselves in our lives are not because we claim them, but because we meet the qualifications to receive them. SELAH! His promises are not all of a positive and beneficial nature. Many of them are of a consequential nature, whether positive or negative they are primarily the result of our own behavior.

I have heard the religious teachers explain how to claim God's promises to their students for themselves, but rarely are the instructions accompanied by the actual qualifications the Lord has given in order to receive them. The many "ifs" and "becauses" are usually left out and passed over.

The actual promises are nearly all obtained in Christ, but how many actually abide in Him? *For all the promises of God find their yes in Him (Jesus). . . . No one who abides in Him keeps on sinning; no one who keeps on sinning has either seen Him or known Him.* Where does this leave the person who claims to be a believer yet confesses that he is still a sinner? The dichotomy here is so obvious that even the one who has embraced the two-nature and the perpetual sinner doctrines should be able to see the impossibility of claiming the promises of God for themselves.

This is a call to those who have believed in false doctrine to seek the truth and fulfill the qualifications that permit a person to take part and receive the promises the Lord has made to those who love and obey Him. To confess to believing God and asking the Lord into your heart does not mean that He actually resides there or that you abide in Him. The reality is in embracing His nature and His image and actually living according to His Spirit. The person who does this is the one who can expect to partake of the promises God has made to those who love Him.

Who are you going to believe?

719 LEARNING

The source of what we learn is critical in regard to our overall health and well-being. Our spiritual well-being is most important. There are countless voices vying for our ears, but there is only one source of truth. Whenever the instruction of man enters the learning process, so does the likelihood of pollution.

Watch yourselves so that you may not lose what you have worked for but may win a full reward. Everyone who goes ahead and does not abide in the teaching of Christ does not have God. . . . However, when He, the Spirit of Truth, has come, He will guide you into all truth; for He will not speak on His own authority, but whatever He hears He will speak; and He will tell you things to come. He will glorify Me for He will take of what is Mine and declare it unto you. . . . But there were also false prophets among the people, even as there will be false teachers among you who will secretly bring in destructive heresies. . . . These things I have written to you concerning those who try to deceive you. But the anointing which you have received from Him abides in you and you do not need that anyone teach you; but as the same anointing teaches you concerning all things and is true and is not a lie and just as it has taught you, you will abide in Him.

If a person does not examine what he is learning at the hand of mortals in the light of the whole of scripture guided by the Spirit of Truth, what would keep such a person from being deceived?

This is no small matter, and every one of us is ultimately responsible to our Lord and Savior for what we have allowed ourselves to be taught and what we have learned.

Purity is what matters!

720 RIGHTEOUS JUDGMENT

The righteous judgment so often promised by the Lord has been and is occurring as these words are written. What we are experiencing as a nation as well as the whole world is a manifestation of the righteous judgment of God. His actual wrath is not far off, and the time to prepare for the end is at hand. The whole earth is near the limit of the Lord's long suffering and patience. How much worse can the perversion of everything in culture and society get?

In spite of the voices calling for justice, the voices of anarchy are prevailing. The judgment that begins with the house of God has been happening throughout the age, and the polarization of good and evil has reached the point of light and darkness. Anyone who has eyes can see it. Only those oblivious and without discernment are left without comprehension. The signs of prophecy and the signs of nature both reveal the critical point of time in which we find ourselves. The whole world is near the point of embracing the Antichrist spirit that has been waiting to manifest himself in a man. Though his time will be short, it will be devastating for those who love the Lord and are faithful to Him. The warning has been given throughout the Bible and is being given now by the true servants of the Lord. Anyone caught unaware has done so by their own lack of spiritual awareness.

Are you ready?

721 THE ANSWER

When each of us stands before the judgment seat of Christ, whether we are actually able to stand remains a question. This I know. No words will be exchanged. The answer given will be the one written in the book of each person's life. There will be no pleading or excuses made for our deeds and our words. *There is nothing hidden from the eyes of Him with whom we must give account.*

If we have indeed been saved, the vague question of "from what" or "to what" will suddenly be answered without any more ambiguity, and the delicacies and leaven of the religious leaders will be exposed. Those who have believed their lies will not be able to remain standing. *Therefore, the wicked will not stand in the judgment nor sinners in the congregation of the righteous. . . . Then I saw a great white throne and Him who was seated on it. From His presence earth and sky fled away and no place was found for them. And I saw the dead, great and small, standing before the throne and books were opened. Then another book was opened which is the "Book of Life". And the dead were judged by what was written in the book according to what they had done. And the sea gave up the dead who were in it, Death and Hades gave up the dead who were in them and they were judged each one of them according to what they had done. Then Death and Hades were thrown into the lake of fire. This is the second death, the lake of fire. And if anyone's name was not found written in the "Book of Life", he was thrown into the lake of fire.*

There are those of the religious hierarchy who have told you that your works are of no significance, and only your confession and beliefs will be in question at the final judgment. Faith is all that matters. Is your faith not demonstrated by your works and your belief not confirmed by your deeds? How is your confession established as true without obedience to the Lord's commands?

It is advisable to prepare your answer before your final debut. Leaven will not save you.

722 BEYOND CARNALITY

The voice of God is calling those who love Him and His truth to a place beyond the one where we were originally born. Those who are living according to the flesh cannot perceive this land beyond the veil and the clouds where Jesus has ascended and is calling us to dwell with Him. This place is beyond the delusion sent to those who have not received the love of the truth and find pleasure in unrighteousness and the indulgence of their lusts.

This revelation is for those who hunger and thirst for righteousness and truth and have sacrificed their own life to gain the life of Christ. There are no liars and no sinners in this land where only the righteous can enter and dwell. This is the real promised land beyond the earthly promised land where the biological descendants of Abraham, Isaac and Jacob have made their home, and where the armies of the enemies of God are gathered to destroy the people God has chosen to bear His name and give testimony to His will.

We are nearing the hour of trial that is coming upon the whole earth to try those who dwell on the earth. Those of us who have heard and responded to the voice of God have moved beyond the natural dwelling where we were born and are now seated with Jesus at the right hand of our Father in heavenly places. This is not just a figurative or hypothetical place but a Spiritual land where we who love the truth have been raised with Jesus to inhabit.

If you cannot hear the voice of God and cannot see the Spiritual land, there is still hope if you seek the Lord diligently with all your heart, soul, mind and strength and are willing to sacrifice your self-life for His life.

Now is the time.

For those who live according to the flesh set their minds on the things of the flesh, but those who live according to the Spirit the things of the Spirit. For to be carnally-minded is death, but to be Spiritually-minded is life and peace.

723 WHO WILL STAND?

Some trust in chariots and some in horses; but we will remember the name of the Lord, our God. They have bowed down and fallen; but we have risen and stand upright. . . . Therefore, the ungodly shall not stand in the judgment nor sinners in the congregation of the righteous. . . . Who may ascend into the hill of the Lord? Or who may stand in His holy place? He who has clean hands and a pure heart who has not lifted up his soul to an idol nor sworn deceitfully.

Those who are able to stand are doing so now. Those who remain sinners cannot stand in the presence of God now, nor will they be able to stand in the final judgment. The teachers of unconditional eternal security and the ongoing sin of believers have made a dreadful error that will cause many who follow them to be ashamed and condemned in the "Day of the Lord".

The misappropriation of the blood of Jesus dishonors God and makes His great sacrifice of no effect for *the person who continues to sin after receiving a knowledge of the truth. For if we sin willfully after we have received a knowledge of the truth there no longer remains a sacrifice for sins but a certain fearful expectation of judgment and fiery indignation which will devour the adversaries. Anyone who has rejected Moses' law dies without mercy on the testimony of two or three witnesses. Of how much worse punishment do you suppose he will be thought worthy who has trampled the Son of God under foot, counted the blood of the covenant by which he was sanctified a common thing and insulted the Spirit of Grace.*

These blind leaders who are exploiting the gospel to enlarge their own kingdoms will not stand in the judgment. Neither will the sinners who follow them. The doctrines of future sin being forgiven without repentance and true contrition is the mark of deception and lies.

Only the blameless and pure of heart will stand on that final day.

724 INSTITUTIONS

The institutions built by man, whether religious or secular, eventually become corrupt. SELAH! Even the ones which seem to be pure at their inception and true to their mission and purpose are eventually infiltrated by people who are not in agreement.

The true "Body of Christ" was not instituted by man, nor is it under the headship of man. Its origin is Spiritual as is its headship. It is a pure functioning entity that cannot be seen by the natural eye nor corrupted by the natural man. As with its headship so its members are spiritual. The only way to become a member is to be born into it. Only this reborn, new creation with a new nature is recognized as part of this Spiritual body. Every member has taken on the image and nature of their originator. There are no exceptions, and impostors are quickly identified as such.

While the earth is covered with religious organizations, governments and partisan groups, there is only one true Church of Jesus Christ, and all others are counterfeit. It is not possible for this true Church to be corrupted, because it is not of this world nor are any of its leaders or members. They all dwell in heavenly places and are not of the world. *You are not of the world just as I (Jesus) am not of the world.* If we were of the world, the world would be able to find our identity and meeting places by searching the internet and all the other sources of information. But we are outside their realm of observation.

This is a wake-up call to all who believe they are members of the "Body of Christ" because they are members of a church or a denomination or an institution that claims to represent Jesus.

The truth and the life are in the Spirit!

725 REAL TREASURE

A careful, honest examination of a person's most valued treasure will reveal where the person's heart is. Our Creator has revealed His treasure to His chosen people and to all mankind by giving us His only begotten Son, His greatest treasure. To really contemplate and realize the love God has for His created treasure requires revelation that exceeds a man's natural capacity. That the Almighty sent His Son to earth as a man to sacrifice Himself in order to redeem us to our Creator is the proof of His love and His treasure.

If this diligent search of our individual heart reveals that we also value Jesus above all other treasure, we have become one with our Creator and share His passion. This treasure cannot be lost or stolen if it is carefully guarded.

Solomon was given earthly treasures without measure and also the wisdom that exceeded that of all who had come before him, but he was robbed of his greatest treasure by the false gods and the idols of his many pagan wives, which he allowed to distract him from his greatest treasure of all. It can happen to anyone who allows himself to yield to worldly temptation.

Jesus has shown us how to resist temptation and also promised us *God will not allow you to be tempted beyond what you are able to bear but with the temptation will provide a way of escape.* This certainly sounds like there is no need for us to sin or abandon our greatest treasure for something of less value.

The spokesmen of the tempter and adversary of our souls have told us that we cannot lose the treasure God has given us, but we know he is a liar and desires to rob us of our great reward. We have been warned, and the preservation of the greatest treasure anyone can possess is left for us to keep under vigilant watch.

There can be no greater commission given to mankind. Love will give us the victory and preserve our greatest treasure.

726 CHOICE AND PREDESTINATION

How can choice and predestination be reconciled by scripture? Absolute determinism leaves no place for free will and choice. We are constantly faced with decisions that appear spontaneous and left for us to make choices. The choices we make are the product of who we are. The actual determination of who we are as individuals is determined by our response to truth and light. If we respond positively to the light given to us, more will be given. If we respond negatively or wrongly, we have put ourselves in a destiny of predictable outcome.

If we walk in the light as He is in the light, we have fellowship with one another. The person who walks in the light loves the truth. The person who walks in darkness does so because he prefers darkness, because his deeds are evil. God has given light to every human being born on the earth and left the response to it up to the individual. Once we make a choice, whether consciously or unconsciously, we begin on a journey where truth and integrity will guide us, or deception and lies will guide us.

Unless there is an intervention in a person's life, there will be no change, and the course is set. By the grace of God we are all called back to reasonable and righteous behavior. Only those who sear their conscience will continue on a path of destruction. *God is not willing that any should perish but that all would come to repentance.* It is God's will that we not sin, and He is able to keep those who love Him and obey Him from the sin that separates us from Him. If you believe Him and trust Him, your destiny will be to spend eternity with Him.

Are you able to see the choice He is giving us? Our actual predestination is to become chosen in Christ, who is the One who has been chosen before the foundation of the world. The real choice is to become one with Him or not.

727 ORIGINS

In the beginning God created. There is no place for a rational person to question how everything originated, but there remain questions with regard to the origins of things like truth, lies, sin, death, right, wrong, responsibility, as well as eternal destiny. God is also the source of all truth, and it is impossible for Him to lie. Whatever He says is so. Lies originated in the spiritual realm by the one who was known as Lucifer. He also initiated lies in the natural realm disguised as a serpent. The first woman of earth believed his lies and, along with her husband, introduced the first sin on earth which, in turn, introduced death in the natural creation. These things are all elementary. Any person who does not know them does not know much.

The introduction of sin on earth brought with it the separation of fellowship of man from his Creator. This was the origin of both spiritual and physical death. The spiritual death came first, and the physical followed. We now live in a land where everything dies in the natural realm.

The great Creator has not left mankind without a way to re-establish fellowship with Himself and a path back to eternal life. Sin is what caused the separation of mankind from God, and sin is what maintains the separation. If the fallen angel, Satan, is able to keep mankind separated from the Lord and eternal life the same way he first initiated sin and death into the Lord's perfect creation, he succeeds.

While our Creator has provided redemption for fallen man and salvation from sin, Satan has devised lies and introduced them into religious institutions that are teaching the descendants of the first Adam that they can continue to sin and still have eternal life. This is the big lie that has permeated the modern church that claims to represent Jesus Christ the Savior. The salvation God has provided is negated and made ineffectual by their lies.

The denial of the truth God has spoken is the same as the lie Satan told Eve in the garden. *You will not surely die.* Those who are telling you that you are saved but that you can continue to sin are condemning those who believe them to the same spiritual death that our first parents experienced in Eden. If you believe Satan's lie and live according to your flesh, you will die just as they did.

All the controversy over the age of earth and the reliability of the word of God pales in significance to the truth of salvation from sin and the absolute need for obedience to the Lord and personal holiness. Everything else is peripheral.

I hope you are listening.

728 THE MIRROR

What can be seen in a mirror? The answer to the question mostly depends on a person's source of vision. *Nevertheless, when one turns to the Lord the veil is taken away. Now the Lord is the Spirit and where the Spirit of the Lord is, there is liberty. But we all with unveiled face beholding as in a mirror the glory of the Lord are being transformed into the same image from glory to glory just as by the Spirit of the Lord. . . . For whom He foreknew He also predestined to be conformed to the image of His Son that He might be the firstborn among many brethren.*

The person who has been given eyes to see will see the image of his Savior in the mirror of God's word and certainly not a sinner. *All have sinned and fallen short of the glory of God.* But those who have been reborn and become new creations and given the nature of their Creator are indeed new creatures with the image of the One who created them. The person who continues to sin will not see the image of Jesus in any mirror. What we see in a mirror is who we really are; if we can only see with natural, fleshly eyes it is because we are living according to the flesh. The image of Jesus is the image of God Himself. Anyone who has been crucified with Christ and been raised with Him bears His image, and He is living His life through them. He does not sin. SELAH!

I have been crucified with Christ; it is no longer I who live but Christ lives through me. The life I now live in the flesh I live by faith in the Son of God who loved me and gave Himself for me.

We see what we see. Only through the eyes of faith do we see the truth in the mirror.

729 TESTIMONIES

The testimonies of the Lord God are sure and reliable. *Your testimonies are also my delight and my counselors.* The whole Bible is a record of the testimonies of God. Its value is beyond any other thing that mankind can lay hold of. The Psalmist who wrote Psalm 119 speaks over and over of the testimonies of the Lord and their value. The testimonies of man are not so sure; even his recorded history is not reliable and cannot be trusted.

If not for the testimonies God has preserved and given to us, watchmen would have little to say and no foundation on which to stand. All things are measured by the testimonies the Lord has given us. Those who do not give them heed are fools who stumble in darkness and don't know what they are doing or where they are going.

The value of the Creator's testimonies cannot be overstated. They are the road map to everlasting life and the identifier of the many pitfalls and snares that would cause His believers to stumble and fall. Without the counsel of the Spirit of God that quickens the testimonies He has inspired to be written, death would have victory over all those who put their confidence in the carnal understanding of what the Lord has said. *The written letter kills but the Spirit give life.* Confidence in the carnal understanding of what God has said is a formula for becoming an enemy of God and the estrangement that results. The Spirit who has provided the testimony of the Almighty is also the counselor who administers their life-giving truth.

As great as the written testimonies of God are, they serve to convict those who disobey them of sin and judgment to come. The testimonies of God are a blessing to those who obey them and revere them, but at the same time a judge of all those who don't.

730 NOWHERE

A hurry to the nowhere that leads to emptiness and despair seems to be the destination of most of the traffic that can be observed on the roadways. The endless vanity and grasping for valueless commodities are the signs of the person who is going nowhere. Some believe that the faster they go, the sooner they will arrive somewhere, but they do not understand that the road they are on only leads nowhere.

Those of whom are being spoken are attempting to satisfy themselves and their fleshly lust while being ignorant of the fact that these things cannot be satisfied and only lead to death. If those who are being called by God are caught up in this frenzy heading nowhere, they too will end up in the same place.

Once a person is called by the Spirit of God, the response they give will determine their destiny and the destination where they will arrive. There is a fork in the road, and the right choice on the way to go is critical to the person's eternal well-being. The road to nowhere leads to a bottomless pit and outer darkness. The righteous road leads to a place of rest and peace in the arms of our Savior.

It is truly amazing that so many have made the wrong turn without considering the consequence. There is truly a right way and a wrong way and a choice to be made.

He who keeps the commandment keeps his soul, but he who is careless of his ways will die.

731 FEEL GOOD PROPHETS

The flattering words and the message of peace and safety to a people unable to cease from sin and rule over their flesh is the mark of the prophet who has not stood in the presence of God. These prophets give people temporary solace and a false sense of well-being. They, nevertheless, only encourage the disobedient to continue to seek refuge outside the will of God and the bounds of righteousness and holiness.

These false prophets have teamed up with the teachers of ongoing sin in the lives of those who call themselves Christians. These things are an abomination to the Lord who gave His life to free people from sin and death. The total hypocrisy of such doctrines and empty promises of well-being are painfully lacking in substance and Biblical support. These self-proclaimed ministers of the gospel are actually denying that Jesus came in the flesh. While they proclaim Jesus with their mouths, their actual lives deny the reality of what He accomplished as a man.

If any person who claims to know the Lord does not exhibit His life, they are in fact denying the reality of Him living His life through them. He came in the flesh to put away sin in the flesh. The person who is unable to cease sinning is, in reality, denying what Jesus has done.

The spirit being described is actually the spirit of Antichrist and has no part in Jesus. *The one who abides in Christ does not sin.* Jesus Christ certainly did not sin as a man, and neither do those who have become One Spirit with Him.

The question must be asked of those who preach, teach and prophesy that the salvation of those who continue to sin is secure while they deny the very words of scripture. "What spirit do they really represent?"

732 BOASTING

Whoever falsely boasts of giving is like clouds and wind without rain. The constant drumbeat of the flesh merchants is a boasting of how much they give and how much they do for the Lord. It is a stench in the Lord's nostrils and a slap in the face to those who love truth. Those who preach about Spiritual things and boast of being filled with the Spirit are the fruitless, empty storms that plague the earth.

From what has the Lord redeemed Israel if not its iniquities? For what did He come to earth as a man if not to deliver His people from their sin? Do you hear Me, says the Lord? Have you read the gospel? This is more than a gentle rebuke to those who give to the prognosticators of the sinful nature and the deniers of freedom from sin. The truth could not be clearer to anyone who loves the Lord. The empty wind of the preachers who claim to know the Lord while denying what He actually accomplished as a man are the scourge of the true gospel.

So, boast on you tele-evangelists and religious scholars. Your day of reckoning is forthcoming. Your false boasts of giving are being exposed to the whole world, while your faithful followers remain mesmerized by your boasts of serving God.

There is greater condemnation for those who set themselves as teachers and then cause those who listen to them to stumble into sin. What will save you from the execution of the truth when it is revealed? Boast on, and build your own earthly kingdoms! The truth will be exonerated, and those who love it will rejoice. Amen!

733 MONEY, POWER, GREED

This title describes the essence of the world system under which mankind is dominated. All the institutions that control the activities of society including religion come under the basic influence of money, power and greed. What can be expected of such wicked influence? The fact is that the fruit of such corrupting forces is exactly what we are experiencing throughout the world.

There is one place, although not of the world, where God is displaying His absolute control. It is a Spiritual nation known as the "Israel of God", not to be confused with the state of Israel in the Middle East. *For He established a testimony in Jacob and appointed a law in Israel which He commanded our fathers that they should make them known to their children; that the generation to come might know them, the children who would be born, that they may arise and declare them to their children, that they set their hope in God and not forget the works of God, but keep His commandments; and that they not be like their fathers, a stubborn and rebellious generation, a generation that did not set its heart aright, and whose spirit was not faithful to God.*

We who are of the generation that was to be born are those who are the true offspring of Abraham and of the generation of Christ; the true Israel of God. If you are comprehending what is being said you are one of the few whom the Lord has chosen and are not part of the corrupt system that dominates the world. Money, power and greed are not motivating factors in the Spiritual nation known as Israel.

No citizen of the Spiritual Israel is influenced by the lusts of the flesh, the eyes, or the pride of life. The love of God has taken priority over the lust for money, power and greed. The will of God and its fulfillment are the motivation of every one of His chosen people in His chosen nation.

The cost of becoming part of the nation that is separate from the world is your life.

734 KINDNESS

What is desired in a man is kindness, and a poor man is better than a liar. Kindness is the companion of love and always tells the truth. The idea that telling a lie in order to make someone feel better or not hurt their feelings is, nevertheless, a lie and an abomination to God. What is being spoken of is particularly true when it comes to sin and salvation.

There are absolute facts with regard to the salvation of a soul. To tell a person they are saved from damnation and forgiven of all their sins for all time is not a kindness but a formula for eternal separation from God. It is good to pity a sinner and to try to snatch them out of the fire and the grip of Satan, but to try and comfort such a person is not kindness but, in reality, sentencing them to death. There are many well-meaning souls who engage in such foolishness, as well as a host of religious opportunists who see these lies as a means of benefitting themselves.

The true gospel makes provision for forgiveness of sin and deliverance from its penalty but requires repentance, contrition, and a total turning away from it. To tell a person who is following the lusts of his flesh and living according to the flesh that God understands and forgives them anyway is the lie that denies the truth of the gospel. *If you live according to the flesh, you will die.* No amount of ignorant kindness can change this absolute proclamation of scripture. A carnal mind and its ignorant, well-intentioned misinterpretation of the gospel is a tool of the adversary of our soul.

Truth is the genuine expression of love and kindness.

735 CONTRAST

Contrasting the attributes of the heavenly and the earthly will yield the true heart and nature of the human being. The Lord, of course, is the maker and God of both, and He does whatever He pleases. Heavenly riches consist of the knowledge and wisdom of God, while the earthly consist of silver and gold. The heavenly-minded person is most concerned with the kingdom and glory of the Lord while the worldly-minded is most concerned with things of earth, such as self-interest and worldly influence. This contrast could go on indefinitely, but you can see the reality of a person's treasures and values are quickly revealed by the contrast.

Every person is either carnal or spiritual, and the contrast of the two natures reveals the condition of a person's soul. Surely the Lord can see these things, and He rewards each individual person accordingly. Is this not a simple concept? The whole Bible records a series of contrasts between those who love and serve the Creator and those who love and serve this present world. The world is passing away along with all those who love it, but those who love, serve, and do the will of God abide forever. Again, this simple concept reveals the simplicity of the gospel and the works of God.

The choices we make and the work we do also fall into the categories being contrasted. Every person will be judged and rewarded according to their deeds. Those who have told us otherwise are badly mistaken. Our works and deeds reveal the true condition of our hearts and who and what we love. If we say one thing and do another, do you suppose the Lord is fooled or oblivious? He knows our hearts, and only those who love Him with all their heart, soul, mind and strength have obeyed His command and done His will.

The contrast is certainly a valid test. In the end we have judged ourselves.

736 WORDS OF LIFE

In a flood of empty words, meaningless conversation, false and worthless information and lies being spewed out of the mouth of the adversary of our souls, there is a refuge and a place where words of life may be found. The secret place of the Most High God is only a secret kept from those who refuse to listen to His voice. This secret place is where the words of life and truth are being heard. This is where the flood of ungodliness that is covering the earth is unable to reach.

This is a call from the Spirit of the Lord to flee from the chatter of religious confusion and the false promises of sinners to the place where only the righteous may enter. If you love the truth, you will be able to find the way into the secret place where Jesus dwells. If you love the truth, you know there will be no sinners there.

Has the Lord not promised such a place to those who love Him with all their hearts? There is no need to be caught in the flood that is overtaking the earth and all those who dwell on it. The secret place is a heavenly place for heavenly people, those who have truly become citizens of heaven. It is the kingdom where Jesus is King, and everyone there bears His image. This is the promise He has made to those who love Him above all others and also love their brethren as themselves.

He is calling us to join Him in the joy of His chosen nation that the world cannot see or partake in. All are invited, but there are only few who respond to the call.

These are words of life, says the Lord!

737 A SPECIAL NATION

There is but one nation on earth that is unique, whose people walk blamelessly before the Lord apart from the law while fulfilling its righteous requirement. It is a nation consisting of members from every other nation and tribe on earth. Every individual is chosen by the Lord to represent Himself. There are no sinners or liars, no murderers or adulterers, no idolators or hypocrites, no greedy or coveters, only those who have forsaken the sinful nature of their parents and taken on the nature of their Creator.

This is the nation whose members are no longer citizens of the world but of heaven; no longer of the generations that perish but of the eternal generation that has walked by faith throughout history. These special people are born of the Spirit of God and follow Him wherever and however He leads. By so doing they glorify the Lord and fulfill His laws.

These chosen ones are no longer controlled by fleshly desire and lust but have gained control by subjecting themselves to the Holy Spirit and the will of God. They remain human beings but have regained what Adam and Eve lost through their disobedience. This special people are the ones who prove what the salvation of God and the sacrifice of Jesus, His Son, accomplished on the earth where the disobedience of man has prevailed throughout the ages.

This is the nation that know their God and do not shame themselves or Him through sin.

Many are called but few become chosen to this generation and this very special nation.

738 COMPULSION AND VOLITION

The compulsion to do what is right or wrong is the result of exercising our volition and choosing the way we will go. The power to make righteous choices and to carry them out is provided by the Spirit of God to those who submit to Him. The compulsion to make unrighteous choices and to sin by doing them is the result of yielding to the nature of the flesh. In either case, the processes of sowing and reaping apply.

Sowing to the Spirit yields eternal life. Sowing to the flesh yields separation from God and eternal death. This seems simple, but it is amazing how theology has complicated it to the point where yielding to the lusts of the flesh can result in eternal life; and how making wrong choices can still result in abiding in the kingdom of heaven. Of course, these theological concepts are mistaken, and those who subscribe to them will perish with them. But the number of souls that embrace these unscriptural perversions of the gospel is truly amazing.

Really, is there any evidence that Jesus condones or legitimizes ongoing sin? Does His blood sacrifice cleanse and cover the future sins of the person who has received forgiveness and the knowledge of the truth? From where do these lies originate? Only those who are deluded are compelled to preach and teach such foolishness.

God will not be mocked, and those who continue making wrong *choices* that result in sin will reap death. Only those who follow the Holy Spirit and make right choices will reap the promises God has made to those who love Him—AMEN.

Ultimately, what we are compelled to do is the result of the choice we have made.

739 THE POOR AND THE NEEDY

The poor and the needy are often spoken of in the Bible. Both are made reference to with regard to the Lord's awareness of their plight and His love for them. What seems to be widely unknown about them is the two distinctly different classes they represent. One is for regarding worldly possession and provisions, and needy with regard to needing physical help. The other class is the one that is poor regarding the spiritual heavenly riches and the need for help from the Lord to guide them to the truth.

The church that Jesus spoke to in Revelation was rebuked by Him, saying, "*I know your works; you are neither cold nor hot! Would that you were either cold or hot! So because you are lukewarm and neither hot or cold, I will spit you out of My mouth; for you say 'I am rich. I have prospered and I need nothing' not realizing that you are wretched, pitiable, poor, blind and naked. I counsel you to buy from Me gold refined by fire so that you may be rich, white garments so that you may clothe yourself and the shame of your nakedness may not be seen, and salve to anoint your eyes so that you may see.*"This is indeed the condition of most of the churches that can be seen proclaiming the gospel of prosperity and the ongoing sin of what they call "believers".

The poor and needy of the kingdom of heaven are well aware of their utter dependence on the grace and mercy of God. They are the people who the Lord has chosen to be His inheritance and reveal Himself to.

The well-educated, socially revered, the economically wealthy and the politically powerful, along with the celebrities of the world do not even register on the scales of heaven.

God knows who His poor and needy are, and He loves us.

There is one who makes himself rich that has nothing; and one who makes himself poor yet has great riches.

740 THE GREATEST BLESSING

To know and experience the Creator of everything is the greatest blessing any human being can receive. There is nothing greater. The Person who is the Creator and the source of every blessing and every good thing is Himself the reward to those who love Him. *He is all and in all.*

He is true, and we who know Him know the truth. He is love, not just in concept but in essence. Is there anything that we can experience that surpasses this love? It is everywhere! There is no place we can hide from it. Those who do not know Him are to be pitied indeed. Everything we can see declares His greatness and the multitude of His attributes. Even mankind itself is a testament to the greatness and wonder of the works of the Lord.

Only a fool can deny God. The evidence of His existence and His intelligence is everywhere. The human brain alone defies the possibility of chance evolution.

To count blessings is like counting stars. Where does it end? God has counted the stars and named every one of them. How's that for greatness? It is good that we who love our Creator have eternity to explore His greatness and majesty.

This discourse is just an acknowledgement of who and what the Lord has come to mean to this lowly servant.

741 THOUGHTS

Seek the Lord while He may be found; call upon Him while He is near; let the wicked forsake his way and the unrighteous man his thoughts; let him return to the Lord that He may have compassion on him and to our God for He will abundantly pardon. For my thoughts are not your thoughts; neither are your ways My ways, declares the Lord. Whereas the heavens are higher than the earth, so are my ways higher than your ways and my thoughts than your thoughts.

The question arises: Can a man's thoughts coincide with God's? And can their ways also be the same? Certainly not while a man is subject to his sinful nature and his flesh, but the Lord has made a way for man to be reconciled to Him and take on His very nature, and even become One Spirit with Him. This is the essence of the gospel. God became a man that man may become one with Him.

It is impossible that the carnal mind of man that is God's enemy could be in harmony with the mind of the Lord, but what does the gospel tell us? *You are not in the flesh but in the Spirit if the Spirit of God dwells in you. . . . Spiritual things must be spiritually discerned. . . . For who has understood the mind of the Lord so as to instruct Him? But we have the mind of Christ.*

If we actually receive what God says He has given us, are we not able to walk as Jesus walked, free from sin? This, of course, requires faith, not the faith of the religious leaders and the teaching of a two-natured man, but faith in the truth of what the Lord has spoken. If there are alarms going off in your spirit, perhaps you have not actually become one with the Lord and are still dominated by carnality.

There is a way that seems right to a man but it ends in death. . . To be Spiritually-minded is life and peace, but to be carnally-minded is death.

There is no place in the thoughts of the spiritual person for the thoughts and ways of carnality.

742 THE GREAT DIVIDE

The gulf that separates heaven and earth consists of a veil that has been removed by the sacrifice of the Son of God. The divide that is the barrier between God and man is a moral and spiritual one brought about by sin. The removal of sin and the rebirth of man is the bridge that spans the gulf of separation. The body of the man, Jesus Christ, is the veil through which a human being must pass in order to experience the reality of the heavenly realm.

When sin is eliminated from a person's life, and his spirit becomes reconnected with the Spirit of God, the ability to maintain this relationship is the absolute abandonment of the old life and the absolute embrace of the new life the Spirit of God has given the person who believes Him. The re-introduction of sin into this new life has the potential of re-establishing the divide that sin caused in the beginning.

There is no place for sin in the life of any person who abides in Christ and follows His Spirit. *He who abides in Christ does not sin.* Faith consists of hearing, believing and obeying the voice of God. His word is His voice when ministered by His Spirit and obeyed by the one who has ears to hear. Faith is the vehicle by which a man can ascend into the Spiritual realm on the other side of the great divide.

It is unbelief or misinformation that keeps a person from crossing over and continuing to sin. The success or failure of the soul on this journey depends on obedience to the voice of the Lord. His commandments are the same on both sides of the great divide. The difference is that on the earthly side the nature of the person living according to the flesh is unable to keep them. On the heavenly side of the gulf, the person who has received the nature of God and lives according to the Spirit is able to overcome his flesh and obey God's righteous commands. *If you live according to the flesh you will die. . . . If you live according to the Spirit you will live.*

The Lord is knocking.

743 COMFORT

The pursuit of comfort is similar to that of pleasure. The flesh craves comfort as does the carnal mind. The Lord has promised His people a Comforter, although His mission is not to comfort those who seek to comfort themselves and their own pleasures. The comfort the Lord gives is to those who love Him and serve Him. He metaphorically pours burning coals of fire on the heads of the wicked.

The act of trying to comfort a sinner who is suffering because of his sin is like trying to console the drunkard who is on a binge. A certain level of physical comfort is not sinful nor is a reasonable amount of biological pleasure that is enjoyed by anyone as a result of his labor.

The real comfort the Lord gives is to the heart, soul and mind of the person who knows Him and trusts Him. The comfort of the world is but for a moment and ends in misery. Here again is a contrast of spiritual and natural. Our character and our values can be evaluated by our own pursuit of comfort and pleasure.

Surely Jesus and His apostles, along with the early believers, have left us an example of righteous levels of comfort. In the words of the writer of Hebrews: *Keep your life free from the love of money and be content with what you have, for He (Jesus) has said, "I will never leave you nor forsake you."*

Finally, brethren, rejoice. Aim for restoration, comfort one another, agree with one another, live in peace; and the God of love and peace will be with you.

There is a difference in the two types of comfort, isn't there? Comfort and pleasure can be an idol.

744 COMMON MAN

Who has believed our report? And to whom has the arm of the Lord been revealed, for He shall grow up before Him as a tender plant and as a root out of dry ground. He has no form or comeliness; and when we see Him there is no beauty that we should desire Him. This is God's only begotten son. But the Lord has also spoken of other sons raised up from the masses. Is there a way for a common man to become such a son and be distinguished from the billions of people on the earth? The answer and the ability come from the Father. *For as many as are led by the Spirit of God, these are sons of God. . . . For whom He foreknew, He also predestined to be conformed to the image of His Son that He might be the firstborn among many brethren.* These many brethren taken from the masses are indeed sons of God and joint heirs of Jesus.

These sons are they who have believed the prophet's report and have followed the Spirit of God and put to death the deeds (sins) of the body. This is no small thing and no small act of faith. It is the thing that separates the average common man from all others. It is the act of faith that enables a person to confess with his spirit that Jesus Christ has come in the flesh. It is also the act of faith that allows the risen Savior to live through and carry out the Father's will on the earth today.

Is this not the true message of the gospel and the doctrine of Christ? There are but few who can actually believe it and walk in it, but they are the ones who have become the saints of God and bring delight to His soul. *As for the saints who are on the earth, they are the ones in whom is all My delight.*

They are not sinners!

745 BEING BORN

Being born is the process of becoming a person who is alive in the world. Every person who is born has a father who produced the seed from which he originated. We all have the nature of the one from whom we have descended. This is an indisputable truth. Unless there is a supernatural intervention in a person's life, everyone will live out his existence on earth with the nature with which he is born.

Jesus Christ has told us that we must be "born again" in order to see the kingdom of heaven and to know His Father. This Jesus did not have the same father as the rest of humanity, nor did he have the same nature. His Father was God, and He inherited that nature. The great miracle of the ages is the new birth of the person who have been given a new life, and along with it, a new nature and a new Father.

Some believe that even though being born again the old nature of the old life still exists and has control over this new creation. This is a lie and contrary to what God has said. The Holy Spirit has told us *Old things have passed away; all things have become new.* The truth is what matters, and the difference between faith and unbelief is the difference between life and death.

The one who is born of God now has the opportunity and the ability to be His son and fulfill the purpose for which all mankind was originally created before sin entered God's perfect creation. The Father's purpose in the sacrifice of His Son is not merely to forgive the past sins and the consequence of them, but to restore the relationship with mankind that existed before the introduction of sin into God's perfect creation.

The person who continues to sin is denying what God has done and the salvation He has provided. The one who is born of God and has been forgiven and received the knowledge and love of the truth is the one who has been truly united in the Lord.

Being born again is truly taking on a new existence.

746 NAME

A good name is to be chosen rather than great riches, loving favor rather than silver and gold. The name of the Lord, of course, is the greatest of all, whether YHWH, of the Old Testament, or JESUS of the New. There is no other name and no other God called Jesus that exists in heaven or on earth that compares. *Nor is there salvation in any other; for there is no other name under heaven given among men by which we must be saved. . . . Therefore, God has highly exalted Him and given Him the name which is above every name, that at the name of Jesus every knee should bow of those in heaven and of those on earth and of those under the earth, and that every tongue should confess that Jesus Christ is Lord to the glory of God the Father.*

Every name has meaning and carries with it significance. The Lord has directly given names to many people, cities and nations all by design. None of them compares to the many names He has given Himself in order to exemplify His greatness. They are all included and brought to fulfillment in Jesus Christ. SELAH!

Our Creator has performed mighty miracles and raised up kings and nations and then destroyed them for His name's sake. So He is doing even as these words are written. In the end every person who has ever lived will see and know the truth and the power of His Name. Those who know and revere His Name now are the ones who will be glorified with Him when He appears to the world that has rejected His person and the name that represents who He is.iH

There is infinitely more that could be said, but the point is made and the message is delivered. To know the person is to know the name in every language.

The Lord also will be a refuge for the oppressed, a refuge in time of trouble. And those who know Your name will put their trust in You; for You Lord have not forsaken those who seek You.

747 FEELINGS

Even God has feelings. *Then those of you who escape will remember Me among the nations where they are carried captive, because I (the Lord) was crushed by their adulterous heart which has departed from Me and by their eyes which play the harlot after their idols. . . . Now as He (Jesus) drew near, He saw the city and wept over it saying, "If you had known, even you especially in this, your day the things that make for your peace! But now they are hidden from your eyes."*

While feelings are valid, and everyone has them, the person who is controlled by them will surely shipwreck. Feelings cannot be relied on as a guide any more than the heart can be trusted to know the ways of God. *He who trusts in his own heart is a fool, but he who walks wisely will be saved. . . . There is a way that seems right . . . but it ends in death.*

Everyone likes feeling good, but what are you willing to give for that feeling? The counsel of God and the guidance of the Holy Spirit is based on trust, obedience, and faith apart from feelings and emotions. *The person who knows what is right and does not do it to him it is sin.* Knowing God and His ways and obeying Him is the way to please Him. Good feelings may follow, but they do not lead the way.

Bad feelings may hurt, but they too, cannot dictate what the saint of God does in reaction to them. Obeying the voice of God may very well result in unpleasantness, and suffering is often a consequence of doing the will of God. Surely Jesus has shown us that. The man, Jesus Christ, was indeed an emotional man with intense feelings, but they did not cause Him to take His eyes off what His Father sent Him to do.

Love, of course, is far more than a feeling, and feelings are subservient to true love. The love of God surpasses feelings by being a choice of the will. Feelings may or may not follow right choices, but the fulfillment of the command to love will render good feelings in the end, says the Lord.

748 DECEIT

Blessed is the man to whom the Lord does not impute iniquity and in whose spirit there is no deceit. . . . Who is the man who desires life and loves many days that he may see good? Keep your tongue from evil and your lips from speaking deceit. . . . Everyone will deceive his neighbor and will not speak the truth; they have taught their tongue to speak lies; they weary themselves to commit iniquity. Your dwelling place is in the midst of deceit; through deceit they refuse to know Me, says the Lord.

This watchman has heard and seen the deceit of the preachers and teachers of the electronic media from nearly every professional representative of every religious institution. The Holy Spirit has directed me to make commentary on what I have seen and heard. The people who follow these deceitful charlatans are being led to the grave of lost salvation. Sin is the main issue, and deceit is sin. The denial of the penalty of ongoing sin after the redemption from sin is among the most diabolical forms of deceit being propagated.

Awake to righteousness and do not sin for some do not have the knowledge of God. I speak this to your shame. To whom does the apostle speak? To whom is the Lord speaking now? From what did the Lord come to save his people? These questions are not presented lightly or in jest. Eternity is not something to be lackadaisical about. If there is a way to be sure of salvation from sin, certainly every diligent and conscientious person would want to know the truth. *He who is careless of his ways will die.* The person who believes lies and loves their sin more than God will certainly be allowed to indulge in gratifying the lust of his flesh.

The deceit of the professional flesh merchants is the delusion God has sent to those who have not received the love of the truth that they might be saved. Now is the time to examine what you have believed and to make your calling and election sure.

Now by this we know that we know Him, if we keep His commandments. He who says, "I know Him" and does not keep His commandments is a liar, and the truth is not in him. But whoever keeps His word truly the love of God is perfected in him. By this we know that we are in Him. He who says he abides in Him ought himself also to walk just as He walked.

749 DESIRES OF THE HEART

Delight yourself also in the Lord and He shall give you the desires of your heart. As I meditated on the desires of my heart, I came to the realization that my greatest desire is to delight in the Lord. It has not always been so, but He has brought me to the place where my soul delights in His ways and desires to please Him. Could there be anything more meaningful than for a man to please His God? Is this not what Jesus did as a man? He told us *I always do the things that please My Father.* To please our heavenly Father is to walk as Jesus walked and to do the things He did. He said: *I only do the things I see My Father doing.*

Is His Father our Father? Are we led by His Spirit? If not, why? Has He not *given us everything that pertains to life and godliness through the knowledge of Him who called us by His glory and virtue by which have been given to us exceedingly great and precious promises that through these you may be partakers of the divine nature having escaped the corruption that is in the world through lust?* It is all about belief and obedience resulting in the faith needed to do the things Jesus did and to walk as He walked. This is what every person who has been called by the Spirit of God has been called to do.

So, what are the desires of our heart? An on what do we think and meditate? Surely the Lord knows the heart of every person and rewards each one according to his deeds. *Commit your way to the Lord; trust also in Him, and He shall bring it to pass. He shall bring forth your righteousness as the light and your justice as the noon day. . . . The steps of a good man are ordered by the Lord and He delights in his way.* Each of us surely has a part in *working out our own salvation.*

Our individual desires are of our own choice, and if we follow the Holy Spirit in the ways of God, our journey here on earth will end with the One whom we have desired to please.

750 A TIME TO MOURN AND WEEP

To everything there is a season; a time for every purpose under heaven . . . a time to weep . . . a time to mourn. My heart is heavy, not for my own loss, but for the great nation that has given way to wickedness, greed, bribery, vileness, lies, corruption and treason. The forces of evil have prevailed over righteousness, truth, and justice. There seem to be more people in our nation that have forsaken God than those who remain faithful. The nation seems to have run its course as so many great nations before it.

What we are witnessing is the judgment of God on a people who have turned their backs on the Lord and His ways in favor of a multitude of idols and false gods. The nation has elected leaders who they think will satisfy the lust for easy living and will supply their needs apart from personal responsibility. The cost is a loss of freedom and liberty to a once-independent and God-fearing population.

We are not left without hope. At least those of us who still trust the Lord. He has told us: *Do not fret because of evil doers or be envious of the workers of iniquity. For they will soon be cut down like the grass and wither as the green herbs.* I could very well copy down all of Psalm 37, but the truth is there for all to read. *The Lord raises up and casts down.*

Nevertheless, we are in a time of turmoil that has engulfed the whole world and could very well be the beginning of the climax of the world as we have known it. It is faith in God and His word that will carry the righteous through the flood just as the Ark carried Noah and his family through the flood of that age. *The Lord sat enthroned at the flood, and the Lord sits as King forever. The Lord will give strength to His people; the Lord will bless His people with peace.*

As we mourn let us remember that our God knows what is going on, and He does have a plan.

751 FACT OR FANTASY

Wherein lies the truth? Does the Lord speak exclusively in metaphors and fiction, allegories and fables? Or, does He speak the truth regarding a place where those who love Him are seated with Him and abide in Him? These are questions that separate belief and faith from unbelief and fears. Can a human being actually inhabit a biological body on earth and, at the same time, dwell in a spiritual land?

The one who has been given eyes to see and faith to believe does indeed dwell with and in the Lord while he walks the earth. This is the one who walks as Jesus walked and knows what his heavenly Father is doing. It is not so with unbelievers and those who have not passed through the veil that separates the natural and the supernatural realms. What you are hearing is not fable or fantasy but the truth of the gospel and the word of God.

The idea that the spiritual man must be continually bound by his biological human nature and dominated by his flesh is the lie propagated by those who are unable to see Spiritual reality. They speak of Spiritual things and places from a natural perspective that does not come from the place where Jesus dwells.

The whole issue of the trustworthiness of the gospel and the whole Bible is weighed on the balance of perspective and belief. Only those who see and interpret from the Lord's perspective are able to discern the truth and reality of what He has said. Can any of the voices coming from the institutions of man be trusted? Did Satan and the leaders of the institutions of man really gain the victory when they crucified Jesus? The answer is obvious, and only the Spirit of God is able to minister the truth with regard to what God has said.

Salvation and eternal life are in the Spirit. *For to be carnally-minded is death, but to be Spiritually-minded is life and peace.*

752 SEDUCTION

The person vulnerable to seduction is the one who does not fear the Lord and does not have the knowledge of God or know His ways. A person may go to Bible studies and attend church services religiously and yet lack the ability to resist temptations and the seduction of sin. Abiding in Christ is not the same as being religious, and following the Holy Spirit is not the same as trying to follow rules. The one who is attempting to please the Lord by such activity has missed the power of the gospel and the life of Jesus.

The deceitfulness of sin and the lure of seduction is the product of a life that remains uncrucified. The person who has died in Christ and risen with Him and been seated with Him in heavenly places is the one who is able to resist the temptation that is able to capture the one living according to the flesh. Can you hear Me, asks the Lord?

Blessed is the man who endures temptation; for when he has been approved, he will receive the crown of life which the Lord has promised to those who love Him. Let no one say when he is tempted, "I am tempted by God," for God cannot be tempted by evil nor does He Himself tempt anyone. But each one is tempted when he is drawn away by his own desires and enticed. Then, when desire has conceived it gives birth to sin; and sin, when it is full grown, brings forth death.

The seducer uses the seductress to lure the simple from whatever steadfastness they may possess. *And I find more bitter than death the woman whose heart is snares and nets, whose hands are fetters. He who pleases God will escape from her, but the sinner will be trapped by her. . . . For the ways of man are before the eyes of the Lord, and He ponders all his paths. His own iniquities entrap the wicked man, and he is caught in the cords of his sin. He shall die for lack of instruction and in the greatness of his folly he shall go astray. . . . For the commandment is a lamp and the law a light; reap fruit from instruction by the way of light to keep you from the evil woman, from the flattering tongue of a seductress. Do not lust after her beauty in your heart nor let her allure you with her eyelids; for by means of a harlot a man is reduced to a crust of bread; and an adulteress will prey upon his precious life.*

There are an abundance of professional instructors and Bible teachers promoting the notion that ongoing sin is normal for a Christian and we all do it. Run! Flee for your life from such an instructor. He represents "Mystery Babylon the Harlot Who Sits on Many Waters".

The wages of sin are still death, and those who teach otherwise are liars.

753 ESCAPES

Escapes from death belong to God. The wise will deal directly with the One who has the power over life and death. There are many mediators who will tell people how to escape the consequence of sin in an attempt to exploit the fear and guilt produced by knowingly doing wrong. They devise religious rituals, ceremonies, penances, sacrifices, traditions and prayers that they teach their followers, telling them that these things are the way to escape damnation.

The Creator himself has provided the way to escape the death that results from sinning against Him. Many people spend their whole lives following the lead and direction of professional clergy and never reach the point of actual faith and salvation promised in the gospel. It is because they are not able to cease from the sin that has caused the separation from God. Hear Me says the Lord. *No temptations have overtaken you except such as is common to man; but God is faithful who will not allow you to be tempted beyond what you are able, but with the temptation will also make a way of escape that you may be able to bear it.* Does the word of the Lord not negate all the excuses and illegitimate justification for ongoing sin?

Hear Me says the Lord. *For if we sin willfully after we have received the knowledge of the truth there no longer remains a sacrifice for sins but a certain fearful expectation of judgment and fiery indignation which will devour the adversary.*

In whom are you going to place your trust and faith? Do these professional, religious leaders really speak for the Lord? Do the countless religious institutions actually possess the knowledge of the escapes from death that they claim to have?

Could anything be more crucial? *Come out of her, my people!*

754 DEBT

Who among us is not a debtor? There is little doubt that we all came into this world with nothing, and what we have has been given to us. The acknowledgement of our indebtedness to our Creator produces humility. SELAH! Any person who has not come to this realization is proud and foolish and lacks understanding. We are told to: *Owe no one anything except to love each other, for the one who loves has fulfilled the law.* Fulfilling this command is but the acknowledgement of the debt we owe the One who loves us and gave Himself for us. He paid the debt we could not pay.

The greatest thing any person can do is to obey the Lord's commandments to love Him and to love our neighbor as ourselves. The one who is unable to fulfill this debt has fallen short of the love God has given those who love Him. SELAH! Regardless of the biological and worldly gifts we have been given, the command of God remains the same. *To whom much is given much is required. And to whom little is given little is required.* Nevertheless, *we are all debtors—not to the flesh to live according to the flesh. For if you live according to the flesh you will die; but if by the Spirit you put to death the deeds of the body you will live. For as many as are led by the Spirit of God these are sons of God.* Can you see how our indebtedness transcends the physical and moves into the spiritual realm?

Our debt goes beyond this earthly existence and on to eternity; there is no end. Our Creator does not expect us to do what He has not given us the ability. In reality our debt is continually paid, and our obligation fulfilled by obeying Him.

The Lord has not asked us to do anything that He was unwilling to do as a man. SELAH!

755 AWAKENING

Awake, you who sleep. Arise from the dead and Christ will give you light. . . . Awake to righteousness and do not sin for some do not have the knowledge of God. I speak this to your shame. The person who continues to sin after having his sins forgiven and washed away is walking among the dead and has fallen asleep. No one who abides in Him (Christ) keeps on sinning; no one who keeps on sinning has either seen Him or known Him. Could scripture be clearer or more precise?

The person unable to cease from sin has either believed a lie or fallen asleep. Therefore, do not be foolish but understand what the will of the Lord is. It is surely the Lord's will that we not sin, and He is able to keep the one who loves Him from it. The truth of the gospel is quite simple. The confusion and the problem are in unbelief and the lies that Satan has succeeded in introducing into the gospel to negate the salvation God has provided. The love of God and the love of the truth will overcome the lies, but those who are not awake to righteousness and holiness will remain in delusion.

Wholehearted abandonment of the self-centered life of the flesh and the pleasure of unrighteousness is the way of salvation. It is the way Jesus has shown us to walk and the path on which the Holy Spirit leads. All liars will be cut off, and all those who continue to sin will share the fate of those who have not received the love of the truth.

Are you awake?

756 THE FOOLISHNESS OF A MAN

The Lord hides His face from the person whose heart is not blameless before Him, whether he calls himself a Christian or not. Foolishness can be discerned by the words of a man's mouth and the labor he engages in. The foolishness of a man twists his way, and his heart frets against the Lord. Believing a lie will not yield righteousness and associating with fools will not yield peace. Fretting against the Lord is the fruit of hypocrisy and disobedience. That is to say, there is no real confidence and assurance of eternal well-being for the one who does not fear the Lord.

The foolishness of a man causes him to act hastily and to speak rashly. It causes him to search endlessly for the truth for which he has no heart. Do not fret-- It only causes harm. How can a fool trust the Lord and walk in His ways if he follows his own heart and chooses friends who are not wise and have no sense of uprightness? The one who follows after his own heart is a fool. . . . The righteousness of the blameless will direct his way aright, but the wicked will fall by his wickedness. . . . The righteousness of the upright will deliver them, but the unfaithful will be caught by their lust . . . the righteous should choose his friends carefully for the way of the wicked leads them astray.

What security does the person who cannot cease from sin have if he has received the knowledge of the truth yet continues to sin? This behavior will surely cause a person to fret against the Lord. It is foolishness to believe that God will maintain fellowship and oneness with a person who refuses to believe Him and obey Him and is carried away by every wind of doctrine.

Fretting is evidence of a lack of faith and trust and not having a love of the truth.

757 MEDITATION

SELAH! Meditation is a process of thought directed by the will to reach a deeper understanding of a subject. This book of the law shall not depart from your mouth, but you shall meditate in it day and night that you may observe and do according to all that is written in it, for then you will make your way prosperous, and then you will have good success. Have I not commanded you? . . . Blessed is the man who walks not in the counsel of the ungodly nor stands in the path of sinners nor sits in the seat of the scornful; but his delight is in the law of the Lord and in His law he meditates day and night. . . . Meditate on these things; give yourself entirely to them that your progress may be evident to all. Take heed to yourself and to the doctrine; continue in them, for in doing this, you will save both yourself and those who hear you.

Meditation is a discipline that yields understanding, knowledge, discernment, revelation, and a multitude of blessings. It requires time and effort. To study and meditate on the works of God produces trust and confidence in Him.

The truth has been violated by those who have put their trust in the commentary of human understanding apart from the wisdom that only comes from God. Institutional, denominational Bible studies promote their own bias and false doctrines. It is incumbent upon the individual to seek God with all his heart and meditate on His ways revealed in His word apart from the influence of partisan spokespeople.

Meditating on the whole counsel of God and His ways produces an overall understanding of His motives and purpose.

If you have the desire to take hold of the deep things of God, meditation may be in order.

758 THE TESTIMONY OF ISRAEL

The God who created heaven and earth has chosen a people and nation to give testimony of Himself. Truth is exemplified by a spiritual people who are chosen from among all nations and compose the true and heavenly Israel of God. The early biological Israel is the one the world can see, where conflict never ceases. Nevertheless, the Lord has preserved this earthly people to give testimony to His word and His faithfulness. The rulers of earth have tried to destroy the nation of Israel from its inception.

The heavenly Israel, like the heavenly Jerusalem is a place of peace where all its people enjoy peace and agreement. The world, along with all the bloodthirsty, has no access or place in this land where righteousness dwells. The heavenly throne of David and his spiritual descendants remain on the thrones of heaven, just as the Lord has promised. Justice and mercy have never failed in this heavenly nation where the will of God is always done. We are all waiting to see the will of God done on earth where the Israel the world can see exists.

Is this land on earth really holy? Is the Jerusalem where Christ was crucified really a place of peace? It is high time for us to make the distinction between the heavenly and the earthly Israel and the testimonies of each. While they both give testimony to the God of heaven, only one actually dwells with Him and knows Him.

Are not the ways of the Lord wonderful? We are given a choice to where we dwell and what we can see.

Blessed is the nation whose God is the Lord; the people He has chosen as His own inheritance.

759 WILLFULNESS

Our thoughts, our words, and our ways reveal the status of our will. A person's will controls the heart and soul of the person. Humility is the fruit of a will given over to the control of the Spirit of God. SELAH! The one who cannot cease from willful sin is the one who denies that Jesus Christ has come in the flesh and has not been baptized into the Holy Spirit. The person who has been crucified, buried and risen in the Lord and become one Spirit with Him is the one whose will is no longer his own. This is not some far-fetched platitude but the reality of the gospel.

The work of God goes far beyond the natural experience of the carnal mind and the biological flesh. Jesus Christ came to earth in the flesh to put away sin in the flesh. Everything He said and did demonstrated what the will of a man whose life is given to God is and does. *He who says he abides in Him (Christ) ought himself to walk just as He walked. . . . Whoever abides in Him does not sin; whoever sins has neither seen Him nor known Him.*

The Lord is asking us the condition of our will. The truth is absolutely crucial with regard to our standing in His sight. This is no longer religious ritual or tradition but absolute truth and reality. This is where we either see the face of God or not. Anyone who is content to continue on in carnal, fleshly religious hypocrisy is free to do so, but at the risk of eternal separation from our eternal Creator and Savior.

Free will and choice have been given to us by a God who loves us and desires us to love Him in return.

The world is passing away and the lust of it; but he who does the will of God abides forever.

760 THE FIELDS OF SCRIPTURE

The resting place of the Lord is not in a place built by the hands of man. His garden is not a place on earth where thorns and thistles grow, or a field where wars are fought. This special holy place is in the heart of the person who has prepared it for the Spirit of the Creator to dwell. The fields of the Lord are the people He has chosen to inhabit. *He who plants and he who waters are one, and each will receive his wages according to his labor, for we are God's fellow workers. You are God's field.*

We have heard that we are God's temple, but how many actually know it experientially? *In Him (Christ) you are also being built together into a dwelling place for God by the Spirit. . . . Christ is faithful over God's house as a Son and we are His house if indeed we hold fast our confidence and the rejoicing of the hope firm to the end.*

Our Father is a husband man, and we are the garden and the vine which His Spirit tends. Dead and unfruitful plants are pruned off and burned. *For the earth which drinks in the rain that often comes upon it and bears herbs useful for those by whom it is cultivated receives blessing from God; but if it bears thorns and briars, it is rejected and near to being cursed whose end is to be burned. . . . I am the true vine and My Father is the vine dresser. Every branch in Me that does not bear fruit, He takes away; and every branch that bears fruit He prunes that it may bear more fruit . . . If anyone does not abide in Me he is cast out as a branch and is withered; and they gather them and throw them into the fire and they are burned.*

Of what do all these metaphors speak? The dwelling place of the Spirit of God is His temple. *Do you not know that you are the temple of God and that the Spirit of God dwells in you? If anyone defiles the temple of God, God will destroy him, for the temple of God is holy which temple you are.*

Where does this leave the one who is unable to cease from sin?

761 WHICH WAY?

How can a young man cleanse his way? By taking heed according to Your word. . . . As for God, His way is perfect; the word of the Lord is proven; He is a shield to all who trust in Him . . . It is God who arms me with strength and makes my way perfect. God's ways remain mysterious to those who have not devoted themselves to knowing them. Even to those who have discovered God's ways, there remains the challenge to walk in them. Knowing is not the same as doing. Whole hearted obedience is the path leading to eternal life. *He who trusts in his own heart is a fool, but whoever walks wisely will be delivered.*

The Almighty makes His ways and His will known to those who love and obey Him and follow His Spirit. He gives eyes to see and ears to hear to those who seek His way whole heartedly. The one who makes a casual attempt at congregational meetings and Bible studies only reaches the limits of carnality. Those who have passed through the gates of righteousness and become One Spirit with the Lord are the elect , whose spirit confesses that Jesus came in the flesh and are able to walk as Jesus walked

The ways of the world and the flesh are totally incompatible with the ways of God. Political correctness is diametrically opposed to Spiritual correctness and righteousness. The laws of man are not the laws of God, and following man's laws will save no one. The true saints of God have the "Mind of Christ" and thus walk in the ways of God. Anyone not able to do so who believes he is a Christian has fallen into the delusion sent by God to those who do not love the truth.

The ways of God are not past finding out, and those who diligently seek the face of God will find them.

762 THE CAUSE OF THE POOR

The cause of the poor is as the cause of the needy. They are both kin to those who hunger and thirst for righteousness and truth. Who are they and what is their cause? Are they not the ones who are close to the heart of the Lord? How can we know them? If any person is one of them, surely that person knows their cause. They are in spiritual reality the people chosen in Christ to inherit the Spiritual land.

The righteous considers the cause of the poor, but the wicked does not understand such knowledge. . . . Blessed are those who hunger and thirst for righteousness for they shall be filled . . . Ho! Everyone who thirsts, come to the waters; and you who have no money, come, buy and eat. Yes, come, buy wine and milk without money and without price. Why do you spend money for what is not bread and your wages for what does not satisfy? Listen carefully to Me and eat what is good and let your soul delight itself in abundance. And incline your ear and come to Me; hear and your soul shall live; and I will make an everlasting covenant with you—the sure mercies of David . . . Seek the Lord while He may be found; call on Him while He is near. . . . He shall regard the prayer of the destitute; he shall not despise their prayer. . . . . Bow down your ear, O Lord, hear me; for I (David) am poor and needy; preserve my life for I am holy; You are my God; save your servant who trusts in You.

There is one who makes himself rich, yet has nothing; and one who makes himself poor yet has great riches. Earthly and worldly wealth or lack of it is not the point here. The real point is how desperate a person is for the living God and the knowledge of Him. There are no greater riches than fellowship and oneness with our Creator, and it is those who realize their utter dependence on Him who also realize how poor and needy they are.

Blessed are the poor in Spirit, for theirs is the kingdom of God.

763 REALITY OR ILLUSION?

The salvation of God is most certainly real as portrayed in the true gospel. The illusion of salvation as presented by the modern-day preachers and teachers is what is in question. From what is a sinner saved? What does the word of God say? *Behold, an angel of the Lord appeared to him in a dream saying, "Joseph, son of David, do not fear to take Mary as your wife, for that which is conceived in her is from the Holy Spirit. She will bear a Son and you shall call his name Jesus, for He will save his people from their sins."* Is there any ambiguity as to what Jesus came to earth to do?

But now, having been set free from sin and having become slaves of God, you have your fruit to holiness and the end everlasting life, for the wages of sin is death but the gift of God is eternal life in Christ Jesus, our Lord. . . . And you know that he was manifested to take away our sins and in Him there is no sin. Whoever abides in Him does not sin. The doctrine being presented by the religious professionals as the gospel is an illusion of salvation without the reality of it. In this delusion, sin has become the normal life experience of the person who has embraced the lies of those who do not love the truth.

Illusions will not save the one who entertains them, no matter how popular and widely accepted they are. It is not the many, but the few, who are actually chosen in Christ. The reality of what Jesus Christ has accomplished through his death, burial and resurrection is the creation of a new race of human beings that have been given the ability to walk as He walked and fulfill the righteous requirements of the law by following after His Spirit.

Yes, this is a miracle and a reality, not the illusion of the unbelievers and the faithless. Freedom from sin is in the reality of what God has done, not the illusion.

Therefore, if anyone is in Christ, he is a new creation, the old has passed away; behold, the new has come.

764 ADDING AND SUBTRACTING

What person can add something to the Lord's salvation? Or, what person can take away anything from the Lord's salvation? Who is the person that is entitled to a new name written on a white stone? And, what person is entitled to have his name preserved in the "Book of Life"?

Every word of God is pure; He is a shield to those who put their trust in Him. Do not add to His words lest He rebuke you and you be found a liar. . . . For I testify to everyone who hears the words of the prophecy of this book: If anyone adds to these things, God will add to him the plagues written in this book; and if anyone takes away from the words of the book of this prophecy, God shall take away his part from "The Book of Life", from the "Holy City", and from the things written in this book.

There are many who have considered themselves entitled to add their own biased commentary and interpretation of what God has said and many more who have subverted and taken away from His words. Any person who belongs to a denomination or religious cult has most likely participated in the heresy described by the prophets. The words and the salvation the Lord has given us are perfect and complete. Those who consider themselves entitled to add or subtract from either have entered a very dangerous place. It matters not how pious these religious leaders may appear. If they have violated the word and commandments of God, they have sealed their own destiny.

There is but one remedy and one hope of redemption for the person who has committed such a violation. It is a change of heart, true repentance, and genuine contrition. God's mercy endures forever, but man's opportunity to avail it lasts only as long as he is breathing air and his biological heart is beating. Do you believe Him?

765 DEFENSE

The righteous walk in defense mode at all times. The enemies of our souls are around every person on earth continually. Unless the Lord shields us, there is little defense against the forces of darkness that cover the earth. Awareness of our enemies is, in itself, a strong defense. The discernment of evil forces that are disguised as righteous is a gift to those who love the truth.

The Lord has given his saints weapons of defense as well as offense against the demonic forces and those who are controlled by them. Truth, righteousness, the knowledge of God, faith and the word of God, along with the fellowship of the Holy Spirit, are among the defenses supplied to those who love the Lord. These things may seem elementary, but implementation of them is the way to defeat our enemies.

Bloodthirsty men of the earth, flesh merchants, along with pious religious counterfeits are all around those who are being called by God. Deception and lust are their favorite devices of destruction. The unsuspecting and the careless are the ones who fall victim to these enemies.

You may have heard it said, "I am my own worst enemy,". This is true of the person who has not learned to take control over his flesh and its desires. This includes the mouth, the eyes, the ears and all the biological senses. Jesus has shown those who love Him how to defeat our enemies; and His Holy Spirit is showing us how to do it right now.

Our defense is of God. To abide in Christ is the summation of all the defensive tools we have been given. Abiding in Him is not a theoretical aspiration but the reality of victory.

He is *the Way, the Truth and the Life. No man comes to the Father but through Him.*

P.S. These things are actually common knowledge to many, but how many actually practice them?

766 IDLE SPEECH

Idle speech surrounds meaningless endeavors and worthless activity. SELAH! The proud speak endlessly about their opinions and their desires, of things that have no eternal value and only lead to more emptiness and frivolity. Are the saints of God really a part of all this foolishness and nonsense? The degradation of righteousness and spirituality is highlighted by all the idle speech and endless talking about nothing.

The vile become wealthy and the wicked become prosperous by talking about and exalting perverts and scoffing and slandering those who have integrity and walk uprightly. They have no fear of God, and He is in none of their thoughts. To talk of His wonderful works and His ways would be grievously offensive and banned from popular, mainstream discussion.

The truth regarding any subject is questioned and usually relegated to relativism and merely subjective. Those who speak truth and of true justice are discredited, slandered and cancelled from the public forum. We are truly living in the time where *evil is called good and good is called evil. . . . An unjust man is an abomination to the righteous and he who is upright in the way is an abomination to the wicked.* In order to abide in Christ, it is critical to discern where we stand in the controversy. *The wicked prowl on every side when vileness is exalted among the sons of men.*

The Spirit of the Lord is still calling out to all the inhabitants of the earth, but the day is coming when the time of the Gentiles will be fulfilled and the final judgment of God will come. The proud will be silenced, and the idle speech will no longer find a voice. Those who have rejected God and His truth will be put to shame and silenced, and the vanity will end.

Even so, come Lord Jesus!

767 THE GENERATION

There is a chosen generation that spans the record of time as a bridge over the history of nations and civilizations. This generation has produced kings, prophets and saints. It is the generation of the people of earth that have known and served their Creator. This generation has not ended and will not end until time itself has come to an end. Even then, it will continue on throughout eternity. It is the generation of the Last Adam, the younger Son who is the Man who descended from the heavenly realm to save His people from eternal separation from their Creator.

The mystery of the generation that precedes the appearance of God Himself coming to earth as a man is revealed to those He has called and chosen to be one with Him and reveal Himself through. They are a peculiar people who, though inhabiting the world, are not of it. They are the "New Creation" created miraculously in their Savior from heaven and have taken on His nature and walk in His ways. The world does not recognize this nation of spiritual beings, because it did not recognize the Creator when He appeared on earth Himself as a man.

There are many impostors among the people of earth who pretend to be the generation of Christ and sons of God, but they are counterfeit impostors of the Spiritual. These counterfeit followers of truth speak of spirituality, but, in reality, live their lives according to the flesh and are incapable of escaping the carnal, biological realm to which they were born. They are the descendants of the first Adam that chose to disobey God and follow the lies of the serpent.

Those of the first Adam's race who are called by the Spirit of God are given a choice pertaining to the way they will go and the nature of the one they will assimilate. The choice will determine each one's eternal destiny and the generation which they inhabit.

PSALM 24

768 SPIRITUAL DECEIT

Blessed is the man against whom the Lord counts no iniquity and in whose spirit there is no deceit. . . . By this you know the Spirit of God: Every spirit that confesses that Jesus Christ has come in the flesh is from God, and every spirit that does not confess Jesus is not from God. What is being spoken of is the spirit of man. The one whose spirit embodies deceit is not able to confess with his life the life of Jesus.

Only the one who has truly and experientially lost his own life for Jesus' sake is able to confess with his spirit that Jesus Christ has come in the flesh. A person's mouth may make the confession, but without the reality of the Spirit of Christ living in and through that person's life, the confession is a lie. The delusion that God has sent to those who have not received the love of the truth is the lie that the religious person believes will save them by confessing Jesus with their mouth, while the reality of his spirit does not bear witness.

The spirit of Antichrist is the religious spirit that attempts to deceive the hypocrite into believing he is right with God, because he makes a verbal confession, when the reality of Jesus living in and through that person does not exist. God surely knows the truth, and it is actually He who tests the spirits. What hope does the person living in delusion really have?

The time is here to examine and to know if we are walking in the truth, if we are conformed to the image of Jesus and have taken on the nature of God. If not, we remain mere descendants of the first Adam and bear his mark on our forehead and hand. SELAH! The mark of God is the image of Jesus, and every person bears the mark of the man of the earth or the Man from heaven.

The honest person who loves the truth knows the truth and has no deceit in his spirit.

769 ADULTERY

The Lord has spoken. Faithfulness is required of everyone who would be one with the Lord. The Lord speaks most often metaphorically to bring awareness of spiritual unfaithfulness and betrayal. The adulteress and the harlot are the people who have known the Lord but have turned to idols and the ways of the world rather than remaining faithful to the One with whom they have entered into covenant.

The Lord is totally faithful and continues to call those who have been deceived and have forsaken Him for their desire of carnal and temporary gratification. There is an end to God's striving with every individual who refuses to turn from his carnal indulgence. At the end of every person's life there comes a reckoning from which no one can escape. The mercy of God is everlasting, but the person (or a people) who continue in adultery to the end of their earthly existence will be separated from the One who has loved them and given Himself for them.

God does not make idle threats. His patience and long-suffering do have a limit which endures only as long as a person inhabits his biological flesh. Second chances only last while a person is breathing the air of the natural realm and taking nourishment from the earth.

The harlot and the immoral woman called Babylon are the ones who pretend to be the "Church" and the "Bride of Christ" but are, in reality the unfaithful, immoral harlot and her illegitimate offspring who have committed adultery and are fornicating with the princes and kings of the earth along with all their flesh merchants.

The faithful "Body of Christ" is a spiritual, chosen people the Lord calls saints. They are the virgins who serve Him faithfully and follow Him wherever He goes. They are the ones who obey Him and are waiting patiently for the return of their Savior. Everyone who has this hope knows who they are and has the assurance of eternal life.

Anyone who does not have the witness of the Holy Spirit in his spirit should certainly be seeking the truth of the Lord with all his heart.

Little children, keep yourselves from idols.

770 THE QUEEN OF HEAVEN

Who is the king in the kingdom of God and of heaven? Is His wife not the queen? In the harlot's house, we are told that the mother of Jesus is the queen of heaven. Is this not a lie perpetrated and dispersed from the chamber of death? There is but one queen of heaven and one "Bride of Christ" and one true Church. SELAH!

Who are you going to believe? There is but one truth. All other queens whose names are given among men are counterfeits and idols. To trust in them is to deny God's truth. The "Mother of Harlots" is the one who has claimed authority on earth, but she is not the "Bride of Christ", and she is not righteous. In fact, she is the chamber of death and the embodiment of the one who *rides the beast with seven heads and ten horns. . . In her was found the blood of prophets and saints and of all who were slain on the earth.*

Who can tell me these things are not so? The illegitimate offspring of this "Mother of Harlots" have covered the earth with their flesh merchants who deal in doctrines of death. The scarlet beast on which she rides is one whose mark is on the forehead and hand of everyone whose name is not written in the "Book of Life". She has made the inhabitants of the earth drunk with the wine of her fornication. The perverts and the vile of humanity congregate in her haunts of cruelty which trap her victims within the shadow of death.

The holy scriptures are full of warnings and exhortations to avoid the path to her house. If anyone has been lured into her snares and traps, he is being shown the way of escape by the exposure of her ways as you read these words.

Come out of her, my people lest you share in her sins and lest you receive of her plagues. . . . For she says in her heart, "I sit as a queen and am no widow and will not see sorrow." . . . Therefore, her plagues will come in one day—death and mourning and famine, and she will be utterly burned with fire for strong is the Lord God who judges her.

771 SPIRITUAL THINGS

Spiritual things must be Spiritually discerned. *But the natural (carnal) man does not receive the things of the Spirit of God . . . nor can he know them because they are spiritually discerned.* The Lord is speaking of the one who has been taught that he remains a sinner after being born of the Spirit. The one who remains in Romans, Chapter 7 rather than passing through the "*gate of righteousness*" into Chapter 8 remains in the flesh. *Who will deliver me from this body of death? I thank God—through Jesus Christ our Lord . . . There is therefore now no condemnation to those who are in Christ Jesus who do not walk according to the flesh but according to the Spirit. For what the law could not do, in that it was weak through the flesh, God did by sending His own Son in the likeness of sinful flesh on account of sin: He condemned sin in the flesh that the righteous requirement of the law might be fulfilled In us who do not walk according to the flesh but according to the Spirit . . . For if you live according to the flesh you will die, but if by the Spirit you put to death the deeds of the body (flesh) you will live.*

The flesh merchants of religion have told us that while we remain in our biological flesh, sin is inevitable. They lie. The person who has died in Christ to his flesh is no longer subject to it. He is a new creation in Christ. *Old things have passed away. All things have become new. . . . Whoever commits sin also commits lawlessness, and sin is lawlessness. And you know that He (Jesus) was manifested to take away our sins, and in Him there is no sin. Whoever abides in Him does not sin.*

The carnal, religious teachers and preachers have discounted and perverted the truth of the gospel, because they have chosen to trust their carnal understanding of Spiritual things rather than follow the "Spirit of Truth". Their ways lead to death and eternal separation from God.

This is no small error in judgment and spiritual discernment of the truth of the gospel. Consequently, they have received strong delusion from God and believed the lie.

772 IN THE EYES OF THE LORD

Who is blameless in the eyes of the Lord? How can a person please Him? These are certainly legitimate questions. *For not the hearers of the law are just in the sight of God but the doers of the law will be justified. . . . But be ye doers of the word and not hearers only deceiving yourselves . . . That the righteous requirement of the law might be fulfilled in us who do not walk according to the flesh but according to the Spirit.*

Without faith it is impossible to please God. Is faith exercised by the one who follows the instructions of an evangelist to invite Jesus into his heart only to walk away with the same heart as before? The demonstration of faith requires works. *Show me your faith without works and I will show you my faith by my works.* The person who stands blameless before the Lord is the one who obeys Him.

How deep into the totality of the words of the Lord are we willing to go to see what He has said about those who actually please Him and are righteous in His eyes? Some believe that the Father only sees us looking through Jesus. His word clearly says that He looks at and tests every heart individually. It is only the pure in heart that will know Him when He appears, because they will be like Him. *For the eyes of the Lord are on the righteous and His ears are open to their prayer. . . . But the Lord looks on the heart. . . . I was also blameless before Him, and I kept myself from my iniquity. Therefore, the Lord has recompensed me according to my righteousness according to my cleanliness in His eyes.*

At the final judgment, every person will be judged by the works recorded in the books. *So then, each of us will give an account of himself to God.* True righteousness is not theoretical or imaginary. It is actual and is demonstrated by works and deeds, and these are the things by which all mankind is judged.

The one who has lost his own life in Christ and has ceased his own works and his sins is the one who does the works of God and is blameless in His eyes. This is the one who bears the mark of God on his forehead and hand. The one who bears the mark of the beast is the one who serves his flesh. The marks are symbols of a person's thoughts and works.

773 WE ARE WHAT WE DO

You may have heard the saying: We are what we eat. This little saying has some validity in the physical realm, but in the spiritual realm, the reality of spiritual food a person consumes goes beyond anything in the natural and influences what we think, believe and ultimately what we do as inhabitants of earth.

There has been a long-standing controversy regarding the salvation of the human soul. Some say that it is exclusively that of grace, while others believe it is of works. The truth lies in the application of the grace God has endowed on each person He calls. In the final analysis, it is what a person has done with what he has been given that is the measure of who he really is. In other words, who a person is is what that person has done while walking the earth.

Jesus said, "*I always do the things that please My Father.*" . . . *And I only do the things I see My Father doing.* The apostle tells us: *Now by this we know that we know Him if we keep His commandments. He who says "I know Him," and does not keep His commandments is a liar and the truth is not in him. But whoever keeps His word truly the love of God is perfected in him. By this we know that we are in Him. He who says he abides in Him ought himself also to walk just as He walked. . . . Most assuredly I say to you, "He who believes in Me, the works that I do he will do also; and greater works than these he will do, because I go to My Father." . . . I have been crucified with Christ, it is no longer I who live but Christ lives in me, and the life which I now live in the flesh I live by faith in the Son of God who loved me and gave Himself for me.*

Faith without works is dead. Can you see the need for works to be done in order for grace to be established in your life? We will be judged by God for the works we have done. Only what has been done in obedience to Him will follow us to the hereafter. The one who has not lost his life for Jesus' sake does not even have the life or nature of God in him.

And they were judged, each one according to his works.

So the controversy over the salvation God has supplied really is a matter of what each person has done with the grace God has given. While there is no salvation apart from grace, there is neither salvation apart from what we do with what we are given. SELAH! The parable of the talents exemplifies the truth of how the Lord judges and rewards every person.

You are what you do, and what you do will determine not only who you are but with whom you will spend eternity.

774 INTENTIONS

Good intentions are not the same as good deeds, just as the knowledge of the truth is not the same as walking in it. The Lord does test the heart and the motives of man, but he nevertheless judges each person according to his works. The mind of man often substitutes his intentions in place of actually carrying them out. The heart of man is deceitful, and without the love of the truth, can easily be deluded into thinking that he can please the Lord with noble intentions.

While the Lord clearly condemns the man of wicked intentions and favors the one of good intentions, His blessing is on the one who fulfills the good. We are constantly presented with opportunities to carry out what we say that we believe, but it seems like most of the time many of us do not see them through. This is not meant to condemn anyone, but to encourage the reader who loves the Lord to do what is right and pleasing to Him. *A good man obtains favor from the Lord, but a man of wicked intentions, He will condemn.*

Intentions are linked to belief and faith. A person who claims to believe what God has said nearly always intends to obey His commands, but actual faith goes beyond good intentions and requires the reality of obeying them. The Lord, of course, knows the truth of every person's heart and will. *Behold, You desire truth in the inward parts . . . Lord, who may abide in Your tabernacle? Who may dwell in Your holy hill? He who walks uprightly and works righteousness and speaks the truth in his heart.*

The delusion of good intentions taking the place of actually putting them into practice is much like thoughts of grandeur entertained by a fool who has no reality of nobility in his life.

Intentions are only as valuable as the works they inspire.

775 MASS DELUSION

Mass delusion is a mark of a people who have lost their way and are no longer able to distinguish truth from lies. It is the judgment of God on nations and people that have ceased to know the difference between righteousness and wickedness. There have been many nations and cultures that have flourished and prospered only to be destroyed and forgotten. We are living in a time when this mass delusion has come upon the whole world, and there are only pockets of sound reasoning and soundness of mind left on earth.

We have come to the place where the darkness is overtaking the light that the Lord has endowed on every person who has been born on earth. *Righteousness exalts a nation but sin is a reproach to any people.* Even the people who call themselves Christians have succumbed to the delusion caused by loving lies more than truth. The time when a place of peace on earth may be found is vanishing, and the dark clouds of universal oppression of humanity are showing themselves.

The Bible has told us of such a time as this, but there remains a place of shelter and peace for the people who know their God and have put their trust in Him alone. Those who have found this place of rest are the ones who have lost their own lives in favor of the Lord's. The mark of His people can be identified by their love for one another in the midst of the hatred that is overtaking the whole world. *By this all will know that you are My (Jesus') disciples if you have love for one another. . . . Then they will deliver you up to tribulation and kill you and you will be hated by all nations for My name's sake, and then many will be offended, will betray one another and will hate one another. Then many false prophets will rise up and deceive many, and because lawlessness (sin) will abound the love of many will grow cold. But he who endures to the end will be saved.*

The time is very near. The mass delusion is here. SELAH!

776 THE EYES OF THE LORD

The eyes of the Lord are in every place keeping watch on the evil and the good. . . . The wicked in his proud countenance does not seek God . . . He has said in his heart, "God has forgotten; He hides His face, He will never see. . ." But You have seen for You observe trouble and grief to repay it by Your hand. The Lord sees everything, and it is also recorded that every person will receive the just reward for what he has done. The Lord is an impartial judge and cannot be bribed. We who trust Him know He will make every person give an account of what he has done while on earth.

Blessed is he whose transgression is forgiven whose sin is covered. Blessed is the man to whom the Lord does not count iniquity and in whose spirit there is no deceit. The one who has come to a knowledge of the truth yet believes he can continue to sin with impunity because of the grace God has shown him in forgiving past sin has been deceived and is dangerously near rejection. *For if we sin willfully after we have received the knowledge of the truth there no longer remains a sacrifice for sins but a certain fearful expectation of judgment and fiery indignation which will devour the adversaries.*

The person who believes that the Lord no longer sees his disobedience and willful rebellion has been deceived into the way that leads to death and eternal separation from the One who sees and knows all things. Jesus died once for the remission of past sins, and He requires holiness and purity from those who have been redeemed. The one who continues to sin is putting to shame the One who gave His life to save him from sin and death. *Of how much worse punishment, do you suppose, will he be thought worthy who has trampled the Son of God under foot, counted the blood of the covenant by which he was sanctified a common thing and insulted the Spirit of Grace?*

Do the eyes of the Almighty not see all these things or does He just overlook them?

777 THE CHOSEN ONE

There is One who was chosen before the foundation of the world. He is the One in whom all those who become chosen also are one with Him. He is the beginning and the end. In Him all things in heaven and on earth consist and are upheld. How great and awesome is this Chosen One who has all power and authority in heaven and on earth? There is only one God who is in all and by whom all things have been created. *He was in the beginning with God. All things were made through Him, and without Him nothing was made that was made. In Him was life and the life was the light of men . . . But as many as received Him, to them he gave the right to become children of God. To those who believe in his name: who were born not of blood nor of the will of the flesh nor of the will of man but of God.*

The journey of becoming children of God and on to becoming chosen in Christ and being conformed to His image and being brethren and joint heirs with Him goes beyond attending church services and listening to religious sermons. Those who become chosen in Christ and become One Spirit with Him have lost their own lives and allowed Jesus to live His life through them. We who have actually become chosen in the Chosen One have been crucified with Christ, and the life that we now live is His life living through our mortal bodies.

To actually be chosen is the choice an individual makes to allow Christ to have total control of his will and his life. There are few who actually do this. *Many are called but few are chosen.* What the religious professionals have told us is wrong, and there are in fact no carnal Christians in the kingdom of heaven. Only those who follow the Spirit of God are sons of God and chosen in the Chosen One. SELAH!

778 FOOTSTEPS

Yes, the Lord will give what is good; and our land will yield its increase; righteousness will go before Him and shall make His footsteps our pathway. The footsteps of the Lord are surely hidden from the world, and those who can see them are the righteous ones to whom they are revealed. The path that has been laid down for the righteous to follow is that of the Holy Spirit. *In the way of righteousness is life and in its pathway there is no death. . . . The path of the just is like the shining light that shines ever brighter unto the perfect day; the way of the wicked is like darkness; they do not know what makes them stumble.*

Trust in the Lord with all your heart and lean not on your own understanding; in all your ways acknowledge Him and He shall direct your paths. The path of the religious professionals and the way of tradition has departed from the footsteps the Lord has laid down for those who love Him to follow. Endless, meaningless prayers and petitions along with ritualistic religious traditions are not the ways of the Spirit. The living God has put forth footsteps and a path that leads past the carnal understanding of religion and into a living relationship with our Creator. The person who actually knows the Lord and walks with Him walks as He walked as a man in the footsteps of our heavenly Father.

These things may seem elementary, but how many who have been called by God actually are able to walk in them? *The kingdom of God is not eating and drinking but righteousness and peace and joy in the Holy Spirit.* The flesh is not in God's kingdom. Hence, the human body is not included in the fellowship with God that is going on there in spite of the fact that earthly beings are able to experience its reality through the Spirit. Our earthly bodies are indeed blessed by God when we are connected to Him in spirit, but flesh and blood cannot enter His kingdom nor will it.

Following the footsteps of the Lord is a spiritual journey to a spiritual land.

779 DEFINITIONS

The truth is ALWAYS true. The workers of iniquity often change the meaning and definitions of words in order to hide their sin, so that it appears acceptable. Without common acceptance and understanding of the definition of words, the truth can be lost. So it is with the homosexual and the sodomite who have succeeded in perverting and changing the meaning of the word gay. The bloodthirsty murderers of unborn babies have succeeded in calling them by other names and covered their wickedness by telling us that abortion is a woman's right to have control of her own body. Only a fool can believe that a baby is not a human being with a body of its own.

The list goes on. The theologians have taken sin and freedom from sin and turned those who have been born again and cleansed of all sin into sinners who cannot cease sinning. A sinner is, by definition, one who sins. How, then, can a person be set free from sin and continue in it? And how can a newborn baby be a sinner; having no knowledge of right and wrong and unable to make the choice to sin or not. SELAH!

The truth IS the truth, and those who love the truth know the truth when they hear it. It is only those who have not received the love of the truth that are sent the strong delusion from God and believed the lies. The perversion of the definition of words by pop culture, which has changed good to bad and righteousness to evil, is like the religious leaders who have called those who have received the righteousness of God perpetual sinners. To be delivered from the power of sin is to be free from it.

Those who have bought into all these lies are certainly not true disciples and followers of Jesus Christ and do not walk as He walked. Even the definition of Christian has been perverted and compromised to include anyone who uses the name as being Christ-like and a member of the "Body of Christ". This is pure foolishness and an abomination to the Lord.

Nevertheless, the solid foundation of God stands having this seal: The Lord knows those who are His, and let everyone who names the name of Christ depart from iniquity.

780 FOUNDATIONS

Truth is the foundation of the faith that gives life. *If the foundations are destroyed, what can the righteous do?* The princes of Ecclesia have presented to us a misrepresentation of truth that allows them to rule over whoever believes their lies. They have, in effect, made the truth powerless in the lives of those who believe them. They have built their own kingdoms on foundations of sand that are not sure and will not last into eternity.

The foundation of the Lord's throne is righteousness and justice. Everyone who is seated with Him in heavenly places must have partaken of that righteousness. There are certainly no sinners there. The truth that makes up the foundation of faith makes no provision for willful, ongoing sin in the life of anyone who aspires to walk with and dwell with the Lord.

The kingdoms of this world are kingdoms of the flesh and will not suddenly be transformed into a Spiritual kingdom at the coming of the Lord. Nor will those who are of the world suddenly be transformed into the image and likeness of Jesus Christ. *All the foundations of the earth are unstable* including its great religions and denominations.

We are being called to a heavenly land and a heavenly kingdom where only the righteous dwell. The walls of this holy city are constructed of pure and holy saints of God who have lost their own lives for His. Jesus Christ, who is the Truth, is the cornerstone of the foundation on which the whole kingdom rests. There are no building blocks in the heavenly Jerusalem that do not bear the image of Jesus. The delusion that unrepentant, carnal sinners are part of this kingdom is what the religious leaders of the world would have us believe.

Without holiness no one will see God. . . . That which is born of the flesh is flesh, and that which is born of the Spirit is spirit. . . . Flesh and blood cannot inherit the kingdom of God nor does the perishable inherit the imperishable. Those who are telling us that we will be raptured out of sinful bodies and sin are lying to us. If we are not part of the kingdom of God already when Jesus appears and bear His image, we will not be among those who are caught up to meet Him.

781 EVANGELISM

I remember well the moment that the Holy Spirit came into my heart and lifted the burden of guilt and sin from my soul and filled me with the love of Jesus. I could not wait to tell the nearest person what my Savior had done. Everything changed, and my life was set on a new course. This is the testimony of many who have truly been born of the Spirit.

In the following days, there were numerous voices of well-meaning people telling me to go here or there and to listen to this and that and to read this book or that instruction manual. Religious people can be very aggressive in trying to recruit a newly regenerated, blameless babe into their franchised brand of Christendom. I truly was pushed around, but the Holy Spirit gave me a love and a hunger for the Bible itself. He has been faithful to this day.

To see a newly reborn babe who has experienced the redemption of Jesus is a pure delight, but this watchman has seen many such newborns recruited into cults, denominations, and even totally false organizations. Those who yield to these "separatarian" groups usually lose their genuine enthusiasm for Christ and His gospel in exchange for denominational doctrines and dogma. Once they become thoroughly indoctrinated, they are sent out as professional missionaries to disseminate the form of oftentimes false doctrines they have learned. Is this not a tragedy?

Hear Me, says the Lord. My doctrine is pure, and the one who actually serves me must be able to discern between the true and the false. There can be no compromise. The true evangelist chosen and sent by Me must be able to see what I am doing and hear My voice and not the voice of an organized religion. The salvation for which I gave My life is salvation from sin and death and Oneness with Myself, not an institution of man. The evangelism of the Spirit adds members to My kingdom and not the kingdoms of mankind's organizations. Man's organizations and denominations are of the world and will likewise perish with the world.

If you can hear Me, says the Lord, then surely you know what you must do and the message you must carry to those who have gone astray.

This is the final hour. I am coming for a spotless Bride.

782 GATES OF BRONZE AND BARS OF IRON

The Lord has already broken the prison gates and cut the prison bars. Those who remain in the prison of fear and fret against the Lord because of their foolishness and their transgressions do so because of ignorance and a lack of knowledge. *My people perish because of a lack of knowledge. . . The foolishness of man twists his way and his heart frets against the Lord . . . Fools, because of their transgression and because of their iniquities are afflicted . . . Oh, that men would give thanks to the Lord for His goodness and for His wonderful works to the children of men! For He has broken the gates of bronze and cut the bars of iron in two. . . . And Jesus answered them, "Truly, truly I say to you: Every one who practices sin is a slave to sin" . . . So if the Son sets you free you will be free indeed. . . . But now having been set free from sin and having become slaves of God you have your fruit to holiness and the end everlasting life . . . And having been set free from sin you became slaves of righteousness.*

Those who the Lord has called who remain prisoners of fear and sin have not believed the truth of the gospel or are ignorant of the knowledge of God. *And you know that He was manifested to take away our sins and in Him there is no sin. Whoever abides in Him does not sin. Whoever sins has neither seen Him nor known Him.*

If a person actually believes what God has said and is willing to obey Him, there remains no reason to continue to live in the prison of fear and dread and fret.

There is no longer any justification for remaining ignorant about what the Lord has done or to believe those who are telling you that you are still a sinner.

Whom the Lord sets free is free indeed.

783 THE OTHER SIDE

There are many who can see the other side, but only a few who pass through the veil into the "holy place" where the Creator dwells. All whose bodies die here on earth do pass on to the other side where spirits dwell, but again, there are few who actually ascend to the throne of God and dwell in his heavenly kingdom. Those who are able to see and enter that kingdom while abiding in their mortal bodies are the ones who pass through the veil into the most "holy place" in their immortal bodies.

The Bible describes these few as chosen, saints, overcomers, faithful and joint heirs with Jesus. Active sinners are not named among this group. The upright and righteous, the just and the holy are the ones who dwell in the presence of the Lord on the other side. Those who have neglected the Lord's call and have defiled their garments and have disobeyed the Lord's commands will not see His face or receive the blessing of His right hand. *He has given us everything that pertains to life and godliness through the knowledge of Him who called us to His own glory and excellence by which He granted to us His precious and very great promises so that through them you may become partakers of the divine nature having escaped from the corruption that is in the world because of sinful desire.*

Anyone who cannot see the Lord's face while walking on the earth will not see Him when he passes to the other side. These are serious matters that deserve serious consideration. God will not compromise His truth for anyone who does not believe and obey him. Our God is merciful, but He does not make provision for anyone who continues to ignore the truth in favor of lies that make them feel good and allow them to continue their sinful ways.

The flesh merchants are willing to sacrifice the souls of their followers in order to build and maintain their own kingdoms and their own recognition and wealth. They and their followers will pass on to the other side with no guide.

784 WHOLEHEARTEDNESS

Nothing less than wholeheartedness may enter through the gates of righteousness. The windows of heaven are open to those who seek the Lord with all their heart, but any less cannot enter through the veil that separates the land where the Lord dwells and the land where the natural man dwells. There is no magical, carnal formula or procedure by which the person who lives according to his flesh can pass into the place where only the righteous live.

The Spirit of God shows us many portals through which a soul can pass into the Spiritual land, but a choice must be made to resist the self-gratification of the flesh and have a wholehearted willingness to follow after and obey the Spirit. When temptation to indulge the desire of the flesh and the carnal nature shows itself, we must avail ourselves of the escape from temptation the Holy Spirit provides. The choices are constant, and the victory over sin is the result of wholehearted obedience to the commands of God and the leading of His Spirit.

There are no double minded and halfhearted Christians who abide in Christ and are seated with Him in heavenly places. This revelation is no less than overwhelming and life changing. This is the reality of the "New Creation" and walking in newness of life. There can be no newness of life apart from the wholehearted commitment to seeking the Lord and His ways.

Wholeheartedness is not some religious endeavor to improve the natural man. It is an absolute change of existence and a total abandonment of self as the center of the universe. Jesus Christ has made it all possible and real for every person who believes what the Lord has said and is willing to obey Him. This is the faith that comes to the person who wholeheartedly seeks the truth.

785 THE WHOLE COUNSEL OF GOD

Whether or not the Lord will allow me to speak the whole counsel of God, I am not sure, but I am sure that those who have been educated and trained in the great theological institutions have not given us the whole counsel of God. They have both added to and taken away from God's counsel, and even worse, they have changed it to suit their own purpose. This is frightening and true and has made the truth difficult for the common believer to discern.

We can take solace in knowing that God does watch over His word, and He has given us "The Spirit of Truth" to guide us into all truth. Unless a person has received the love of the truth, there is little hope of receiving more than delusion and the lies of Ecclesia. *The carnal mind is enmity against God; for it is not subject to the law of God nor indeed can be. So then those who are in the flesh cannot please God.* Is there really any question as to whether the religious leaders of the churches that have formed the multitude of denominations and factions that the world recognizes as "the church" are operating in the carnal realm and dominated by the flesh?

Really, is it possible that these flesh merchants could be giving us the whole counsel of God? It is very unlikely that a person who is telling us that we remain sinners after the Lord has set us free from sin is sharing the whole counsel of God. The essence of the gospel is salvation from sin. It is sin that has estranged mankind from God. The only one who benefits from convincing those whom the Lord is calling to Himself that they cannot cease from sin is the one who wants to take the pasture of the Lord for himself.

The Spirit of Truth is clearly speaking the counsel of God that is not heard from the pulpits and platforms of sinners.

786 WORDS

The power of words should not be overlooked or underestimated. Truth and lies as well as life and death are contained in words. The person who speaks the words and the words which are used can carry immeasurable significance. While idle words do little more than pass time, words wisely crafted are able to shape the course of history.

When the Lord speaks, the words He uses are always true and pure and carry the weight and depth of eternity. His words have the power to create and to destroy. The person who does not regard the words the Lord has spoken is a fool with no wisdom or understanding. The words anyone speaks reveal that person's heart and who they really are. SELAH! The words you are reading right now are a wake-up call to choose your words carefully, both when you speak and when you listen. Yes, the words that a person listens to have the power to guide that one to heaven or hell.

Whatever words we put our trust in are the words that guide our journey on earth and the works we do while we are here. This is no small thing when one considers that every person will be judged by his works. God does not show partiality to anyone, though He does bless those who fear Him and obey His words. Those who follow the words of the enemies of the Lord and those who hate Him obviously will suffer His rejection.

We are in deep water here, and only words of truth can guide us to high ground and plant our feet on the rock. Those who reject words of truth have sealed their own destiny, and it is not pleasant.

Diligence is man's precious possession, and the one who shows diligence in choosing his words is the one who will attain the highest prize.

The Lord has spoken!

787 DEMOCRACY

While the kingdom of God is clearly a monarchy as is the Church of Jesus Christ, many, if not most, treat her as a democracy. In most of the so-called churches of the world today, the elected hierarchy of these institutions have taken on the role of a ruling magistrate or a president. In the true "Body of Christ" Jesus is *head over all things to the church which is His body, the fullness of Him who fills all in all . . . But to each one of us grace was given according to the measure of Christ's gift . . . And He Himself gave some to be apostles, some prophets, some evangelists and some pastors and teachers for the equipping of the saints for the work of the ministry for the edifying of the Body of Christ til we all come to the unity of the faith and of the knowledge of the Son of God to a perfect man to the measure of the stature of the fullness of Christ. SELAH!*

The idea that the Body of Christ is a democracy where the leaders are chosen because of carnal and fleshly attributes and gifts by popular consensus and the doctrinal solidarity with denominational beliefs and traditions is a grave error. Every faction of false Christianity is the result of leaving the true understanding and principles laid down and given to us by the Holy Spirit. *Now you are the Body of Christ and members individually. And God has appointed these in the Church: first apostles, second prophets, third teachers; after that, miracles, then gifts of healing, helps, administrations, varieties of tongues.* Are these people elected through democratic process?

The true Church is not of the world and does not conduct herself as part of the world.

If you desire to be part of a social club that makes mention of God and Jesus, then one of the multitude of democratic denominations may be right for you. But if you desire to be part of the "Body of Christ" with all your heart, diligently seek the face of God and obey His voice.

788 CAUSE AND EFFECT

What we see happening universally throughout the world today is not a mystery for those who understand the principle of cause and effect. The effect of sin has never changed, just as the cause of the curse that has come upon the whole natural creation is the direct result of disobedience and rebellion against our Creator. So is the pain, death, suffering, and hopelessness that the world is experiencing. This fact is true for individuals as well as nations, cultures, and all of humanity. All of creation has been made subject to the death brought on by the willful disregard of man for his Creator.

God has established laws in the natural realm and has made them known to man intuitively. When these laws are violated, there is a consequence to be paid by every perpetrator, whether they are aware of it or not. Sometimes the effects are not realized for generations, but the Creator forgets nothing.

Cause and effect can be associated with sowing and reaping. Whatever a man sows that he will also reap. . . . He who sows to the flesh will of the flesh reap corruption. Hear Me, says the Lord, As righteousness leads to life, so he who pursues evil pursues it to his own death. Our Creator came to earth as a man to save the world from sin, not only the consequence and effect of sin but from sin altogether.

Who are these teachers telling us who Jesus has freed from sin that we are still sinners? Who do they represent? Surely, not the Creator who came to earth as a man and gave His life to free His people from their sin and the curse that was placed upon creation. For we know that the whole creation groans and labors with birth pangs together until now. Not only that, but we also who have the firstfruits of the Spirit even we ourselves groan within ourselves eagerly waiting for the adoption, the redemption of our body. When Jesus appears again the second time, it will be our mortal bodies that will be changed, not our souls that have already been saved from sin.

The sting of death is sin, and the strength of sin is the law, but thanks be to God who gives us the victory through our Lord, Jesus Christ. Therefore, my beloved brethren, be steadfast, immovable, always abounding in the work of the Lord, knowing that your labor is not in vain in the Lord.

The victory that we have is the victory over sin, the flesh, and the world. Jesus did not come to save His people in their sin but from their sin!

789 RADICALISM

Is the Lord radical? Have you read the account of Nebuchadnezzar whom the Lord raised up and sent to Jerusalem and the devastation that the king of Babylon brought on the city that God had once said is the place where the name of the Lord dwelt and was honored. If what the Almighty wrought there was not radical, what is? Certainly, we have not yet seen how radical the Lord is or can be. His judgments prophesied in Revelation go beyond anything the world has ever seen since the curse that He put on the whole creation because of Adam and Eve's disobedience in Eden.

We are nearing the consummation of the prophesies that have been made throughout scripture. They are, indeed, radical and are coming soon to pass. There are but two groups of people who live on earth, one is redeemed and the other is lost. The first is a people who have been saved out of the world and are, even now, seated with Christ in heavenly places. The second is a people who dwell on earth and are subject to all that has been prophesied to come upon the earth. All have been given a choice as to whom they will serve and obey, just as the Jews in the days of Nebuchadnezzar.

In the final analysis of humanity and the world in which we live, there can be no excuse for rebellion against the loving and merciful Creator who would have all men come to repentance and a knowledge of the truth. The radicalism demonstrated by the Lord is to bring about His view of sin and the seriousness of it. Those who consider sin as sport and take a lackadaisical attitude toward sin will be among those on whom all the plagues coming upon the earth will fall.

It is pointless to argue or make excuses for those who are unwilling or unable to cease from sin and disobedience to the voice of God.

This is a plea to those who have been deceived by those who are serving their own bellies and peddling the gospel for selfish reasons. It is time to flee for your lives from Babylon and the coming judgment of a radical God.

790 MIND CONTROL

Mind control is a tactic and a discipline used by people and spirits who desire to control others. This tactic is employed by a host of power-seeking and domineering personalities that find their satisfaction in the dominance and the ability to convince their victims to submit to them.

Mind control has been used throughout history by a list of perpetrators that is far too extensive to name or recognize. Politicians, kings, religious leaders, media personalities, celebrities, businessmen, military leaders and innumerable, common people who want to have power over others. Educators are also prominent on the list along with scientists.

There is a worldwide effort as these words are written that is working to enslave not only nations but the entire population of the world. It is truly a conspiracy that has nearly succeeded. The Bible makes reference to "MYSTERY BABYLON THE GREAT, THE MOTHER OF HARLOTS AND OF THE ABOMINATIONS OF THE EARTH". She is the harlot who sits on many waters with whom the kings of the earth committed fornication, and the inhabitants of the earth were made drunk with the wine of her fornication.

The controllers who are attempting to create a one-world government in order to enslave the inhabitants of earth have conspired with Babylon to carry out their wicked plot. They are the enemies of God, and though they may have some measured success, they will all be destroyed in the end.

The true Church of Jesus Christ is the force that stands against this conspiracy and is not subject to their mind control. *God has not given us (His people) a spirit of fear but of power, love and a sound mind.* Our God is mightier and more powerful than all the forces of hell arrayed against us, and *there can be no counsel against Him that can succeed.* Those who have received the love of the truth cannot be overcome by any of the forces of darkness that try to control their minds.

The end of the story is already written, and those who love the Lord and are faithful and steadfast to the end will appear with Him when He comes and defeats all the mind controllers who would rule the world.

791 THE BEAST FROM THE SEA

I saw a beast rising up out of the sea . . . the dragon gave him his power, his throne and great authority . . . and all the world marveled and followed the beast. So they worshiped the dragon who gave authority to the beast; and they worshiped the beast saying, "Who is like the beast? Who is able to make war with him? . . . Then he opened his mouth in blasphemy against God to blaspheme His name, his tabernacle and those who dwell in heaven. It was granted to him to make war with the saints and to overcome them. And authority was given him over every tribe, tongue and nation; all who dwell on the earth will worship him whose names have not been written in the "Book of Life" of the Lamb slain from the foundation of the world. SELAH! . . . If anyone has an ear to hear, let him hear; he who leads into captivity will go into captivity; he who kills with the sword must be killed with the sword. Here is the patience and the faith of the saints.

Where do you dwell? Can you see the beast? He has appeared, and his assault on righteousness and truth and those who love God is underway. The mystery of ungodliness is being revealed to those who are seated with Christ. The flesh merchants, false prophets and prognosticators are still selling books and making movies that depict the saints of God escaping the great tribulation and being raptured out of their sinful flesh and their sin. It will not happen that way, brethren.

The number of the beast is that of a man, and his mark is on the soul of every person who lives according to the flesh and follows the man of earth who is himself a beast of the earth. Only those who live according to the Spirit and follow the Lamb are the children, sons and daughters, of God.

Jesus Christ died as a man to put away sin in the flesh, even though He had not sinned. He died for the sins of all who trust and believe Him. Those who abide in the risen Savior no longer sin against Him, because they died with Him and have risen with Him to newness of life and are now seated with Him in heavenly places. Those who live according to their carnal flesh are following the beast and the false prophet and are receiving his mark as they walk according to the lust of their flesh, the lust of their eyes and their pride.

The truth being shared here is not really complicated for the person who has Spiritual discernment and loves the truth. We are being called to a higher realm of existence where only the righteous dwell.

792 RULES

Have you heard the rules laid down by the flesh merchants trying to achieve holiness by following after rules to try and subdue the flesh? Well, they are the ones who remain sinners. Their brand of Christianity does not promote the freedom that following the footsteps of Jesus and the leading of the Holy Spirit produce. Rules only conform a person to the image of those who make them. The sin that is produced by those who live according to the flesh can only be suppressed without the true freedom from sin that the gospel promises. The rule makers of modern Christianity are really no different than the Jewish religious leaders of Jesus' time who crucified Him.

Unless a person dies to his flesh experientially and learns to live according to the Spirit, there is no hope of overcoming sin and the carnal nature. A person can only overcome sin by dying to it and putting on Christ. *How can we who died to sin still live in it? Do you not know that all of us who have been baptized into Christ Jesus were baptized into His death? We were buried therefore with Him by baptism into death in order that just as Christ was raised from the dead by the glory of the Father, we too might walk in newness of life.*

Those who are governed by rules are still walking according to the flesh and remain in bondage to it. *If you live according to the flesh you will die, but if by the Spirit you put to death the deeds of the body, you will live. For as many as are led by the Spirit of God are sons of God . . . I have been crucified with Christ. It is no longer I who live but Christ who lives in me. And the life I now live in the flesh, I live by faith in the Son of God who gave Himself for me.*

It is by faith we please God, not by following rules. It is by faith we overcome the sin that rules have no power over.

The so-called holiness churches that believe their rules can make them holy have misinterpreted the gospel.

793 HIGHER

How far into heaven can we go without leaving our mortal bodies behind? We know Paul was caught up to the third heaven, but he was not sure if he was still in his body or had left it behind. Pain has surely been left behind, and the body has lost its relevance. When we are conscious of being seated with Christ in heavenly places, what level of heaven are we in? When looking at the things of earth from this heavenly place, they look much different. Are these things not scriptural?

There is a way to experience the reality of the things the Lord has said that a believer can experience while still walking the earth. These are things that draw us closer to our Savior and allow us to see the things that can only be revealed by the Spirit of God. We are all being called to this place where the Lord dwells. There is no sin in this place. The flesh does not have preeminence in the life that is lost in Christ. The mind that is set on things above is not caught up with things of the world.

The journey we are on here on earth is just a test and preparation for what God created us to be. He designed us to have continual fellowship and oneness with Himself. God is a Spirit, and He dwells in a Spiritual land. If we can believe what He has told us, our lives here on earth are to prove if we will obey Him and walk in His ways. How are we doing? If not so good, it is time for the change that will allow us to be conformed to the image of Jesus Christ and thus bear the mark of God.

If the life of the flesh is the primary form of life we experience, we will bear only the mark of the man formed from dust.

We have been given the choice to follow and live according to the flesh and the carnal mind or to follow and live according to the Spirit.

Eternal life is in the Spirit!

794 TOMORROW

There is a promise of tomorrow, but not for the inhabitants of earth. Today is the day the Lord has given us, and no man knows what tomorrow may bring. What kind of people ought we to be in light of the temporary nature of our being. Tomorrow only comes until time ends. When a man takes his last breath, time ceases, and he must face eternity. Why does a person worry about tomorrow or of any of the things that can be imagined? Though we may plan for the future, none of us have a guarantee of being on earth to see it. *Do not boast about tomorrow for you do not know what a day may bring.*

The fear of man brings a snare and fear of the future causes torment. Those who have learned to trust the Lord do have hope, and the end of time for them is a promotion. *Let what you heard from the beginning abide in you. If what you heard from the beginning abides in you, then you too will abide in the Son and in the Father. And this is the promise that He made to us—eternal life.* Faith and obedience to the voice of God is the root of the security of tomorrow that only we who believe Him have. Tomorrow will come whether we are ready for it or not. We can be ready. Jesus has told us to be ready. To have a pure heart and the assurance that we stand blameless in the sight of God is how we remain ready.

When Jesus appears, whether for an individual or for His whole Church, the formula is the same. Those who are ready will go with Him, and those who are not ready will be lost.

The Lord is not slow to fulfill His promise as some count slowness but is patient toward you not wishing that any should perish but that all should reach repentance. But the day of the Lord will come as a thief and then the heavens will pass away with a roar and the heavenly bodies will be burned up and dissolved, and the earth and the works that are done on it will be exposed. Since all these things are thus to be dissolved, what sort of people ought you to be in holy conduct and Godliness looking for and hastening the coming of the day of God because of which the heavens will be dissolved being on fire, and the elements will melt with fervent heat? Nevertheless, we according to His promise look for a new heaven and a new earth in which righteousness dwells. Therefore, beloved, looking forward to these things, be diligent to be found by Him in peace without spot and blameless; and consider that the long suffering of our Lord is salvation.

How significant is tomorrow? *Today is the day of salvation. SELAH!*

795 THE FUTURE

The devil will have his day, and the destroyer will overtake the world. The prophets of God have told us of such a day before the second coming of Messiah. Those who are promising a better day and prosperity for all are liars and deceivers. Murder and mayhem are predicted for those who dwell on earth in Satan's day. Personal freedom, independence, liberty and privacy will be lost. It is happening as these words are written.

Those who do not know and trust the Lord will have no place to turn for refuge. The futility of religion will be exposed, and the empty promises of its leaders and promoters will be seen for what they have always been. The spirits of defilement will roam the earth unchecked, and demons will control the lives of those who are not protected by the angels of God. If what you are hearing sounds too negative and pessimistic, you must not have read what Jesus and the prophets of God have told us. There is no hope for the world that now exists, nor is there hope for those who remain of it. A change is possible for any person who can believe the truth and repent of their own ways that have left their Creator a stranger and an anomaly to them. A living and real relationship with the Lord is the only way to escape the hopelessness and darkness coming upon the earth. If you reject this message because you refuse to yield to fear, I counsel you to yield for the sake of love of the truth. The truth can save your soul, but lies will cost you everything.

When the final trumpet sounds, truth and righteousness will be what is left standing. All the enemies of God will be consumed by the breath of His mouth and the brightness of His coming. Amen!

796 IN THE WORLD

I (Jesus) have said these things to you that in Me you may have peace. In the world you will have tribulation. But take heart, I have overcome the world. It is evident that overcomers are the ones who abide in Christ, not only the world but also sin. *No one who abides in Him keeps on sinning.* These statements of the Holy Spirit are not complicated or ambiguous. *For everyone who has been born of God overcomes the world.* We are talking about those to whom the promise of eternal life applies. *He who overcomes shall inherit all things and I will be his God and he shall be My son.* What can we say to these things? Can we remain sinners and still avail ourselves of the promises of the Lord?

The promises Jesus has made to the churches in Revelation, Chapters 2 and 3, are all made to the overcomers and conquerors. The question being raised is about whether we are merely sojourners passing through the world or are we part of it? Jesus told his disciples: *I have chosen you out of the world.* Through John He says: *Love not the world or the things in it. If anyone loves the world the love of the Father is not in him. For all that is in the world—the lust of the flesh, the lust of the eyes, and the pride of life—is not of the Father but is of the world. And the world is passing away and the lust of it; but he who does the will of God abides forever.*

This whole issue which is argued by theologians and scholars is foolishness that anyone who actually loves the truth is able to understand and accept. There is no place for worldliness or sin in the life of the person who abides in Jesus Christ and walks in the Spirit.

The case is made, and the truth is told. The world is not our home; we are only passing through.

797 SPIRITUAL INSIGHT

Spiritual insight is a gift from the God of heaven. A person with this form of insight understands the ways of the Lord and has the knowledge of God. Righteousness is not a mystery for the one who has insight into the mind of the Lord. Spiritual insight is the incorporation of wisdom, knowledge, understanding and discernment. Insight into the purpose of creation and the nature of man allows one to navigate the world without being caught up in it.

A person may have insight into the biological makeup of God's creation and yet be void of the Spiritual dimension from which it originated. The insight that produces common sense and the ability to successfully walk the earth peacefully without being caught up in the snares of the wicked is the result of the insight given by our Creator to those who fear Him.

Insight that transcends the natural human intelligence is the source of life and peace that a person of faith is able to see with spiritual eyes that only those who hear the voice of God and believe Him are endowed with. The ability of a person to enter into a relationship with his Creator is the real gift that allows him to become a child and a son of God. This insight is not based on natural giftedness, but supernatural.

Spiritual insight is available to the one who will choose it over the instruction of the world and the carnal instruction of the religious clergy.

What you are hearing is the insight given to a common man gifted by his Creator with the anointing to make known to his brethren the ways of God.

798 THE LORD'S FLOCK

The Lord had Ezekiel write down His view of the shepherds (pastors) that holds true to this very day and is up to the minute. Chapter 34 of Ezekiel is an enlightening read. Who are the shepherds being addressed by the Lord? Who are the sheep of His pasture and who are the goats? Surely the Lord knows these things and desires those who love Him and love the truth to know them as well.

All the preaching and all the teaching being put forth as the gospel today is the same as it was in the days of Ezekiel. The message has been refined and the deceivers have grown worse and worse, but the truth has never changed nor have the hearts of the eternal generation whose hearts are blameless in the sight of God.

Jesus Christ's great sacrifice has made a way and opened a door for all mankind, Jew and Gentile, to be redeemed, renewed and set free from sin and death. The leaders, shepherds and pastors of our day are proclaiming peace and safety to a people who flatter God with their lips while their hearts are not faithful to Him, and the law of God does not reside in their hearts. To them, the love of the truth is but an empty slogan uttered by deceitful tongues.

The clergy has grown fat, while the flock of the Lord are starving for the truth. The goats have mingled with the sheep, and the shepherds love to have it so, that their herds may be large and their wealth will be great. The wheat and the tares grow together in the great denominational, sectarian houses of religion, while the true flock of the Lord are scattered and left to fend for themselves. The Lord is aware and is, even now, making the separation and gathering those who really love Him to Himself.

If you can hear His voice, you know what is being said is true, and it is each individual's responsibility to respond to the voice of the Holy Spirit.

799 THE SELLING OF ONE'S SOUL

What does it profit a man if he gains the whole world yet loses his soul? This question is more than rhetorical and deeper than the sea. The person with insight has seen countless celebrities, musicians, politicians, businessmen, religious leaders, educators, scientists and common folk sell their souls in order to gain the prosperity of the world. To compromise truth, integrity, justice, righteousness along with the love of thy neighbor are some of the things a person can exchange for his soul. An honest evaluation of one's own heart will reveal the condition of one's own soul.

What is being spoken of here is the value each individual person places on his own soul and where he will spend eternity. Yes, it is that serious. Believing a lie may seem like a small thing, but it becomes much larger when one considers that it could cost the loss of his soul. A person may very well sell his soul for a lie that causes him to feel good in his flesh. The truth is sometimes difficult to accept but is certainly better than the loss of one's soul. Just how far can we carry this line of thought? Jesus has told us: *Truly, truly I say to you, unless a grain of wheat falls into the earth and dies it remains alone; but if it dies, it bears much fruit. Whoever loves his life loses it, and whoever hates his life in this world will keep it for eternal life. If anyone serves Me, he will follow me; and where I am there will my servant be also.* The point being, the salvation and preservation of our souls depend on the choices we make with regard to compromising with the world or serving God. SELAH!

800 PORTALS

There are many portals through which a soul may pass into the Spiritual dimension. There is danger lurking on the spiritual side of most of them, and there are some through which a soul may not be able to return. Through some of these portals, there are phantoms of defilement lurking to capture unsuspecting victims.

There is a carefully guarded portal where those who hunger and thirst for righteousness and truth are guided. It is the portal through which those who are allowed to pass see the face of the righteous Creator, and if obedient to Him, may abide. Where else would a righteous soul desire to go? This is the Spiritual land where those who love the Lord are able to fellowship with Him without interruption.

Those who are lured through one of the many unguarded portals that lead to death are bribed and drawn through them by lust and greed and pride, none of which are allowed where the Creator dwells. There are few who actually love truth and righteousness and are willing to sacrifice their lives in order to obtain it. These are the ones who pass through the portal and the veil into the most holy place and the kingdom of God.

Certainly, the Spirit of God is calling out to all the inhabitants of earth to join Him in the kingdom where righteousness dwells, but it is amazing how few actually respond. Most of mankind really don't want to enter the spiritual realm at all and choose to make the earth and the world their permanent home. Unfortunately, this natural realm is passing away along with those who have chosen to remain citizens of it.

While many choose to pass into the realm where spirits do dwell, there are few who choose the portal into and through the gates of righteousness where there are no sinners.

801 QUESTIONS

There are questions that every person should answer for himself. These questions deserve thought and introspection. Who am I? How do I know? There are many who satisfy themselves with answers given to them by other people, but every person must know in his heart the things that only God can answer. The Lord has recorded many things for us, but most of them have qualifications and require certain participation by an individual to apply to oneself.

Am I a child, a son, a saint? Am I called, chosen, or saved? There are multitudes who will offer answers to the questions, but can they be trusted to speak for the One who holds eternity and our very souls in His hand? Am I a sinner? If so, why? Is it possible to be a holy sinner? Do I really have two natures? Or, must I choose one or the other? God Himself has the answers, and every individual must have a direct, personal relationship with his Creator in order to have the questions answered and settled.

We have entered deep waters here, and there is only One who is able to save us. The questions must be answered with the certainty of truth, and no man can be trusted. Those who have trusted professional clergy that have a biased and vested interest in the souls they wish to control are not trustworthy or honest. The person who embraces their lies will not know the true answers to the questions that have been asked.

Hear Me, says the Lord. The one who hungers and thirsts for righteousness and truth and speaks the truth in his own heart is the one who will hear from Me.

802 FULFILLMENT

Fulfillment of life designed by our Creator depends on our response to the light that is given to every person born into the world. The fulfillment one experiences is not the exclusive result of the gift or ability a person may have, but living up to and making the most of what has been given. Fulfillment comes from knowing that we have done the best we can with what we have been given.

God is not willing that anyone should perish. We know that many do perish and that most people never even find the will of God for their lives. The call of God has gone out, and it can be heard throughout the earth. Nevertheless, those who respond to it are far fewer than those who don't. Those who do respond to Him are given more light. *In God's light we see light; if we walk in the light as He is in the light, we have fellowship with one another and the blood of Jesus cleanses us from all sin.*

In this fellowship is where our lives are fulfilled and purposeful. This is where peace and rest and fulfillment are found. This is where assurance of salvation and freedom from the grasp of the world can be realized, knowing the love of God overcomes all the fear that would rob us of the fulfilling lives that the Lord has meant for us to have.

If fulfillment seems out of reach, perhaps it is because we have not believed the voice of God or obeyed Him. The person of faith is the one who is able to find his place of fulfillment even in the chaos that surrounds us and tries to rob us of the fulfillment God has planned for us to have.

The choice is ours. The Lord is for us.

803 ORDER

The one who offers thanksgiving as his sacrifice glorifies Me. The one who orders his way rightly I will show the salvation of God. . . . Consequently, He (Jesus) is able to save to the uttermost those who draw near to God through Him since He always lives to make intercession for them. Is the salvation of God really complete and attainable for the person God shows it to? Or are we left here on earth as sinners who are not yet saved to the uttermost?

The modern congregations that are misnamed as churches have violated the order of the true Church the Lord established on earth to represent Him. How is it that pastors are as CEO's of corporations, and women have authority over men and are not only teachers but have assumed the role of the pastor and even the apostle?

What then, brethren? When you come together each one has a hymn, a lesson, a revelation, a tongue or an interpretation. Let all things be done for building up . . . For God is not a God of confusion, but of peace, as in all the churches of the saints the women should keep silent in the churches for they are not permitted to speak but should be in submission as the law also says . . . For it is shameful for a woman to speak in church or was it from you that the word of God came? Or, are you the only one it has reached? If anyone thinks that he is a prophet or spiritual, he should acknowledge that these things I am writing to you are a command of the Lord . . . But all things should be done decently and in order.

I do not permit a woman to teach or have authority over a man; but to remain quiet. For Adam was formed first, then Eve; and Adam was not deceived but the woman was deceived and became a transgressor.

The order of conduct in the Body of Christ has not changed because the people and the women of the world have been liberated. The commands of God, and His established order remain for us who believe Him.

Commit your works to the Lord, and your thoughts will be established.

804 MARRIAGE

The Lord is speaking of marriage. *He who is joined to the Lord is one Spirit with Him.* The essence of marriage is oneness of being. The foundation of marriage is steadfast love, faithfulness and trust. The marriage of man and woman is a type and a symbol of the Spiritual union of the spiritual man and his Creator.

Marriage of a man and woman was initiated by God. It is the basis of procreation for which the human race is constituted. The person who lives according to the Spirit is able to understand these things and is also given the ability to live according to the Creator's plan for His chosen people. The Lord Himself is the husband of the true Israel of God and the eternal generation of which the true Body of Christ is the wife.

The person who does not believe or understand these things is the one who cannot fulfill the purpose for which he was created, nor is he able to fulfill the will of God. The church that believes that they can continue to walk as sinners on the earth are the adulterers and adulteresses that actually inhabit Babylon. She is the one that is recognized by the world as the church, but is not the true Body of Christ or the chosen people of God or the spiritual offspring of Israel.

Can you hear Me, says the Lord? You are hearing the truth regarding righteousness and the purpose of your existence. Marriage was and is the basis of ongoing life and the meaning of all the created things that exist in the natural realm. Surely, all nature is giving testimony to this truth.

What God has joined together, let no man put asunder. . . . For the Lord God of Israel says He hates divorce.

Does the God of all creation have any purpose or pleasure in the union of same-sex couples? What do you think? Civil marriage is man's invention to begin with and was only meant to reinforce what God does.

The one who would fulfill God's will in marriage will certainly obey Him! The prophet, Malachi, has certainly expounded on this subject.

805 REALITY CHECK

Does the Lord no longer rule over the nations? And does He no longer give to the people the leaders and rulers they deserve? Are the doors of the churches really synonymous with the gates of the kingdom of God? The educated fools who fill the pulpits and the airwaves with their pious absurdities do not seem to realize that the judgment of God has come upon the world—including the USA.

Who are the people who actually understand the ways of the Lord? They don't seem to be the ones who are making all the noise and proclaiming revival in the congregations of their followers whom they deem sinners. Jesus most certainly came to save sinners from their sin, but sinners are not included among the true saints of God who have forsaken and been set free from sin.

It is a truly amazing thing that these sinners are not able to see that the corruption and degradation that has come upon people from all tribes and nations that have forsaken truth and righteousness in favor of lies and wickedness has not come from the hand of God. Really, where can the righteous be found on the earth? When the foundations have been destroyed and truth has been compromised and perverted by religious and political leaders, where can those who really love truth and righteousness turn but to the Lord Himself? This is what is taking place around the world today.

The Lord is turning the hearts of those who love Him to Himself and away from those who claim to represent Him but do not know His ways or the salvation He has provided to those who have received a love of the truth.

806 HANDS

And let the beauty of the Lord, our God, be upon us and establish the work of our hands for us; yes, establish the work of our hands. The majority of the earth's inhabitants do not know their right hand from their left and have given their minds and their hands to vanity. Even among those who claim to know the Lord, there seem to be few who understand that God judges every person according to the work of his hands.

The beasts of the earth that live according to the domination of their flesh and do the work of its nature have not known the ways of God or followed after His Spirit as Jesus has shown us. This is the mark of the beast of the earth whose works demonstrate his true nature and who he serves. This mark has been here since Adam (the first) chose to follow after his flesh and disobey the command of God. He died as a result, just as those who choose to live according to the flesh die to this very day.

Many of us are watching and waiting for the Lord to come and judge the earth and are not aware that He is doing it right now. Can we not see that what is taking place in the world and even in our nation today is God's judgment on a people who have forsaken His ways and His commandments? This is not delusion on the part of this writer but the actual revelation of the truth. We are in the last days, and the Lord's second coming is near.

Those who claim to know the Lord yet continue to be sinners are proving that they do not have the true knowledge of God and are bringing shame on his name and upon themselves.

Who is it that will mount defense of those whom the Lord has called, yet continue to follow after the nature of the first Adam that chose to live according to his flesh?

Who may ascend into the hill of the Lord? He who has clean hands and a pure heart who has not lifted his soul to an idol nor sworn deceitfully. He shall receive blessing from the Lord and righteousness from the God of his salvation. This is Jacob (Israel) the generation (eternal) of those who seek Him, who seek Your face.

807 BLESSED

Blessedness is a state of being in which the person who has become chosen in Christ may abide continually. *Blessed are those who keep justice and he who does righteousness at all times!* This person is no longer a sinner and has found eternal life in the Savior who is blessed forever. This is not a platitude or religious jargon but the reality of one who has been joined to the Lord. This is what true salvation consists of and what the normal Christian experience is intended to be.

The Lord has told us *"And to him who orders his conduct aright, I will show the salvation of God."* This blessing is not a once for all event but a continual progressive occurrence that has no end while we walk this earth. Freedom from sin is not something that is experienced only at the point of regeneration but is the reality of the ongoing life that has been lost in Christ and has become one Spirit with Him. This is the blessing that enables the true believer to walk as Jesus walked and do the things that He did.

If we are not Christ-like now, how will we be like Him when He appears at His second coming? The person who knows the Lord in the present moment is the one who is ready to meet Him when He comes for His bride. Is this not what the gospel really teaches us? The true "Body of Christ" is not made up of church-goers and members of religious institutions but of those who know and love the Lord and walk in His ways and keep His commandments.

What you are hearing is the way of blessing and eternal life. *Remember me, O Lord, with the favor you You have toward your people. O visit me with Your salvation that I may see the benefit of Your chosen ones, that I may rejoice in the gladness of Your nation, that I may glory with Your inheritance.*

808 HE WHO RULES HIS SPIRIT

The will of the person subjected to the Spirit of God is able to rule his own spirit through the power of God and subsequently control his flesh. What? *He who is slow to anger is better than the mighty, and he who rules his spirit than he who takes a city.* How does this morsel of truth line up with the doctrine of the ongoing sin of one who has been born of the Spirit of God?

The preparations a person can make in an attempt to preserve the fleshly body seem to be unlimited, but what of the Spirit that gives the body life? What is the Creator's purpose for mankind on earth? To love God with all our heart, soul, mind and strength requires that our spirit rules over all the aspects of our humanity. This seems obvious, but how is it that the religious rulers and teachers tell us that our flesh remains dominant? Was the Man, Jesus, dominated by his flesh?

The flesh lusts against the Spirit, and the Spirit against the flesh. Do not be deceived: God is not mocked, for the one who sows to his own flesh will from the flesh reap corruption (death), but the one who sows to the Spirit will, from the Spirit, reap eternal life. For if you live according to the flesh, you will die, but if by the Spirit you put to death the deeds of the body, you will live.

The professionals have lied to us, whether knowingly or unknowingly, in order to advance their own kingdoms and their own influence and control.

The Lord is calling those who love the truth to disassociate from those who cannot cease from sin and those who love the ways of the flesh more than the ways of the Spirit. In the end, each one of us will be judged according to what we have done in our bodies, not by our intentions.

The one who rules over his own spirit will certainly have control over his fleshly body.

809 ENTANGLEMENT

Passion for the ways of God delight His soul. But, entanglement in the affairs of the world and the cares of this life cloud the ways of God and cause our hearts to become lukewarm. The person who is able to maintain his passion and zeal for the ways of the Lord is the one who dwells in His presence and can see the works He is doing among us.

How can we receive the fullness of His blessings and take part in what He is doing, if our hearts are consumed by the confusion that has overtaken the earth and those who dwell there? *His divine power has given us everything that pertains to life and Godliness through the knowledge of Him who called us by His glory and virtue, by which have been given to us exceedingly great and precious promises that through these you may be partakers of the divine nature having escaped the corruption that is in the world through lust.*

Our part in the maintenance of our own soul is continual, diligently seeking the Lord's face and His righteousness. If our hearts are set in pilgrimage here on earth, and not the establishment of our own claim on it, we are free to walk with God and follow His footsteps. To become entangled in temporal things and overcome by them is the way of the world and leads to death and separation from the Spirit that guards the life of a person's soul.

What does it profit a person if he gains the whole world but loses his soul? The Lord has made it clear that only those who are wholehearted and single-minded can be chosen ones.

Is there really a place in the kingdom of God for those who are entangled in the affairs and cares of this present world?

810 GRIEF

Grief is mental anguish that we humans share as the result of being created in the likeness of our Great Creator. Yes, our Lord also experiences grief as a result of His love for His creation and His own loss at the hands of those who refuse to obey and honor Him. There is a time coming when all tears will be wiped away, but it has certainly not yet arrived.

Misunderstanding and ignorance are sources of grief for us who have love for our fellow humans and are able to see those who live according to the flesh drawn toward death and stumbling to the slaughter. God has made a way for mankind to escape the way of death, but can you imagine His grief for all those who will not listen to Him? This watchman can see what is happening on the earth today, and the grief of being able to do so little to rescue the masses that can be seen perishing produces sorrow of heart.

Even among those who have called themselves Christians, there seem to be few who actually live according to the Spirit and walk in the ways of God. The day of reckoning is drawing near, and the masses are heading full blast toward destruction. Many of our loved ones are among them, and it seems there is little we can do to change the course they are following.

This little discourse is what the Lord has given me to do to try and rescue some of those who have wandered from the path of true godliness and righteousness and are following the path of religion and the way that seems right to them. There is but one true gospel, and only those who have received a love of the truth are able to embrace it.

The way of sinners and the religions of the world will surely go the way of the world.

Is this not a legitimate source of grief?

811 WHAT MATTERS

And now, Israel, what does the Lord your God require of you but to fear the Lord your God, to walk in all His ways, to love Him, to serve Him, to serve the Lord your God with all your heart and with all your soul, and to keep the commandments and statutes of the Lord.

The controversies over things that have nothing to do with righteousness and walking in the ways of the Lord have constituted countless sermons and consumed the time and the minds of many who call themselves Christians yet do not possess the true knowledge of God or His righteousness. This is a serious transgression of the gospel and the relationship that the Lord requires of those who would walk with Him.

Does the age of the earth and all of the physical creation, or the existence of extra-terrestrials really have any bearing on the way we conduct our lives and our consciousness? Truth certainly matters, but speculation and theory are worth little in the light of right standing and blamelessness in the sight of our Creator. It is certain that all we can see and know has been created by an intelligent and thoughtful Creator who has made us in His own image and likeness and expects us to give Him the honor that He rightfully deserves.

The theories and speculation that have consumed the modern so-called church with everything from time and sin are really distractions from the true purpose of the creation and God's desire for His inheritance. All that we can see with our natural eyes will perish along with our mortal bodies and the world we live in, but the one who does the will of God will live eternally. Amen!

812 EVIDENCE

The final judgment is made by an all-seeing, all-knowing, all-powerful Judge who is guided by incontrovertible evidence regarding every person's deeds. There can be no defense against such absolute truth and finality.

The one who has seen and been given the knowledge of such truth and yet turns away and resumes his own fleshly pursuits has confessed with his conduct that Jesus Christ has not come in human flesh. This is the confession of the spirit of the one who confesses not that Christ has come in the flesh. The spirit who confesses that Jesus Christ has come in the flesh is the one who is conformed to His image and walks as He walked.

This is the evidence of a person receiving the Spirit and nature of God. Pleading the blood of Jesus and continuing to live according to the flesh is evidence that this one has refused to obey the Spirit of Christ and walk in the ways of God. The record of every person's works and deeds is contained within, and there is no way to disguise or hide the truth.

The Lord has extended His mercy and forgiveness to all who repent and turn away from sin and rebellion against Him. But those who turn back to their own ways and the way of the world have denied the truth and the love of it.

The evidence of true conversion and rebirth in the likeness of the Son of God is in the way we live our lives and the work we do here on earth. Our works are the evidence of redemption and our love of God.

All the theological commentary and religious jargon have no bearing on the truth or the evidence contained within the spirit of every accountable person.

Let God be magnified!

813 LEFT STANDING

At the final judgment, all mankind of all ages will stand before the face of Him from whom heaven and earth flee away. When the books are opened, every person's works will be revealed, and every person will be judged according to their works. At the end, only those whose names are recorded in the "Book of Life" will remain standing. All others will be cast down into the lake of fire.

I am well aware that this account does not line up with what most of us have been taught by the trained professionals of Ecclesia, but then, sinners will not stand in the congregation of the righteous, either. Should we not examine what God has said about the ones throughout the record of scripture who have stood and can stand in the presence of the Lord and dwell in His holy place? Who is it that will see His face and live? Who is it that may abide on His holy hill? Certainly not anyone who has continued to sin after receiving a revelation of the truth. Truth is the real subject at hand, and no one who has embraced a lie will be among those whose names are written in the "Book of Life" or among those who stand in the presence of God.

The teachers of unconditional eternal security seem to have overlooked or denied the conditions and qualifications the Almighty has placed upon everyone who is able to stand in His presence now and in eternity. His judgment is more severe on those who have come to a knowledge of the truth and turned or wandered away from it than on those who have not known.

To stand blamelessly before the throne of God is the only way one can do so. It is God who has made the way of escape from death, and He requires holiness and faithfulness in order to avail oneself of His provision.

814 HATRED AND MURDER

How can a person who has experienced the love and forgiveness of Jesus hate another who has experienced the same? *If someone says, "I love God" and hates his brother, he is a liar. For he who does not love his brother whom he has seen, how can he love God whom he has not seen? . . . He who says he is in the light and hates his brother is in darkness until now . . . but he who walks in darkness does not know where he is going because the darkness has blinded his eyes. . . . He who does not love his brother abides in death. Whoever hates his brother is a murderer, and you know that no murderer has eternal life abiding in him.*

What does skin color have to do with love? Can love be measured by any of the world's social prejudice and cultural bias? Bitterness is the companion of hatred. *Pursue peace with all people and holiness without which no one will see the Lord: Looking carefully lest anyone fall short of the grace of God; lest any root of bitterness spring up, cause trouble, and by this many become defiled.*

What we have been given is not without qualification and expectation of the Lord for us to maintain and walk in accordance with.

There can be no excuse or justification for the sins of hatred, bitterness or murder. Although the Lord has provided atonement, even for these transgressions, He requires repentance and contrition in order to have fellowship with Him restored and established.

The whole notion of right standing with God without obedience and humility is the false premise of the theologian who believes that any person can be saved without an actual ongoing relationship with our Savior.

Hatred and murder are the denial of the one whose spirit confesses that Jesus Christ has not come in the flesh.

Is this not the spirit of Antichrist?

815 FREEDOM FROM AND TO

Jesus answered them, "Most assuredly I say to you, whoever commits sin is a slave of sin. And a slave does not abide in the house forever, but a son abides forever. Therefore, if the Son makes you free, you shall be free indeed." . . . And she,(Mary) will bring forth a son and you shall call his name Jesus, for He will save His people from their sins.

Is the message not clear enough for even the simplest among us to comprehend? How is it that churches full of people who claim to be "born again" can be duped into believing that they are still sinners? Has Jesus failed? Has God lied? Have the people calling themselves Christians no knowledge of God? *Awake to righteousness and do not sin; for some do not have the knowledge of God. I speak this to your shame.*

The gospel is a message of redemption and salvation from sin and death, here and now. Our adoption and our new birth as children of God and brethren of Jesus is here and now, not after we die. If we are not new creatures created and conformed to the image of God's son, and able to walk as He walked and do the things He did as a man, has the Father lied to us? Someone is certainly lying, but it cannot be the Lord. *It is impossible for God to lie.*

If we have been crucified with Christ and become new creatures, having been raised with Him and seated with Him in heavenly places and given His mind, why would we continue to be sinners and be alienated from our Heavenly Father?

What does the gospel really teach us? Has Jesus not set us free to serve God in true righteousness and holiness? SELAH!

816 PRETENDING SUBMISSION

Have the many assemblies who gather in lavish church buildings and flatter God with pretentious ceremonies and rituals, written sermons and prayers really submitted to His Lordship? Those who have pretended to submit to Him while retaining their lives and their hearts for themselves will not escape the just reward for their hypocrisy.

Does the Almighty not know the secrets of the heart of every person? Who will escape the judgment that is coming upon all who dwell on earth? What of those who serve their flesh while pretending to serve the Lord? Does God not see and will he not reward every person according to their works regardless of the hypocritical confession of their lips?

Every person must answer for himself, and there will be no place to hide and no one to hide behind. Only those who have lost their lives for Jesus' sake and worship Him in spirit and truth will be among those left standing in the congregation of saints. The Lord is speaking to those who have received a love of the truth. His words are a comfort to those who do love the truth, while being a very serious warning to those who prefer the lies of the false prophets who enable them to continue in unrighteousness.

Yes, to pretend submission to the Lord will only land an individual in the congregation of those who have chosen to try and please God without actually obeying Him and giving their lives to Him.

Religious pretense is the way people fool themselves.

817 RIGHT AND WRONG

Truth is the basis of what is right, and falsehood is the basis for what is wrong. The ways of the world will cloud the issue along with the opinions of the natural man. God's word and His ways are always right and trustworthy, whether we can understand them or not. There is a way that seems right to a person, but it ends in death. . . . As righteousness leads to life, so he who pursues evil pursues it to his own death.

Truth always agrees with the word of God, while anything wrong will disagree with what the Lord has said. The deceiver will and does twist and pervert what is right very subtly to cause us to mistake wrong for right. This is the role the false church has taken on to cause those who do not love the truth to be diverted from the path of righteousness and wander onto the wrong path and stumble.

God is not a respecter of persons, and He knows those who obey Him and love His ways. A verbal assent to His commandments is not the same as actually doing them, and there are no liars abiding in His presence.

Those who wrongfully accuse the righteous because of doctrinal bias are an abomination to the Lord and will not go unpunished. The doctrinal biases of the denominations are indeed wrong, along with their erroneous rituals and traditions. Can the God of truth and justice endorse or bless these wrongful religious blasphemies and lies?

If this is not a call from the Lord to forsake what is wrong and turn to what is right and true, then wrong is the way you are heading.

818 RELIGION

Religion is man's attempt to please and pacify gods of his own making and fabrication. The multitude of religious disciplines that fill the earth are figments of the imaginations of men's minds and the inspiration of demons. There are countless denominations calling themselves Christian but are incapable of agreement or unity. The rest of the religions of the world are even further away from the actual truth and person of our Creator.

God has made Himself and His salvation known, but there are few who will actually listen to Him and obey Him. Those who have heard Him and come to know Him are the ones He has chosen to become One with Himself. None of us can take this honor to himself. It is a gift of grace.

The religions of man provide formulas, sacrifices and disciplines that they claim will enable their followers to be able to reach heaven and please God. They have all been deceived and become deluded, because they have not received a love of the truth. We are all subject to temptation and the deception of Satan and his lies about the true God of heaven and earth. It is love of the truth that is able to preserve us along with the knowledge and relationship with the Lord.

The champions of religion are like the giant, Goliath, that challenged the army of Israel. But it was a simple trust in the God of Jacob that enabled David to defeat him. So it is with the Israel of God now. All the fearmongers of the world today are no match for the one who truly knows his God. This is the day spoken of by Daniel: *Those who know their God shall be strong and carry out great exploits. And those, the people who understand, shall instruct many.*

We who have become One Spirit with the Lord and are led by His Spirit are indeed the ones of whom Daniel has prophesied.

819 MERCHANTS AND SERVANTS

The merchants' hands are full of bribes and covered with blood. The servants' hands are clean and pure. We are talking here about those who are paid by the vested interests of religious organizations and institutions in contrast to true disciples of Jesus Christ. The life of the merchant has been purchased by the one who pays his salary, while the true servant of God has been purchased by Jesus' blood and is sustained by His Spirit and His provision.

These things are not complicated or difficult to discern, but they are clouded by the misuse of the gospel and the mask of religion. Many whom the Lord has called have been hired and bribed by the prospect of worldly security and recognition. Those who remain true and faithful to Jesus and His gospel are they who become chosen in Him and are saints of God.

Wisdom, understanding and the knowledge of God do not come from institutional, formal education but from the instruction of the Holy Spirit. Diplomas, degrees, and certification do not necessarily represent the endorsement of the Lord, but the anointing of the Holy Spirit carries the power and authority of God Himself. If a person is able to see these things, he will not continue with those who do not.

This message is but one of the many calling the Lord's people out of Babylon, the false church and the prison of the world. *Jesus is the Way, the Truth, and the Life.* And He has endorsed no institution of which I am aware.

The voices which are calling us are many, but there is only One that can be trusted with our souls. He is a Spirit and cannot be heard with the natural ear.

ABOUT THE AUTHOR

A Testimony. At the age of 25, I had reached a place where I could not see a reason to go on living. I had come to a place of desperation and hopelessness. I did not pray outright to the Lord, but He, nevertheless, heard the cry of my heart and took the initiative to reveal Himself to me by taking me to a place where I was able to see how He had His hand on my life from birth. He showed me how He had been there for me throughout my life in countless situations of near-death and emotional crises where I had no place and no one to rescue me.

It was the Lord's mercy and love that caused me to reach out and cry for His forgiveness at that very moment. This is when He came into my very being and began to speak to me. He has been with me ever since that encounter and has redeemed my soul and given me ongoing testimony of His wonderful works in a personal way.

These publications of "A Watchman Speaks" are but an example of how the Lord has led and instructed His servant over the past 48 years or so.

INDEX

Titles available from Prosody Communications
are found at www.barnesandnoble.com,
and also other online sites where leading books are purchased.

ASSURED

Biblical Poetry Through Other Perspectives
By Deedrick Jaymin
127 pages

Witty and connectable themes throughout: Marriage, Separation, Struggles, Success, Relationships, Unbeknownst Faith, Family, Money & Hope.

Deedrick's familiar understanding and fresh approach to these broad topics make an interesting read and prove a valid resource to committed readers of any age.

ISBN 978-1-951357-00-9 (paperback)
ISBN 978-1-951357-01-6 (e-book)

A WATCHMAN SPEAKS

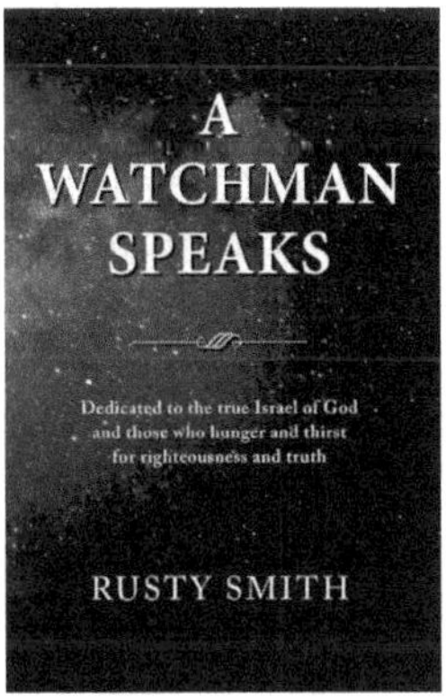

Dedicated to the true Israel of God and those who hunger and thirst for righteousness and truth
By Rusty Smith
894 pages

The revelation of mysteries and metaphors contained in this compilation of writings comes primarily from a Spiritual point of view which originally inspired them before the institutions of carnal wisdom and intelligence were established to train, certify and endorse those who they deemed qualified to lead the less educated.

This book is for those who may not have found the righteousness and truth for which their soul hungers and thirsts that is so frequently described and promised in the Scriptures.

Join the author, Rusty Smith, inside these pages to partake in the journey given to him from the Lord as we view the word together in, A Watchman Speaks.

ISBN: 978-1-951357-02-3 (paperback)
ISBN: 978-1-951357-03-0 (e-book)

5 QUESTIONS

Synopsis of Those Among Us
By Darin Johnson
146 pages

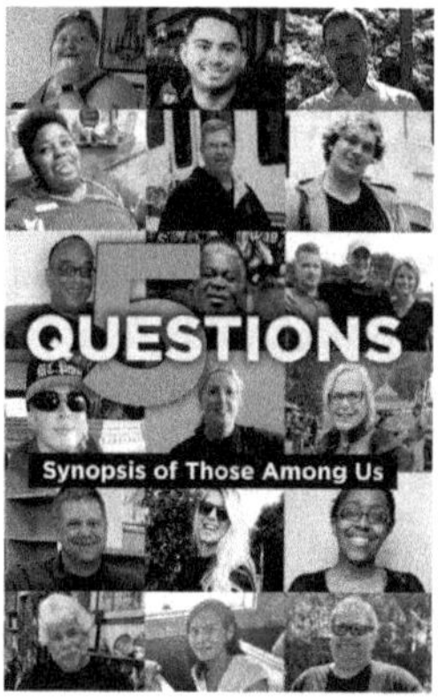

Brought together within these pages is a meeting of many unveiling for all to discover the enduring values that each holds dear. Found out is that to say hello to a stranger or one not well known just may create something of lasting worth. The remembrance of these moments together forever producing a familiarity due to the simplistic approach that **5 Questions** insisted upon.

As you enjoy this compilation, you will meet people across the room, others walking by, persons working at your neighbors, folks enjoying the nearby event, those chatting at a table next to yours, and ones shopping in the local market.

The people that we see.
The people that bring wonder.
The people that are among us.

ISBN 978-1-951357-04-7 (paperback)
ISBN 978-1-951357-05-4 (e-book)

Thank You!

CPSIA information can be obtained
at www.ICGtesting.com
Printed in the USA
BVHW040959210621
610126BV00009B/1823

9 781951 357061